# LARA

ANNA PASTERNAK

# LARA

## THE UNTOLD LOVE
## STORY THAT INSPIRED
## DOCTOR ZHIVAGO

*An Imprint of* HarperCollins*Publishers*

HarperCollins books may be purchased for educational, business, or sales promotional use. For information, please email the Special Markets Department at SPsales@harpercollins.com.

A hardcover edition was published in the U.K. by William Collins in 2016.

Map and family tree © Martin Brown
Picture credits: Page 3 (top) © Mondadori Portfolio/Getty; page 4 (top and bottom) courtesy of the Estate of Boris Pasternak; page 11 (bottom) © ullstein bild/Getty; page 12 (top) © Bettmann/Getty. All other photographs courtesy of the author.

FIRST U.S. EDITION

Library of Congress Cataloging-in-Publication Data has been applied for.

ISBN 978-0-06-243934-5

17 18 19 20 21    RS/RRD    10 9 8 7 6 5 4 3 2 1

In loving memory of my mother,
Audrey Pasternak

Writers can be divided into two types: meteors and fixed stars. The first produces a momentary effect: you gaze up and cry 'Look!' – and they vanish forever. Whereas fixed stars are unchanging, they stand firm in the firmament, shine by their own light and influence all ages equally; they belong to the universe. But it is precisely because they are so high that their light usually takes so many years to reach the eyes of the dwellers on earth.

Arthur Schopenhauer

It is not for nothing that you stand at the end of my life, my secret, forbidden angel, under the skies of war and turmoil, you who arose at its beginning under the peaceful skies of childhood.

Yury Zhivago to Lara, Doctor Zhivago

# CONTENTS

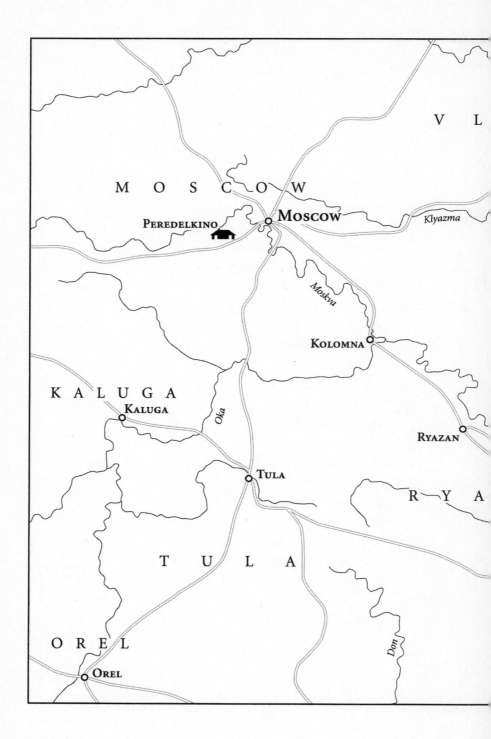

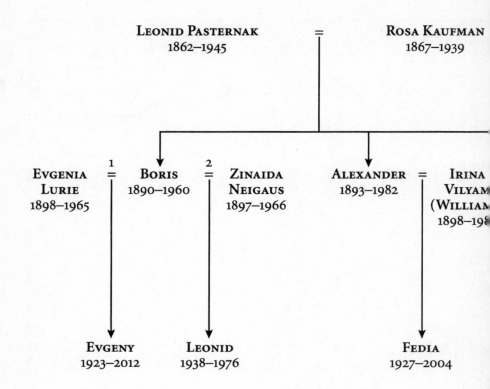

LEONID PASTERNAK
1862–1945
=
ROSA KAUFMAN
1867–1939

EVGENIA
LURIE
1898–1965
= 1
BORIS
1890–1960
= 2
ZINAIDA
NEIGAUS
1897–1966

ALEXANDER
1893–1982
=
IRINA
VILYAM
(WILLIAM
1898–198

EVGENY
1923–2012

LEONID
1938–1976

FEDIA
1927–2004

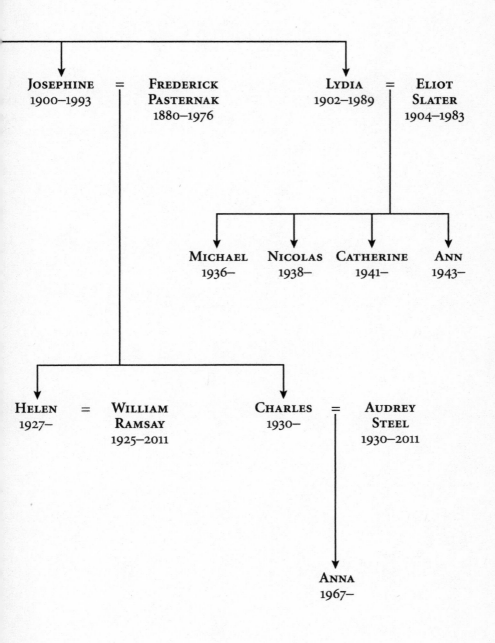

# Straightening Cobwebs

It is almost impossible, by today's standards of celebrity, to comprehend the level of fame that Boris Pasternak engendered in Russia from the 1920s onwards. Pasternak may be most famous in the West for writing the Nobel Prize-winning love story *Doctor Zhivago*, yet in Russia he is primarily recognised, and still hugely feted, as a poet. Born in 1890, his reputation escalated during his early thirties; soon he was filling large auditoriums with young students, revolutionaries and artists who gathered to hear recitals of his poems. If he paused for effect or for a momentary memory lapse, the entire crowd continued to roar the next line of his verse in unison back at him, just as they do at pop concerts today.

'There was in Russia a very real contact between the poet, and the public, greater than anywhere else in Europe,' Boris's sister, Lydia, wrote of this time; 'certainly far greater than is ever imaginable in England. Books of poetry were published in enormous editions and were sold out within a few days of publication. Posters were stuck up all over the town announcing poets' gatherings and everyone interested in poetry (and who in Russia did not belong to this category?) flocked to the lecture room or forum to hear his favourite poet.' The writer had immense influence in Russian society. In a time of unrest, with an absence of credible politicians, the public looked to its writers. The influence of literary journals was prodigious; they were powerful vehicles for political debate. Boris Pasternak was not only a popular poet hailed for his courage and sincerity. He was revered by a nation for his fearless voice.

From his early years Pasternak longed to write a great novel. He told his father, Leonid, in 1934: 'Nothing I have written so far is of any significance. Hurriedly I am trying to transform myself into a writer of a Dickensian kind, and later – if I have enough strength to do it – into a poet in the manner of Pushkin. Do not imagine that I dream of comparing myself with them! I am naming them simply to give you an idea of my inner change.' Pasternak dismissed his poetry as too easy to write. He had enjoyed unexpected, precocious success with his first published volume of poetry, *Above the Barriers*, in 1917. This became one of the most influential collections ever published in the Russian language. Critics praised the book's biographical and historical material, marvelling at the contrasting lyrical and epic qualities. A. Manfred, writing in *Kniga I revolyutsiya*, observed a new 'expressive clarity' and of the author's prospects of 'growing into the revolution'. Pasternak's second collection of twenty-two poems, *My Sister, Life*, published in 1922, received unprecedented literary acclaim. The exultant mood of the collection delighted readers as it conveyed the elation and optimism of the summer of 1917. Pasternak wrote that the February Revolution had happened 'as if by mistake' and everyone suddenly felt free. This was Boris's 'most celebrated book of poems', observed his sister Lydia. 'The more sophisticated younger generation of literary Russians went wild over the book.' They considered that he wrote the finest love poetry, in thrall to his intimate imagery. After reading *My Sister, Life*, the poet Osip Mandelstam declared: 'To read Pasternak's verse is to clear your throat, to fortify your breathing, to fill your lungs: surely such poetry could provide a cure for tuberculosis. No poetry is more healthful at the present moment! It is *koumiss* [mare's milk] after evaporated milk.'

'My brother's poems are without exception strictly rhythmical and written mostly in classical metre,' Lydia wrote later. 'Pasternak, like Mayakovsky, the most revolutionary of Russian poets, has never in his life written a single line of unrhythmic poetry, and this is not because of pedantic adherence to obsolete classical rules, but because instinctive feeling for rhythm and harmony were inborn qualities of his genius, and he simply could not write differently.' In a poem written shortly after *My Sister, Life* was published, Boris bids farewell to poetry: 'I will say so long to verse, my mania – I have an appointment with you in a novel.' Still though, he glorified prose-writing as being too difficult. Yet the two modes of writing actually shared an intrinsic relationship in his work, regardless of the genre. In his autobiography *Safe Conduct*, published in 1931, a mannered account of his early life, travels and personal relationships, he wrote: 'We drag everyday things into prose for the sake of poetry. We draw prose into poetry for the sake of music. This, then, I called art, in the widest sense of the word.'

It was in 1935 that Pasternak first spoke of his intent to fulfil his artistic potential by writing an epic Russian novel. And it was to my grandmother, his younger sister, Josephine Pasternak*, that he first confided his ideas at their last meeting at Friedrichstrasse station in Berlin. Boris told Josephine that the seeds of a book were germinating in his mind; an iconic, enduring love story set in the period between the Russian Revolution and the Second World War.

*Doctor Zhivago* is based on Boris's relationship with the love of his life, Olga Vsevolodovna Ivinskaya, who was to become the muse for Lara, the novel's spirited heroine. Central to the novel is the passionate love affair shared by Yury Zhivago, a doctor and poet (a nod to the writer Anton Chekhov, who was also a doctor) and Lara Guichard, the heroine, who becomes a nurse. Their love is tormented as Yury, like Boris, is married. Yury's diligent wife, Tonya, is based on Boris's second wife, Zinaida Neigaus. Yury Zhivago is a semi-autobiographical hero; this is the book of a survivor.

*Doctor Zhivago* has sold in its millions yet the true love story behind it has never been fully explored before. The role of Olga Ivinskaya in Boris's life has been consistently repressed both by the Pasternak family and

---

* Josephine married her cousin, Frederick Pasternak, hence the continuation of the surname.

Boris's biographers. Olga has regularly been belittled and dismissed as an 'adventurous', 'a temptress', a woman on the make, a bit part in the history of the man and his book. When Pasternak started writing the novel, he had not yet met Olga. Lara's teenage trauma of being seduced by the much older Victor Komarovsky is a direct echo of Zinaida's experiences with her sexually predatory uncle. However, as soon as Boris met and fell in love with Olga, his Lara changed and flowered to completely embody her.

Historically both Olga and her daughter, Irina, have received a bad rap from my family. The Pasternaks have always been keen to play down the role of Olga in Boris's life and literary achievements. They held Boris in such high esteem that for him to have had two wives – Evgenia and Zinaida – and a public mistress was indigestible to their staunch moral code. By accepting Olga's place in Boris's life and affections, they would have had to further acknowledge his moral fallibility.

Shortly before she died, Josephine Pasternak told me furiously: 'It is a mistaken idea that this … *acquaintance* ever appeared in *Zhivago*.' In fact, her feelings for 'that seductress' were so strong that she refused to ever sully her lips with her name. She was in denial, blinded by her reverence for her brother. Even though in Boris's last letter to her, written on 22 August 1958, he tells his sister that he hopes to travel in Russia 'with Olga', underlining the importance of his mistress in his life, Josephine would not acknowledge her existence. Evgeny Pasternak, Boris's son by his first wife, was more pragmatic. He may not have liked Olga, displaying little warmth towards her, yet he was more accepting of the situation. 'It was lucky that my father had the love of Lara,' he told me shortly before he died in 2012, aged eighty-nine. 'My father needed her. He would say "*Lara exists, go and meet her.*" This was a compliment.'

It was not until 1946 that fate intervened, when Boris was fifty-six years old. As he later wrote in *Doctor Zhivago*, 'From the bottom of the sea the tide of destiny washed her up to him'. It was at the offices of the literary journal *Novy Mir* that he met thirty-four-year-old Olga Ivinskaya, an editorial assistant. She was blonde and cherubically pretty, with corn-flower-blue eyes and enviably translucent skin. Her manner was beguiling – highly strung and intense, yet with an underlying fragility, hinting at the durability of a survivor. She was already a dedicated fan of Pasternak the 'poet hero'. Their attraction was mutual and instant, and it is easy to see why they were drawn to each other. Both were melodramatic romantics given to extraordinary flights of fantasy. 'And now there he was at my desk by the window,' she later wrote, 'the most unstinting man in the world, to whom it had been given to speak in the name of the clouds, the stars and the wind, who had also found eternal words to say about man's passion and woman's weakness. People say that he summons the stars to his table and the whole world to the carpet at his bedside.'

Having become fascinated with my great-uncle's love story, I feel passionately that if it were not for Olga, not only would *Doctor Zhivago* never have been completed but it would never have been published. Olga Ivinskaya paid an enormous price for loving 'her Boria'. She became a pawn in a highly political game. Her story is one of unimaginable courage, loyalty, suffering, tragedy, drama and loss.

From the mid-1920s, as Stalin came to power after Lenin's death, it was established that communism would not tolerate individual tendencies. Stalin, an anti-intellectual, described writers as the 'engineers of the soul' and regarded them as having an influential potency that needed to be channelled into the collective interests of the state. He began his drive for collectivisation and with it mass terror. The atmosphere for poets and authors, expressing their own individual creativity, became unbearably oppressive. After 1917 nearly 1,500 writers in the Soviet Union were executed or died in labour camps for alleged infractions. Under Lenin, indiscriminate arrests had become part of the system, as it was believed to be in the interest of the state to incarcerate a hundred innocent people rather than let one enemy of the regime go free. The atmosphere of fear, of people informing on colleagues or former writer friends, was actively encouraged in Stalin's new stifling regime where everyone was fighting to survive. Many writers and artists, terrified of persecution, committed suicide. Where Pasternak's semi-autobiographical hero Yury Zhivago dies in 1929, Boris himself survived, though refusing to kowtow to the literary and political diktats of the day.

Stalin, who had a special admiration for Boris Pasternak, did not imprison the controversial writer; instead he harassed and persecuted his lover. Twice Olga Ivinskaya was sentenced to periods in labour camps. She was interrogated about the book Boris was writing, yet she refused to betray the man she loved. The leniency with which Stalin treated Pasternak did not diminish the author's outrage towards his country's leader; he was, he lamented, 'a terrible man who drenched Russia in blood'. During this time an estimated 20 million people were killed, and 28 million deported, most of whom were put to work as slaves in the 'correctional labour camps'. Olga was one of the millions sent gratuitously to the gulag, precious years of her life stolen from her due to her relationship with Pasternak.

In 1934 Alexei Surkov, a poet and budding party functionary, gave a speech at the First Congress of the Soviet Writers' Union that summed up the Soviet view: 'The immense talent of B. L. Pasternak will never fully reveal itself until he has attached himself fully to the gigantic, rich and radiant subject matter [offered by] the Revolution; and he will become a great poet only when he has organically absorbed the Revolution into himself.' When Pasternak saw the reality of the Revolution, that his beloved Russia had had its 'roof torn off', as he put it, he wrote his own version of history in *Doctor Zhivago*, defiantly criticising the tyrannical regime. In it Yury says to Lara:

Revolutionaries who take the law into their own hands are horrifying, not as criminals, but as machines that have got out of control, like a run-away train ... But it turns out that those who inspired the revolution aren't at home in anything except change and turmoil: that's their native element; they aren't happy with anything that's less than on a world scale. For them, transitional periods, worlds in the making, are an end in themselves. They aren't trained for anything else, they don't know about anything except that. And do you know why there is this incessant whirl of never-ending preparations? It's because they haven't any real capacities, they are ungifted.

In the last century few literary works created such a furore as *Doctor Zhivago*. It was not until 1957, over twenty years after Pasternak first confided in Josephine, that the book was published, initially in Italy. Despite being an instant, international bestseller, and even though Pasternak was then seen as Russia's 'greatest living writer', it was over thirty years later, in 1988, that his book, regarded as anti-revolutionary and unpatriotic, was legitimately published in his adored 'Mother Russia'. The cultural critic Dmitry Likhachev, who was considered the world's foremost expert in Old Russian language and literature in the late twentieth century, said that *Doctor Zhivago* was not really a traditional novel but was rather 'a kind of autobiography' of the poet's inner life. The hero, he believed, was not an active agent but a window on the Russian Revolution.

In 1965 David Lean made film history with his adaptation of Pasternak's novel, in which Julie Christie was cast as the heroine, Lara, and Omar Sharif as the hero, Yury Zhivago. The film won five Academy Awards and was nominated for five more. Lean's Hollywood classic has left millions of viewers with images as magic and endurable as Pasternak's prose. It is the eighth highest-grossing film in American film history. Robert Bolt, who won an Academy Award for the screenplay, said of adapting Pasternak's work: 'I've never done anything so difficult. It's like straightening cobwebs.' Omar Sharif said of it: '*Doctor Zhivago* encompasses but does not overwhelm the human spirit. That is Boris Pasternak's gift.' Of the enduring quality of the story, he concluded: 'He proves that true love is timeless. *Doctor Zhivago* was and always will be a classic for all generations.'

There is a Russian proverb: 'You cannot know Russia through your head. You can only understand her through your heart.' When I visited Russia for the first time, walking around Moscow was like being haunted, as I had the sense not of being a tourist but of coming home. It was not that Moscow was familiar to me but it did not feel foreign either. I marched through the snow one wintry February night, up the wide Tverskaya Street, to dinner at the Café Pushkin restaurant, acutely conscious that Boris and Olga had used the same route many times during their courtship, over sixty years earlier, treading the very same pavements.

Sitting amid the flickering candlelight of the Café Pushkin, which is styled to resemble a Russian aristocrat's home of the 1820s – with its galleried library, book-lined walls, elaborate cornices, frescoed ceilings and distinct grandeur – I felt the hand of history gently resting on me. The restaurant is close to the old offices of *Novy Mir*, Olga's former workplace on Pushkin Square. I imagined Olga and Boris walking past, their heads bowed low and close against the snow, wrapped in heavy coats, their hearts full of desire.

Five years later, on another visit to Moscow, I went to the Pushkin statue, erected in 1898, where Boris and Olga frequently rendezvoused during the early stages of their relationship. It was here that Boris first confessed the depth of his feelings to Olga. The vast statue of Pushkin was moved in 1950 from one side of Pushkin Square to the other, so they would have started their courtship on the west side of the square and moved to the east side in 1950 where I stood, looking up at the giant bronze folds of Pushkin's majestic cape tumbling down his back. My Moscow guide, Marina, a fan of Putin and the current regime, looked at me standing under Pushkin's statue, envisaging Boris at that very spot, and said: 'Boris Pasternak is an inhabitant of heaven. He is an idol for so many of us, even those who are not interested in poetry.'

This reverential view echoed my meeting with Olga's daughter, Irina Emelianova, in Paris a few months earlier. 'I thank God for the chance to have met this great poet,' she told me. 'We fell in love with the poet before the man. I always loved poetry and my mother loved his poetry, just as generations of Russians have. You cannot imagine how remarkable it was to have Boris Leonidovich [his Russian patronymic name*] not just in the pages of our poetry but in our lives.'

---

* Every Russian has three names. A first name, a patronymic and a surname. The patronymic name is derived from the father's first name. The usual form of address among adults is the first name and the patronymic.

Irina was immortalised by Pasternak as Lara's daughter, Katenka, in *Doctor Zhivago*. Growing up, Irina became incredibly close to Boris. He loved her as the daughter he never had and was more of a father figure to her than any other man in her life. Irina got up from the table we were sitting at and retrieved a book from her well-stocked shelves. It was a translation of Goethe's *Faust* which Boris had given her, and on the title page was a dedication in Boris's bold, looping handwriting in black ink, 'like cranes soaring over the page' as Olga once described it. Inside, Boris had written in Russian to the then seventeen-year-old Irina: 'Irochka, this is your copy. I trust you and I believe in your future. Be bold in your soul and mind, in your dreams and purposes. Put your faith in nature, in the spirit of your destiny, in events of significance – and only in such few people as have been tested a thousand times, and are worthy of your confidence.'

Irina proudly read the final inscription to me. Boris had written: 'Almost like a father, Your BP. November 3, 1955, Peredelkino.' As she ran her hand affectionately across the page, she said sadly: 'It's a shame that the ink will fade.'

It was a timeless moment, as we both stared at the page, considering perhaps that everything precious in life eventually ebbs away. Irina closed the book, straightened her shoulders, and said: 'You cannot imagine how knowing Boris Pasternak altered our lives. I would go and listen to his poetry recitals and I was the envy of my friends at school and my English professor and the teachers. "You know Boris Leonidovich?" they would ask me in awe. "Can you get the latest poem from him?" I would ask his typist if we could just have one line of his verse and sometimes he would distribute a poem for me to hand out. That gave me incredible prestige at school and in a way his glory rubbed off on me.'

The Russian people's reverence for Pasternak, which remains to this day, is not just because of the enduring power of his writing, but because he never wavered in his loyalty to Russia. His great love was for his Motherland; in the end, that was stronger than everything. He renounced the Nobel Prize for Literature when the Soviet authorities threatened that if he left his country, he would not be allowed to return. And he never became an émigré, refusing to follow his parents to Germany, then England, after the 1917 Revolution.

When I went to Peredelkino, to the writer's colony, a fifty-minute drive from central Moscow, where Boris spent nearly two decades writing *Doctor Zhivago*, I felt a profound sadness. As I sat at Boris's desk in his study on the upper floor of his dacha, I traced the faint ring marks his coffee cups had left on the wood over fifty years earlier. Icicles hung outside the window, reminiscent of David Lean's film: I was reminded of Varykino, the abandoned estate in the novel, where Yury spends his last days with Lara, dazzling in the sun and snow; the lacework of hoar frost on the frozen window panes; the crystalline magic conjured on screen; Julie Christie, embodying his Lara, effortlessly beautiful beneath her fur hat. I thought of my great-uncle Boris looking out of the window, across the garden he adored, past the pine trees to the Church of Transfiguration. In the distance lies Peredelkino cemetery, where he is buried. Earlier that day, my father, Boris's nephew, and I had trudged through deep snow-drifts in the cemetery to visit his grave, where I was touched to find a bouquet of frozen long-stemmed pink roses carefully placed against his headstone. They must have been left there by a fan. I was struck that no words of Boris's adorn his grave. Just his face etched into the stone. Powerful in its simplicity, nothing more needs to be said.

I leaned back in Boris's chair in his study and considered how often he must have turned back from the undulating view to his page (he wrote in longhand), inspired, to create scenes of longing between Yury and Lara. When I was there the snow was gently falling outside, enhancing the stillness. The room is almost painful in its plainness. In one corner stands a small wrought-iron bed with a sketch of Tolstoy hanging above it and family drawings by Boris's father, Leonid, to each side. With its drab grey patterned cover and the reddish brown cut-out square of carpet close by, the bed would not have been out of place in a monastic cell. Opposite, a bookcase: the Russian Bible, works by Einstein, the collected poems of W. H. Auden, T. S. Eliot, Dylan Thomas, Emily Dickinson, novels by Henry James, the autobiography of Yeats and the complete works of Virginia Woolf (Josephine Pasternak's favourite author), along with Shakespeare and the teachings of Jawaharlal Nehru. Facing the desk, on an artist's easel, a large black and white photograph of Boris himself. Wearing a black suit, white shirt and dark tie, I considered that he looked about my age, mid-forties. Pain, passion, determination, resignation, fear and fury emanate from his eyes. His lips are almost pursed, set with conviction. There was nothing soft or yielding about his sanctuary; he saved his sensuousness for his prose.

I thought about Boris's courage, a courage that meant he could sit there and write his truth about Russia. How he defiantly stared the Soviet authorities in the face, and how persecution and the threat of death eventually took its toll. How, despite outliving Stalin, in spite of his colossal literary achievements, he lived his last years here in imposed isolation, the Soviet authorities watching and monitoring his every move. His study became his personal quarantine: writing upstairs; his wife Zinaida downstairs, chain-smoking as she played cards or watched the clunky antique Soviet television, one of the first ever made.

And I imagined his lover Olga Ivinskaya, in the last years of Boris's life, anxiously waiting for him every afternoon to join her in the 'Little House' across the lake at Izmalkovo, a kilometre away. Here she would soothe and support, encourage and type up his manuscripts. Not visible in his home by way of cherished photograph or painting, her absence is jarring. For what is the love story in *Doctor Zhivago* if it is not his passionate *cri de coeur* to Olga? I thought of her endlessly reassuring him of his talent when the authorities taunted that he had none; how she brought fun and tenderness into his life when everything else was so strategic, harsh, political and fraught. How she loved him but, just as crucially, how she understood him. Many artists are selfish and self-indulgent, as he was. It would be easy to conclude that Boris used Olga. It is my intention to show that, rather, his great omission was that he did not match her cast-iron loyalty and moral fortitude. He did not do the one thing in his power to do: he did not save her.

Looking around his study for the last time, I knew that I wanted to write a book which would try to explain why he performed this uncharacteristic act of moral cowardice, putting his ambition before his heart.

If I could understand why he behaved as he did and appreciate the extent of his suffering and self-attack, could I forgive him for letting himself and his true love down? For not publicly claiming or honouring Olga – for not marrying her – when she was to risk her life loving him? As he writes in *Doctor Zhivago*: 'How well he loved her, and how loveable she was in exactly the way he had always thought and dreamed and needed … She was lovely by virtue of the matchlessly simple and swift line which the Creator at a single stroke had drawn round her, and in this divine outline she had been handed over, like a child tightly wound up in a sheet after its bath, into the keeping of his soul.'

# 1

## A Girl from a Different World

*Novy Mir*, meaning 'New World', the leading Soviet literary monthly where Olga Ivinskaya worked, was set up in 1925. Literary journals such as *Novy Mir*, the official organ of the Writers' Union of the USSR, enjoyed huge influence in the Stalinist period and had a readership of tens of millions. They were vehicles for political ideas in a country where debate was harshly censored, and the contributors held enormous sway in Russian society. The offices in Pushkin Square were situated in a grand former ballroom, painted a rich dark red with gilded cornices, where Pushkin once danced. The magazine's editor, the poet and author Konstantin Simonov, a flamboyant figure with a silvery mane of hair who sported chunky signet rings and the latest style of American loose-fitting suits, was keen to attract 'living classics' to the journal, and counted Pavel Antokolsky, Nicolai Chukovski and Boris Pasternak among its contributors. Olga was in charge of the section for new authors.

On an icy October day in 1946, just as a fine snow was beginning to swirl outside the windows, Olga was about to go for lunch with her friend Natasha Bianchi, the magazine's production manager. As she pulled on her squirrel fur coat, her colleague Zinaida Piddubnaya interrupted: 'Boris Leonidovich, let me introduce one of your most ardent admirers,' gesturing to Olga.

Olga was stunned when 'this God' appeared before her and 'stood there on the carpet and smiled at me'. Boldly, she held out her hand for him to kiss. Boris bent over her hand and asked what books of his she had. Astounded and ecstatic to be face-to-face with her idol, Olga replied that she only had one. He looked surprised. 'Oh, I'll get you some others,' he said, 'though I've given almost all my copies away ...' Boris explained that he was mainly doing translation work and hardly writing any poems at all due to the repressive strictures of the day. He told her that he was still translating Shakespeare plays.

Throughout his writing career, Pasternak earned the bulk of his income through commissioned translation work. Proficient in several languages, including French, German and English, he was deeply interested in the intricacies and dilemmas of translating. Gifted in interpreting, and conveying a colloquial essence, he was to become Russia's premiere translator of Shakespeare, and would be nominated for the Nobel Prize six times for his accomplishments in this area. In 1943 the British embassy had written to him with compliments and gratitude for his efforts translating the Bard. The work provided several years of steady income. He told a friend in 1945: 'Shakespeare, the old man of Chistopol, is feeding me as before.'

'I've started on a novel,' he told Olga at *Novy Mir*, 'though I'm not yet sure what kind of thing it will turn out to be. I want to go back to the old Moscow – which you don't remember – and talk about art, and put down some thoughts.' At this stage, the novel's draft title was 'Boys and Girls'. He paused, before adding a little awkwardly: 'how interesting that I still have admirers ...'. Even at the age of fifty-six, more than twenty years Olga's senior, Pasternak was considered handsome in a strong, striking way, despite the fact that his elongated face was often likened to an Arab horse's – hardly flattering – partly because he had long yellowish teeth. It seems slightly disingenuous that Boris should have questioned that he had admirers – a faux modesty – when he knew perfectly well that he had a hypnotic effect on people, and that men and women everywhere were in awe of him. The Russian poet Andrei Voznesensky, to whom Pasternak would become a mentor figure, was captivated by the poet's dazzling presence the first time he met him, that same year, 1946:

> Boris Leonidovich started talking, going straight to the point. His cheekbones would twitch, like the triangular shaped cases of wings pressed tight shut, prior to opening. I worshipped him. There was a magnetic quality about him, great strength and celestial other-worldliness. When he spoke, he would jerk his chin, thrusting it up, as if trying to break free of his collar and body. His short nose hooked right from the bridge, then went straight, making one think of the butt of a gun in miniature. The lips of a sphinx. Grey hair, cropped short. But, overshadowing everything else, was the pulsating wave of magnetism that flowed from him.

All through his life women pursued Boris Pasternak. Yet he was no quasi-Don Juanesque character; quite the opposite. He revered women, feeling an innate empathy for them because he saw that for women, as for poets, things could often become complex and entangled in their emotional and sentimental lives. His fateful meeting with Olga at *Novy Mir* was to become the greatest entanglement, enmeshing his emotional and creative lives.

After exchanging a few words with Zinaida Piddubnaya, he kissed both women's hands and left. Olga stood there, speechless. It was one of those life-changing moments when she felt the axis of her world tilt. 'I was simply shaken by the sense of fate when my "god" looked at me with his penetrating eyes. The way he looked at me was so imperious, it was so much a man's appraising gaze that there could be no mistake about it; here he was, the one person I needed more than any other, the very one who was in actual fact already part of me. A thing like this is stunning, a miracle.'

In *Doctor Zhivago* the reader is introduced to Lara in chapter two, 'A Girl from a Different World'. Yury Zhivago's first impressions of Lara are based on Boris's early meetings with Olga: '"She has no coquetry," he thought. "She does not wish to please or to look beautiful. She despises all that side of a woman's life, it's as though she were punishing herself for being lovely. But this proud hostility to herself makes her more attractive than ever."'

There was an instant attraction between Boris and Olga, recalled Irina: 'Boris was sensitive to my mother's kind of beauty. It was a tired beauty. It wasn't the beauty of a brilliant victor, it was almost the beauty of a defeated victim. It was the beauty of suffering. When Boris looked into my mother's beautiful eyes, he could probably see many, many things in them.'

The following day, Pasternak sent Olga a parcel. Five slim volumes of his poems and translations appeared on her desk at the offices at *Novy Mir*. His tenacious pursuit of her had begun.

Olga had first set eyes on him fourteen years earlier, when, as a student at the Moscow Faculty of Literature, she went to one of Pasternak's poetry recitals. She was hurrying through the corridor to get to her seat at Herzen House, Moscow, anxious to hear the 'poet hero' recite his famous poem 'Marburg', which chronicled his first experience of love and rejection. Suddenly, as the bell rang to announce the performance, the nervous black-haired poet rushed past her. He had an electric energy, she thought, which made him seem 'dishevelled and on fire'. When he finished his recital, the excitable crowd surged forwards to surround him. Olga watched as a handkerchief belonging to him was torn to shreds and even the remaining crumbs of tobacco from his cigarette butts were snatched up by fans as meaningful keepsakes.

Over a decade later, in 1946, when Olga was thirty-four, she was given a ticket to an evening in the library of the Historical Museum where Pasternak was to read from his Shakespeare translations. The Russian writer had been first introduced to the works of the English playwright by his first love, Ida Davidovna Vysotskaya, when he was at Marburg University; Ida was the inspiration for his poem 'Marburg'. The daughter of a wealthy Moscow merchant, she had been tutored by Boris as a young girl. Ida and her sister visited Cambridge in 1912, where she discovered Shakespeare and English poetry. She spent three days with Boris in

Marburg later that summer, presenting her serious-minded friend with an edition of Shakespeare's plays and indirectly giving birth to a fresh calling.

On 5 November 1939, Pasternak's translation of *Hamlet*, which had been commissioned by the great theatre director Vsevolod Meyerhold, had been accepted for staging at the Moscow Art Theatre. This made Pasternak immeasurably proud, not least because the 1930s had been a decade filled with terror and frustration for him. Just as Pasternak had warmed to the task of writing his novel, external circumstances kept him from fulfilling his creative dream. At first, he was hampered by financial need, later by isolation, depression and fear. In 1933 he had written to Maksim Gorky, the godfather of Soviet letters and the founder of the 'socialist realism' literary style, that he needed to write short works and publish quickly in order to support his family, which after divorce and remarriage had doubled in size. Already, Pasternak's attitude to his work was one of risk-taking. Completely against being any sort of mouthpiece for Soviet propaganda, he believed it a moral imperative that he write the truth about the age. He considered it dishonest to be in a privileged position against a backdrop of universal deprivation. Yet publication of his work was regularly delayed by censorship problems.

In August 1929, the whole literary community were affected by an issue that broke out in the press. During the 1920s it was frequent practice among Soviet authors to publish works abroad to secure international copyright (the USSR was not a signatory to any international copyright convention) and to circumvent official censorship. On 26 August the Soviet press accused two authors, Evgenyi Zamyatin and Boris Pilnyak, who published abroad, of major acts of treachery involving anti-Soviet slander. The party- and state-organised campaign of vilification played out in the press lasted several weeks, leaving the writing community in a state of fear and insecurity. In the end Zamyatin emigrated to France and Pilnyak was forced to resign from the Writers' Union. Pasternak took these cases closely to heart as he shared stylistic features and close personal relations with the two writers. These literary witch hunts coincided with the collectivisation of agriculture. Over the next few years, its violent enactment would devastate the rural economy and destroy the lives of millions.

On 21 September 1932 Pasternak added a note to a collection of poems under preparation at the Federatsiya state publishing house. 'The Revolution is so unbelievably harsh towards the hundreds of thousands and the millions: yet so gentle towards those with qualifications and those with assured positions.' Openly voicing the struggles of this oppressive and cruel period of post-revolutionary Russia through his poetry quickly brought counterattacks and noises of displeasure from Soviet authorities. Boris continued fearlessly. As his son Evgeny commented: he 'had to become the witness to truth and the conscience-bearer for his age'. Perhaps this is because Boris took his own father's advice to heart. 'Be honest in your art,' Leonid Pasternak had encouraged him; 'then your enemies will be powerless against you.'

During the summer of 1930 Pasternak composed the poem 'To a Friend', bravely addressing it 'To Boris Pilnyak' whose recent novella, *Mahogany*, which presented an idealised portrait of a Trotskyite communist, had been published in Berlin and banned in the Soviet Union. Pasternak's poem was published in *Novy Mir* in 1931 and in a reprint that year of *Above the Barriers*. Written as a statement of solidarity with Pilnyak, and as a warning that writers were under assault, it drew damning comment from Pasternak's orthodox colleagues and critics. Paradoxically it caused more controversy than the stance taken by Pilnyak and his novella. In 'To a Friend', Pasternak wrote:

And is it not true that my personal measure
Is the Five-Year Plan, its rise and its fall?
Yet what can I do with my rib-cage's pressure
And with my inertia, most sluggish of all?
In vain in our day, when the Soviet's at work
By high passion all seats on the stage have been taken.
But the poet has forsaken the place they reserved.
When that place is not vacant, the poet is in danger

By 1933, it had become clear that collectivisation – during which at least five million peasants died – had been a terrible and irreversible disaster. As Pasternak would write in *Zhivago*: 'I think that collectivisation was both a mistake and a failure, and because that couldn't be admitted, every means of intimidation had to be used to make people forget how to think and judge for themselves, to force them to see what wasn't there, and to maintain the contrary of what their eyes told them … And when the war broke out, its real horrors, its real dangers, its menace of real death, were a blessing compared with the inhuman power of the lie, a relief because it broke the spell of the dead letter.' At another point Yury says to Lara: 'everything established, settled, everything to do with home and order and the common round, has crumbled into dust and been swept away in the general upheaval and reorganisation of the whole of society. The whole human way of life has been destroyed and ruined. All that's left is the bare, shivering human soul, stripped to the last shred …'

During the Great Terror in the 1930s, during which much of the old Bolshevik elite, generals, writers and artists perished, Pasternak was increasingly forced to retreat into silence, sure that he too would not have to wait long for the late-night knock at his door. His fear and distress were compounded when soon after Vsevolod Meyerhold had invited him to translate *Hamlet*, the director and his wife, Zinaida Raikh, perished at the hands of the secret police. Boris valiantly persisted in his translation, finding in it 'the mental space to escape constant fear'.

His courage paid off. On 14 April 1940 he was asked to read his *Hamlet* aloud at the Moscow Writers' Club. Of the evening, he wrote to his cousin Olga Freidenberg: 'The highest incomparable delight is to read aloud, without cuts, even though it is only half of your work. For three hours you are feeling Man in the highest sense, independent, hot for three hours, you are in spheres you know from the day you were born, from the first half of your life, and then, exhausted, with your energy spent, you are falling back down, nobody knows where to come back to reality.'

\* \* \*

The first time that Olga Ivinskaya saw Boris properly, at close range, and 'feeling Man' and 'hot for three hours', was the autumn evening in 1946 when he read out his Shakespeare translations at the Moscow museum library. She found him 'tall and trim, extraordinarily youthful, with the strong neck of a young man, and he spoke in a deep, low voice, conversing with the audience as one talks with an intimate friend or communes with oneself'. In the interval some of the audience summoned up the courage to ask him to read work of his own, but he declined, explaining that the evening was supposed to be devoted to Shakespeare and not to himself. Olga was too nervous to join the 'privileged people' brave enough to approach the writer, and left. She arrived home after midnight and, having forgotten her door key, was forced to wake her mother. When her mother angrily reprimanded her, Olga retorted: 'Leave me alone, I've just been talking to God!'

Olga had spent her adolescent years, along with her friends at school and 'everybody else of my age', infatuated with Boris Pasternak. As a teenager she frequently wandered through the streets of Moscow repeating the seductive lines of his poetry over and over to herself. She knew 'instinctively that these were the words of a god, of the all-powerful "god of detail" and "god of love"'. When as a teenager she went for her first trip to the sea, in the south, a friend gave her a small volume of Pasternak's prose, *The Childhood of Luvers*. Lilac-coloured and shaped like an elongated school exercise book, the binding was rough to the touch. This novella, which Boris started writing in 1917 and had published in 1922, was his first work of prose fiction. Originally published in the *Nashia Dni* almanac, Pasternak wanted this to be the first part of a novel about the coming-into-consciousness of a young girl, Zhenia Luvers, the daughter of a Belgian factory director in the Urals. Although Zhenia Luvers has typically been viewed as the prototype for Lara in *Doctor Zhivago*, Pasternak based much of the characterisation on the childhood of his sister, Josephine.

Lying on the upper bunk of her sleeping compartment, as the train sped south, Olga tried to fathom how a man could have such insight into a young girl's secret world. Like many of her peers, she often found it hard to understand Pasternak's poetic images, as she was accustomed to more traditional verse. 'But the answers were already in the air all around us,' she wrote. 'Spring could be recognised by its "little bundle of laundry/ of a patient leaving hospital". Those "candle-drippings" stuck on the branches in springtime did not have to be called "buds" – it was sorcery and a miracle. It gave you the feeling of personally discovering something hitherto unknown and locked away by a god behind a closed door.' Olga could now barely believe that the 'magician who had first entered my life so long ago, when I was sixteen, had now come to me in person, living and real'.

Their courtship moved at a furious pace. Not for one moment did Boris attempt to hide his attraction for the beguiling editor, nor fight his desire for her. He phoned her every day at her offices, where Olga, 'dying of happiness' yet fearing to meet or talk with the poet, always told Pasternak that she was busy. Undeterred, her suitor arrived at the offices every afternoon. He walked her home through the boulevards of Moscow to her apartment in Potapov Street, where she lived with her son and daughter, Mitia and Irina, and her mother and stepfather.

As both Boris and Olga had family at home, most of their initial romance was spent walking the wide streets of Moscow, talking. They met at the memorials of great writers; their usual rendezvous was by the Pushkin statue in Pushkinskaya Square, at the crossing of Tverskoy Boulevard and Tverskaya Street. On one of their city walks, they passed a manhole cover with the name of the industrialist 'Zhivago' written on it. The translation of Zhivago is 'life' or 'Doctor Lively' and Boris was suitably inspired by the name. As he fell in love with Olga, finding his true Lara, he changed the working title of the novel, from *Boys and Girls* to *Doctor Zhivago*.

In the new year, on 4 January 1947, Olga received her first note from Boris: 'Once again I send you all best wishes from the bottom of my heart. Wish me godspeed (cast a spell over me in your thoughts!) with the revision of *Hamlet* and 1905, and a new start on my work. You are very marvellous, and I want you to be well. B.P.' Although Olga was pleased to have her first written communication from her esteemed admirer, she was a little disappointed by the tone of cool formality. The romantic in her, hoping for something warmer, worried that this was his way of warding her off. She need not have been concerned. For the obsessive writer wooing his young beauty, soon even daily contact with Olga was not enough.

Because Olga had no telephone in her apartment, and as Boris wanted to speak to her in the evenings as well, she boldly gave him the number of her neighbours, the Volkovas, who lived below them on the same staircase and were the proud owners of a telephone – rare in Moscow at that time. Every evening Olga would hear a Morse code-like knocking on the hot-water pipes, a signal that Pasternak was on the telephone for her. She would knock back on the damp walls of her apartment, before rushing downstairs, eager just to hear the distinctive voice of the man she was falling in love with. 'When she would come back a few moments later, her face would be somewhere else, like it was facing inwards,' remembered Irina. 'For a whole year, their meetings would take place in the midst of reproaches, knocks on walls, constant surveillance until one day, faced with the ineluctability of their passion, it was decided that our family would officially meet Pasternak.'

The day before, Boris had called Olga at her office and told her that he had to see her as he had two important things to say to her. He asked her to meet him as soon as she could at the Pushkin statue. When Olga arrived, taking a quick break from work, Boris was already there, pacing up and down, agitated. He spoke in an awkward tone, quite unlike his usual voice of bellowing confidence. 'Don't look at me for a moment, while I tell you briefly what I want,' he instructed Olga. 'I want you to say "thou" to me because "you" is by now a lie.'

In terms of their courtship, this was a significant step forwards, away from the formality of 'you', to the familiarity of 'thou'.

'I cannot call you "thou" Boris Leonidovich,' Olga pleaded. 'It's just impossible for me. I am afraid still …'

'No, no! You'll get used to it,' he commanded. 'Very well, then, go on saying "you" to me for the time being but let me call you "thou".'

Flattered and concerned by this new intimacy, Olga returned to work, flustered. At about nine in the evening, she heard the familiar tapping on the pipes in her apartment. She raced downstairs to speak. 'I didn't get to the second thing I wanted to tell you,' he said. 'And you didn't ask me what it was. Well, the first thing was that we should say "thou" to each other. The second thing was; *I love you*. I love you and this is my whole life now. I won't come to your office tomorrow but to your house instead – I'll wait for you to come down and we'll walk round the town.'

That night, Olga wrote out a 'confession' to Boris; a letter that filled a whole notebook. In it she detailed her past history, sparing no detail of her two marriages and the difficulties that she had already endured in her life. She told him that she was born in 1912 in a provincial town where her father had been a high school teacher. The family moved to Moscow in 1915. In 1933 she graduated from the Faculty of Literature of Moscow University. Both her previous marriages had ended in tragedy.

Olga's past was colourful and complex, a fact her detractors in Moscow literary circles leapt upon when gossip of her affair with Boris began to circulate. She told Boris every detail, writing in her confessional notebook about the deaths of both her previous husbands. She could not be accused of hiding anything from him. However, it is odd that even her daughter, Irina, was unsure whether Ivan Emelianov was her mother's first or second husband. 'Ivan [Vania] Emelianov is the man I got my name from,' Irina wrote later. 'He was my mum's second husband (or maybe third) and posed as my father. When you look at his face in photographs, it is hard to believe that he was a mere farmer and that his mother, wrapped up in a black scarf, was illiterate. There was something classy about his family, some kind of elegance.'

Ivan Emelianov hanged himself in 1939, when Irina was nine months old, apparently because he suspected Olga was having an affair with his rival and enemy, Alexander Vinogradov. According to Irina, her father was 'a man from a different era, a good family man, a principled husband and difficult to live with. Their marriage was destined to fail.' In family photographs her father was a 'tall man with a sombre face and doleful expression but handsome'.

Although Olga mourned Ivan's death, Irina noted wryly that her sorrow did not last very long. The forty-day mourning period was barely over when a man in a long leather coat (Vinogradov) was seen standing outside the family home, waiting for her mother. Olga and Vinogradov soon married and had a son, Dimitri (known by the family as Mitia). From a large impoverished family 'worn down by diseases and alcohol', Vinogradov was 'brilliant and strong-willed'. He embraced the new Soviet order, working his way up from being in charge of a poor farmer committee at the age of fourteen. He was quickly promoted to run a collective farm, then moved to Moscow, where he gained a managerial position on the editorial board of a magazine called *Samolet*. It was there that he had first met Olga, who was working as a secretary.

Vinogradov died in 1942 from lung congestion, leaving Olga a widow for the second time. 'I had already gone through more than enough horrors,' she later wrote: 'The suicide of Ira's father, my first husband Ivan Vasilyevich Yemelyanov; the death of my second husband, Alexander Petrovich Vinogradov – who had died in my arms in hospital. I had had many passing affairs and disappointments in love.' Olga concluded in her confessional letter to Boris: 'If you have been a cause of tears [she was still addressing him as 'you' as opposed to 'thou'] so have I! Judge for yourself the things I have to say in reply to "I love you" – which gives me more joy than anything that has ever happened to me.'

The next morning, when she went down from her apartment to work, Boris was already waiting for her by an empty fountain in their court-yard. She gave him the notebook and eager to read it, he embraced her and left soon afterwards. Olga was hardly able to concentrate at work all day, jittery inside as to how he would react to the highly personal details she had chronicled. If on some level, her confessional was a bid to push him away, she failed miserably, underestimating Boris's admiration for the plight of wronged womanhood.

That night, Olga was summoned by a knock on the pipe at half past eleven. Her grumpy, long-suffering neighbour, clad in her nightgown, led Olga into her apartment to speak to her amour. Olga felt terribly embarrassed for her neighbour but did not have the heart to tell Boris not to ring at such an unsociable hour as his voice sounded so joyous.

'*Olia*, I love you,' Boris declared. 'I try to spend my evenings alone now, and I think of you sitting in your office – where for some reason I always imagine there must be mice – and of the way you worry about your children. You have come tripping right into my life. This notebook will always be with me, but you must keep it for me – I dare not leave it at home in case it is found there.'

During that call, Olga knew that they had crossed a boundary line and now nothing could stop them from being together, no matter how challenging the obstacles. There was little doubt that they had found each other. Boris needed the miracle of love at first sight as much as Olga did. They were both lonely, full of yearning for romance and in difficult, emotionally unsatisfying domestic situations.

On 3 April 1947 Boris was invited to Olga's apartment, on the top floor of a six-storey building, to meet her family. Irina, who was nine years old, was wearing a smart pink dress with matching ribbons. Used to the 'misery that comes with war and post war time' she felt uncomfortable trussed up. She also felt under considerable pressure, as the night before Olga had read and reread Pasternak's poems to her, which she wanted her daughter to learn and recite to their esteemed visitor. Irina, who did not understand a word she was saying, became flustered: 'Even words I knew like "garage" and "taxi depot" have an unusual meaning in those verses and it felt like I had never seen them before. I became so disarmed; I was incapable of pronouncing them. Mum was distraught, what cou[l]d she do?'

Olga had placed a bottle of cognac and a box of chocolates on th[e] before Boris. According to Irina, her mother had decided to g[o] 'minimalistic option', concerned that the writer would judge t[h] habits, which were 'not really worthy of a man like him'. B[o] oversized wax cloth that covered the table and, as alway[s] black coat on and did not remove his well-worn astrak[han] conversation was a little awkward to begin with, Olg[a] wrote verse too. Irina blushed, embarrassed, especially when Boris promised that he would look at her poetry at a later date.

Irina, however, was smitten. There was 'something remarkable about him. His booming voice interrupting with its famous "yes, yes, yes". He had a magnetic, magic quality.'

Although Irina felt nervous and intimidated in front of her mother's 'idol', their first meeting was to have an equally indelible impact on the burgeoning novelist: 'The day came when my children saw BL for the first time,' Olga later wrote. 'I remember how Irina, stretching out her thin little arm to hold on to the table, recited one of his poems to him. It was a difficult one, and Lord knows how and when she had managed to learn it.' Afterwards, Boris wiped away a tear and kissed her: 'What extraordinary eyes she has!' he exclaimed. 'Look at me, Ira. You could go straight into my novel!'

She did go straight into the pages of his book. In *Doctor Zhivago* Pasternak describes Lara's daughter Katenka: 'A little girl of about eight came in, her hair done up in finely braided plaits. Her narrow eyes had a sly, mischievous look and went up at the corners when she laughed. She knew her mother had a visitor, she had heard his voice outside the door, but she thought it necessary to put on an air of surprise. She curtsied and looked at Yury with the fearless, unblinking stare of a lonely child who ⸴arted to think early in life.'

⸴e moment that Boris entered Olga's family's life, he felt torn ⸴n his love and loyalty to them, and to his wife Zinaida and ⸴id. Just as years before he had previously been torn ⸴ and his first wife, Evgenia, and their son, Evgeny. ⸴rlier, on 1 October 1937, Pasternak had written to his settled air of regret in his home: 'A divided family, le⸴nd constantly looking over our shoulders at that thing⸴.'

⸴rtured by guilt for the suffering he caused ⸴re her), part of him seemed to enjoy – or at ⸴uish. Renouncing Olga was never some- ⸴arly into his affair with Olga he told his artist friend Liusia Popova that he had fallen in love. When asked about Zinaida, he replied: 'What is life if not love? She [Olga] is so enchanting, such a radiant, golden person. And now this golden sun has come into my life, it is so wonderful. So wonderful. I never thought I would still know such joy.'

# 2

## Mother Land
## and Wonder Papa

Pasternak inherited his prodigious work ethic from his father, Leonid, a post-impressionist painter, who exerted the greatest influence on his son's creative life. All Leonid's four children – Boris, Alexander, Josephine and Lydia – grew up acutely aware of their father's 'shining perennial example of artistry' and felt discomfiture that Boris's fame eclipsed their father's.

Before the Revolution, when the family lived together in Moscow, it was Leonid, not Boris, who was the better known. Leonid worked through one of the greatest periods of Russian cultural life. He painted and socialised with Leo Tolstoy, Sergei Rachmaninoff, the composer Alexander Scriabin and the pianist and composer Anton Rubinstein, who founded the St Petersburg Conservatory. The Russian painter Ilya Repin gained such respect for Leonid that he later sent him art students. There was definitely the feeling in the family that Leonid and his pianist wife, Rosalia, were overlooked. There was a silent shame, unspoken by all but Boris, that he had outshone them both.

In 1934, when Boris was forty-four, he wrote to Leonid: 'You were a real man, a Colossus, and before this image, large and wide as the world, I am a complete nonentity and in every respect still a boy as I was then.' In November 1945, a few months after Leonid died, Boris told Josephine:

'I wrote to father that he need not have been dismayed that his enormous services have not received even a hundredth of the recognition they deserve ... that there is no justice in our lives, that he will ultimately triumph, having lived such a sincere, natural, interesting, itinerant and rich life.'

Where Leonid undoubtedly triumphed was in his rich personal life. His marriage to Rosalia was blessed; the couple were genuinely devoted to each other. Leonid was a rare artist in that he was a truly contented man. He considered himself lucky both to pursue a profession he revered and to marry a woman he loved. Unlike many artists, he always had time for his children. Unfortunately, the same cannot be said of Boris. The writer always put his work before his family, while they would not have considered it appropriate to challenge this. 'He was a genius,' Evgeny said of his father, Boris, by way of explanation for the writer's parenting shortfalls. 'He was that rare thing – a free man. He was much ahead of his time and it was not easy for him to follow his dream. It is so sad if you have to sacrifice your genius for your family. We only went to him when strictly necessary. I was glad of his assistance but never asked for it. We didn't bother him. He was a man of power and we knew and respected that.'

None of Leonid's children ever felt that they were secondary to his art or that anything could be more important in their father's life. In fact they became his art. Contemporaries used to joke that 'Pasternak's children were the main breadwinners in the family', as they were his favoured subjects. A master of rapid drawings, capturing characteristic movements and poses, his charcoal sketches of family life are considered some of his most powerful compositions. From these affectionate drawings alone, it is clear that Rosalia was a devoted mother. Her body is always portrayed leaning in towards her children; whether she is sitting with them at the piano or watching them study or draw, her quiet maternal presence is palpable.

Leonid met Rosalia Isidorovna Kaufman in Odessa, where he grew up, in 1885 when he was twenty-three and she was eighteen. The Pasternaks were of Jewish descent, whose forebears had settled in Odessa in the eighteenth century. Leonid had blue eyes, was slender and handsome with a trim goatee beard. 'He always wore a kind of cravat,' remembers his grandson Charles: 'Never a tie but a loose white silk scarf tied in a bow. He was not a vain man but he must have fancied his visage as he never stopped making self-portraits.' Charles had a boyish fascination with the nail on the fourth finger of Leonid's right hand. 'He specifically let it grow long so that he could scrape paint that he didn't want off a canvas.'

Like Leonid, Rosalia possessed precocious talent. She was a concert pianist who, as a child of nine, had made her public debut to great acclaim in a Mozart piano concerto. From the age of five, she would sit under the grand piano and listen to her older sister's piano lessons, then reproduce by memory the pieces her sister was playing. Rosalia was a comforting-looking woman, well padded, with thick chestnut hair always in a neat bun and knowing dark eyes. 'I felt more attracted to Rosa than to her girlfriends and other young women,' Leonid recalled. 'This was not only because of her exceptional musical talent – like any natural gift, this conquered all – but also because of her mind, her rare good nature and her spiritual purity.' Despite Leonid's attraction to her, he initially fought against a relationship, worried that it might impede her career as a pianist. Leonid was also unsure what he, as an impoverished artist, could offer her, as she was already a professor of the Odessa Conservatory. Fate decreed otherwise, as they kept bumping into each other. Before proposing to her (they married on Valentine's Day in 1889) Leonid sank into an uncharacteristic period of reflective apathy: 'One unsolved question did not cease to torment me: was it possible to combine the serious and all-embracing pursuit of art with family life?'

He need not have worried; for him it definitely was. Sadly, less so for Rosalia. After Boris was born on 10 February 1890, she stopped playing in public, although she still played privately and in her spare time earned money giving piano lessons. In 1895 she came out of retirement to play part of a series of benefits for the Moscow School of Painting and Architecture, where Leonid taught. The journal *Moskovskiye Vedomosti* reported that 'the very talented pianist Mrs Rosalia Isidovna Pasternak (wife of a famous artist) played the piano part of Schumann's quintet'. The concerts were a resounding success.

As they grew up, the children bore witness to their mother's career sacrifice and it saddened them. During a family holiday in Schliersee, Bavaria, Josephine overheard her father say to her mother: 'I now realise that I ought not to have married you. It was my fault. You have sacrificed your genius to me and the family. Of us two, you are the greater artist.' The children considered this too noble. 'It would have been better if we had not been born,' wrote Lydia, 'but maybe it was vindicated by the existence of Boris.'

Josephine recalled of their childhood: 'When I think back about our family as it was before we parted (during the Revolution) I see it thus: three suns or stars, and three minor bodies related to them. The minor bodies were: Alexander, Lydia and myself. The suns were father, mother and Boris. Mother was the brightest sun. However outstanding they were, both with father and Boris one could detect endeavour, quest, in their art. Mother never tried to shine: she shone as naturally as people breathe.'

In 1903 the Pasternaks took a summer cottage on an estate in the village of Obolenskoye, 100 kilometres south-west of Moscow. Evenings were spent with Rosalia at the piano, her music flooding through the open windows. While the teenage Boris played Cowboys and Indians with his brother Alexander, they stumbled across the next-door house where the pianist Scriabin was staying. Listening to him compose his *The Divine Poem*, part of his Symphony No 3 in C Minor, Boris was so enchanted that he decided that he too would become a composer. Thanks to Rosalia's tutelage, he was already an accomplished pianist. 'From his childhood, my brother was distinguished by an inordinate passion to accomplish things patently beyond his powers, ludicrously inappropriate to his character and cast of mind,' said Alexander.

Part of what Alexander was referring to was a fantasy of his brother's which ended in disaster. The veranda of the family's rented dacha had a sweeping view across water meadows and every evening peasant girls galloped by on their unsaddled horses, taking the herd to the grazing land for the night. They were illuminated by the setting sun. Its glowing rays captured the bay horses, the motley skirts and shawls and the sunburnt faces of the riders. Boris longed to ride in this romantic cavalcade, despite having no riding experience. When, on 6 August, one of the peasants failed to show up, Boris rode off on a wild horse that bucked him to the ground. The whole family watched, aghast, as he fell under the horse and the herd thundered over him. The accident left him with a broken leg which, when the cast came off after six weeks, remained shorter than the other. This caused a lifelong limp. As a result, he was unfit for military service – which may, in the long run, have saved his life.

The disability rankled. Boris hated failure in anything, and this helps explain why, despite considerable success in composition, he decided to give up his musical aspirations when he realised that he had a 'secret trouble'. 'I lacked perfect pitch,' Pasternak wrote later. 'This was quite unnecessary to me in my work but the discovery was a grief and humiliation and I took it as proof that my music was rejected by heaven or fate. I had not the courage to stand up to all these blows and I lost heart. For six years I had lived for music. Now I tore it up and flung it from me as you throw away your dearest treasure.'

However, when he had abandoned music, fate played her hand: he took up verse and found his true calling. Once he discovered his vocation as a writer, it was his father's working relationship with Leo Tolstoy that was to indelibly influence Boris's creative life and stringent writing ethic.

In 1898 Leonid's career hit a high note when Leo Tolstoy commissioned him to illustrate *Resurrection*, which had taken him ten years to write. Tolstoy had met Leonid five years earlier in 1893 when he attended the regular exhibition of the Wanderers (a show case of distinguished Moscow and St Petersburg artists). Tolstoy was introduced to Leonid and shown Pasternak's painting *The Debutante*. Leonid was invited to Tolstoy's Moscow home the following Friday for tea and told to bring his portfolio. When Tolstoy saw some illustrations that Leonid had done with *War and Peace* in mind, he turned to Leonid and said: 'They offer the squirrel nuts when it's lost its teeth. You know, when I wrote *War and*

*Peace*, I dreamed of having such illustrations. It's really wonderful, just wonderful!'

Working with Tolstoy on *Resurrection* at Yasnaya Polyana, the Tolstoys' country estate situated in the Tula region, was a privileged, immensely enjoyable yet challenging time for Leonid. 'Some of the most memorable and happiest days of my life were spent reading the manuscript in the daytime and conversing with Tolstoy in the evenings.' He would walk up and down the hall with the writer, discussing what he had read and planned to illustrate the following day. Once, when Tolstoy saw one of Leonid's illustrations he exclaimed: 'Ah, you express that better than me. I must go and change my prose.'

Under incredible pressure to meet the deadlines of Tolstoy's St Petersburg publisher and do the writer he worshipped justice, Leonid diligently completed thirty-three illustrations in six weeks, afterwards falling ill, burnt out with exhaustion. This intense collaboration made an enduring impression on Boris. 'It was from our kitchen that my father's remarkable illustrations for Tolstoy's *Resurrection* were dispatched,' he said.

The novel appeared, chapter by chapter, in the journal *Niva*, a periodical edited by the Petersburg publisher Fyodor Marx. Boris was struck by how feverishly his father had to work to meet the deadline. 'I remember how pressed for time father was. The issues of the journal came out regularly without delay,' he wrote. 'One had to be in time for each issue. Tolstoy kept back the proofs, revising them again and again. There was the risk that the illustrations would be at variance with the corrections subsequently introduced into it. But my father's sketches came from the same source whence the author obtained his observations, the courtroom, the transit prison, the country, the railway. It was the reservoir of living details, the identical realistic presentation of ideas that saved him from the danger of digressing from the spirit of the original.'

In view of the urgency of the matter, special precautions were taken to prevent any delay in the sending of the illustrations. The services of the conductors of the express trains at the Nikolayevsky railway were enlisted; the guards on the express trains to St Petersburg acted as messengers.

'My imagination was impressed by the sight of a uniformed guard waiting outside our kitchen door, as on a station platform outside a railway carriage,' wrote Boris. 'Joiner's glue sizzled on the range. The drawings were hastily sprinkled with fixative and glued on sheets of cardboard, and the parcels, wrapped up, tied and sealed up with sealing wax and handed over to the guard.' The whole family was involved in this endeavour – Rosalia used to help with the pressured business of packing and mailing the illustrations, while the children watched, rapt.

Thirty years later, on 21 May 1939, Pasternak wrote to his father: 'Leo Tolstoy's granddaughter [Sofia Andreyevna Tolstaya-Esenina] came to see me with a friend of hers and they talked a great deal about you. She had already spoken to me several times before about how she loved your illustrations. "Of all Tolstoy's illustrators, not one has come close to him or embodies his ideas so faithfully as your father" – "Yes, yes, the drawings for *Resurrection*, they're just brilliant," put in the other. And we all agreed that you have no equal.'

Tolstoy died on 7 November 1910 while 'fleeing the world' at Astapovo train station. The world's press was camped out on the platform. Leonid was summoned to make a drawing of the deceased writer on his death bed and took the twenty-year-old Boris with him. Boris watched as his father drew in pastel the corner of the room where Countess Tolstoy sat 'shrunken, mournful, humiliated' at the head of the iron bed where her husband was lying. Sofia Tolstoy explained to Leonid that after Tolstoy left her, due to antagonisms between her and his disciples, she had tried to drown herself and had to be dragged out of the lake at Yasnaya Polyana. It took Leonid fifteen minutes to complete the death-bed drawing. In his notebook, Leonid wrote: 'Astapovo. Morning. Sofya Andreyevna at his bedside. The people's farewell. Finale of a family tragedy.'

*   *   *

The summer before the 1917 Revolution, Boris Pasternak was visiting his parents at the apartment they rented in a manor house in a Molodi estate, 60 kilometres south of Moscow. It was thought that the house had served as a lodge for Catherine II's journeys to the south of Crimea. The generous proportions of the manor and grand layout of the park, with its converging avenues, suggested royal origins. While his first collection of poetry, *Above the Barriers*, was being prepared, Pasternak went to work as an industrial office clerk to support the war effort. The twenty-seven-year-old poet was given a job in a chemical works in an industrial town called Tikhiye Gory, on the banks of the River Kama in the Republic of Tatarstan. This town, known as 'Little Manchester', was at an important intersection of geographical and trade routes uniting East and Western Russia. While fulfilling his daily filing duties, Pasternak did not cease his literary work. In order to earn money he began translating Swinburne's trilogy of dramas about Mary Stuart, Queen of Scots.

'In March 1917, when news of the Revolution that had broken out in Petersburg came through, I set out for Moscow,' Pasternak later wrote. 'At the Izhevsk factory I was to find and pick up Zbarsky, a fine fellow of an engineer who had been sent there on a work assignment, place myself at his disposal and then continue my journey with him. From the Tikhiye Gory we sped on in a covered wagon on runners, for an evening, right through the night and part of the following day. Wrapped up in three long coats and half buried in hay, I rolled on the floor of the sleigh like some bulky sack, robbed of any freedom of movement.'

The February Revolution was focused around Petrograd (now St Petersburg). In the chaos, members of the Imperial Parliament assumed control of the country, forming a provisional government. The army leadership felt that they did not have the means to suppress the Revolution, resulting in Tsar Nicholas's abdication. A period of dual power ensued, during which the provisional government held state power while the national network of 'soviets', led by socialists, had the allegiance of the working classes and the political left. During this period there were frequent mutinies, protests and strikes as attempts at political reform failed and the proletariat gained power. In the October Revolution

(November in the Gregorian calendar) the Bolsheviks, led by Lenin, overthrew the provisional government and established the Russian Soviet Federative Socialist Republic, moving the capital from Petrograd to Moscow in 1918 out of fear of imminent foreign invasion. The Bolsheviks appointed themselves as leaders of various government ministries and seized control of the countryside. Civil war subsequently erupted among the 'Reds' (Bolsheviks) and 'Whites' (anti-socialist factions). It continued for several years, creating poverty, famine and fear, especially amongst the intelligentsia. The Bolsheviks eventually defeated the Whites and all rival socialists, paving the way for the creation of the Union of Soviet Socialist Republics in 1922.

In *Doctor Zhivago*, Yury Zhivago bears witness to the momentous political upheaval:

The paper was a late extra, printed on one side only; it gave the official announcement from Petersburg that a Soviet of People's Commissars had been formed and that Soviet power and the Dictatorship of the Proletariat were established in Russia. There followed the first decrees of the new government and various brief news items received by telegraph and telephone.

The blizzard slashed at Yury's eyes and covered the printed page with a grey, rustling snowy gruel, but it was not the snowstorm that prevented Yury from reading. He was shaken and overwhelmed by the greatness of the moment and the thought of its significance for centuries to come.

After 1917 life in Moscow was harrowing. Food and fuel were scarce and living conditions poor. Fortunately, Boris's brother Alexander, a budding architect, knew exactly which bits of roof beams could be cut away and sawn up for firewood without causing the whole house to collapse, as a number did in the Moscow winter of 1918–19. Fuel was in such demand that at night Boris broke planks from rotten fences or stole firewood from government places, and guests invited for tea brought a log as a gift instead of sweets or chocolates. In the grey hours before sunrise, the

Pasternak children would set out for the Boloto, a market where villagers sold what vegetables they could. In *Zhivago*, Pasternak recalls the privations and pressures of war, the resulting famine and spread of typhoid:

> Winter was at hand and in the world of men the air was heavy with something as inexorable as the coming death of nature. It was on everybody's lips.
>
> Food and logs had to be got in. But in those days of the triumph of materialism, matter had become an abstract notion, and food and firewood were replaced by the problems of alimentation and fuel supply.
>
> The people in the towns were as helpless as children in the face of the unknown – of that unknown which swept every known usage aside and left nothing but desolation in its wake – although it was the offspring and creation of the towns.
>
> People were still talking and deceiving themselves as their daily life struggled on, limping and shuffling to its unknown destination. But Yury saw it as it was, he could see that it was doomed, and that he and such as he were sentenced to destruction. Ordeals were ahead, perhaps death. The days were counted, and these days were running out before his eyes.
>
> … He understood that he was a pygmy before the monstrous machine of the future. He both feared and loved that future and was secretly proud of it, and as though for the last time, as if saying good-bye, was avidly aware of the trees and clouds and of the people walking in the streets, of the great Russian city struggling through misfortune – and he was ready to sacrifice himself to make things better but was powerless to do anything.

In 1921, to Boris's great distress, his sisters and parents left Russia and travelled to Germany. Unbeknownst to any of them, they would never live in Russia together again. Deprived of her rights for higher education in Russia – just as any offspring of a non-proletarian family in the post-revolutionary climate was – Josephine went to Berlin on her own, keen to enter a university and rent accommodation for her parents, who intended to come after her. She was soon joined by Lydia, Leonid and Rosalia. Boris and Alexander stayed on at the family's studio apartment at 14 Volkhonka Street in Moscow, as they had embarked on their respective careers as writer and architect. Rosalia and Leonid had managed to obtain visas for Germany for a long course of health treatment – Leonid had to have a cataract removed and Rosalia had heart problems. The hungry years of the Revolution had undermined their health, strength and spirit, while Leonid Pasternak was deeply concerned by the threat that he would lose his Moscow apartment to state requisition. However, it never occurred to any of the family that they would not be reunited in Russia after the country's upheavals.

Josephine's last memories of her childhood in Moscow were the gruelling winters when the town was covered in snow and the citizens had to report at labour centres. 'They were given spades and perhaps a day's ration and had to clear the roads,' she remembered. 'Lydia was underage and did not need to report, but she went instead of me as I was not strong enough to shovel the heavy snow. She and Boris were in the same group. It must have been an unforgettable day … A day of such brilliance of sun and snow, of purity of landscape, of concerted effort and of friendliness among the people at work.' In *Doctor Zhivago*, to escape starvation and the political uncertainties in Moscow after the 1917 Revolution, the Zhivago family travels to Varykino, Tonya's ancestral estate in the Urals. When their train is halted by snowdrifts, the civilian passengers are commandeered to clear the rails. Yury Zhivago remembers these three days as the most pleasant part of their journey:

But the sun sparkled on the blinding whiteness and Yury cut clean slices out of the snow, starting landfalls of dry diamond fires. It reminded him of his childhood. He saw himself in their yard at home, dressed in a braided hood and black sheepskin fastened with hooks and eyes sewn into the curly fleece, cutting the same dazzling snow into cubes and pyramids and cream buns and fortresses and cave cities. Life had had a splendid taste in those far-off days, every-thing had been a feast for the eyes and for the stomach!

But at this time, too, during their three days of work in the open air, the workers had a feeling of pleasantly full stomachs. And no wonder. At night they were issued with great chunks of hot fresh bread (no one knew where it came from or by whose orders); it had a tasty crisp crust, shiny on top, cracked at the side and with bits of charcoal baked into it underneath.

Berlin in the 1920s was a period of high productivity for Leonid Pasternak, as the city had become a meeting place of the Russian intelligentsia. Over 100,000 Russians were living in exile. Leonid painted and befriended Albert Einstein, and the opera singer Chaliapin, who was rehearsing for his Berlin recital. He also sketched and painted the Russian composer, pianist and conductor Prokofiev at the piano, painter Max Liebermann and the Austrian poet Rainer Maria Rilke, who was to enjoy an intense correspondence with Boris.

It was an immeasurable source of pain for Boris that after his parents left Moscow, he only saw them once again. He visited them in Berlin in 1922 and lived with them for nearly a year with his first wife, Evgenia. Afterwards, in the ensuing correspondence, lasting over twenty years, the constant ache of his missing them and echo of regret is tangible.

Conditions meanwhile were worsening throughout Russia, with food shortages and ration cards introduced in 1929. Collectivisation was regarded as the solution to the crisis of agricultural distribution, mainly in grain deliveries in Russia. In 1930, there was a decree of the Federation of Soviet Writers' Associations providing for the formation of writers' shock brigades, to be sent out to the collective and state farms.

The conditions that Pasternak witnessed at the state farms stressed and depressed him; he regarded what he saw as inhuman. 'Among them was the war with its bloodshed and its horrors, its homelessness, savagery and isolation, its trials and worldly wisdom which is taught,' he later wrote in *Doctor Zhivago*. 'Here too were the lonely little towns where you were stranded by the war, and the people with whom it threw you together. Such a new thing, too, was the Revolution, not the one idealised in student fashion in 1905, but this new upheaval, today's born of the war, bloody, pitiless, elemental, the soldiers' revolution, led by the professional, the Bolsheviks.' It made you question your loyalty to what mattered in life. Everything and everyone felt deposed. Nothing seemed sacred anymore; not even loyalty to your spouse:

> Everything had changed suddenly – the tone, the moral climate; you didn't know what to think, who to listen to. As if all of your life you had been led by the hand like a small child and suddenly you were on your own, you had to learn to walk by yourself. There was no one around, neither family nor people whose judgement you respected. At such a time you felt the need to entrust yourself to something absolute – life or truth or beauty – of being ruled by it now that man-made rules had been discarded. You needed to surrender to some such ultimate purpose more fully, more unreservedly than you had ever done in the old familiar, peaceful days, in the old life which was now abolished and gone for good.

Josephine Pasternak last set eyes on Boris at Berlin train station in the summer of 1935. On 23 June the Kremlin had insisted that Boris attend an anti-fascist writers' congress in Paris. This summons was a rushed exercise in Soviet propaganda, as the 'Congress for the Defence of Culture' had already commenced in Paris two days earlier. The Kremlin recognised suddenly that Boris Pasternak's absence from a line-up that included the world's leading writers – including Gide, Bloch and Cocteau from France, W. H. Auden, E. M. Forster and Aldous Huxley from Britain, as well as Brecht and Heinrich Mann from Germany – would be a cause of international dismay. Despite suffering from chronic insomnia and depression so debilitating that it had led him to spend months in the writers' country sanatorium outside Moscow earlier that spring, the Kremlin ordered Pasternak to go immediately to Paris. He was, however, granted six hours free to stop off in Berlin.

Boris had telegrammed his family from Russia prior to his departure to say that he dearly hoped to see Josephine and Frederick along with his parents during this fleeting visit. Rosalia and Leonid were in Munich at the time and regrettably were not strong enough to make an impromptu journey to Berlin. But Josephine and Frederick immediately travelled overnight from Munich, arriving at the family's Berlin apartment the following morning to await Boris's arrival.

Josephine was troubled by a new fragility in her older brother's emotional state. He had been unwell for months, exhausted and distressed by Stalin's reign of terror on writers and his own inner torment. Despite being hailed as 'one of the greatest poets of our time' when he was introduced at the writers' congress the following day, he felt ashamed of his esteemed reputation. Afterwards he wrote to his father that the whole event had left him with 'the bitter dregs of a terrible, inflated self-importance, ludicrous over-estimation and embarrassment, and – worst of all – a sort of gilded captivity'. So severe was his nervous exhaustion and depression that when initially requested to go to Paris for the conference, he had rung Stalin's secretary in person to protest that he was too unwell to attend. 'If there was a war and you were called to serve, would you go?' he was asked. Yes, Boris replied. Well, 'regard yourself as having been called to serve', was the reply.

Within twenty-four hours an ill-fitting suit was bought for him and two days later he arrived at midday by taxi at his parents' apartment in Berlin, which Josephine and Frederick had opened up in readiness for his visit. 'I do not remember my brother's first words or his greeting, or how we all embraced each other: everything was overshadowed by the strangeness of his bearing,' recalled Josephine. 'He behaved as if only a few weeks, not twelve years, had separated us. Every now and again he burst into tears. And he had one wish only: to sleep!'

Josephine and Frederick drew the curtains and insisted that Boris lie down on the sofa. They sat with him while he slept for two or three hours. Josephine was increasingly anxious, as she knew that Boris had to be at the Friedrichstrasse train station for around six that evening and as yet they had not had time to talk. When Boris woke up he seemed mildly refreshed; however Frederick tried to persuade him to rest further and continue on to Paris the following morning. The three of them travelled by underground to the Soviet embassy to request permission for an overnight stay in Berlin. Despite Frederick pleading that his brother-in-law was in no fit state to continue the journey, the request was turned down.

En route to the station, they stopped off at a nondescript hotel to have something to eat. Sitting in the visitors' lounge, with guests drifting through, Josephine observed that her brother's face clouded with sadness. Occasionally he would speak in his familiar booming voice, complaining about the journey ahead to Paris. While Frederick went to the train station to make enquiries, Boris at last opened up to his sister during their last precious hour together. Oblivious to the people coming and going around them, they sat huddled close, while the distraught writer tried to control his emotion and suppress his tears.

All of a sudden he spoke with perfect clarity. 'He said: "You know, I owe it to Zina – I must write about her. I will write a novel … A novel about that girl … Beautiful, misguided. A veiled beauty in the private rooms of night restaurants … Her cousin, a guardsman would take her there. She, of course, could not help it. She was so young, so unspeakably attractive …"' Boris, who had not yet met Olga Ivinskaya, was referring to his second wife, Zinaida Neigaus, whom he had married the year before. The marriage was already running into difficulties, which caused Boris fierce guilt and disquiet, not least because he had already left his first wife for Zinaida, who was then married to his friend, the eminent pianist Genrickh Gustavovich Neigaus.

Josephine was stunned: 'I could not believe my ears. Was this the man as I had known him, unique, towering above platitudes and trivialities, above easy ways in art and above cheap subjects – this man now forgetting his austere creative principles, intending to lend his inimitable prose to a subject both petty and vulgar? Surely he would never write one of those sentimental stories which flourished at the turn of the century?'

An hour later, choking back tears as she waved him off from the platform, Josephine tried to take in Boris's anguished face as he stood by the window of the departing train. She clutched the arm of Frederick, who called out to his brother-in-law: 'Go to bed straightaway.' Yet it was only early on a summer's evening. And then, Josephine heard Boris's deep, distinctive voice for the last time in her life: 'Yes … if only I could go to sleep.'

In his personal life Boris was conflicted on many levels. He could not assuage his guilt at the way he had treated his first wife and, feeling emotionally shredded, he was unproductive in his work. His parents were bitterly disappointed that he did not return to Munich after the writers' congress in Paris, en route to Russia, which he had promised them he would try to do. Boris wrote rather defensively to his father on 3 July: 'I'm incapable of doing anything whatever on my own, and if you imagine that a week's stay near Munich is going to put right what's been wrong for two months (progressive loss of strength, sleeplessness every night and growing neurasthenia), you're expecting too much. I don't know how it all came about. Perhaps it's all a punishment to me for Zhenia [Evgenia] and the suffering I caused her at the time.'

If only Boris had known that this visit would be his last chance to see his parents again. In the summer of 1938, Leonid and Rosalia left fascist Germany for London, where they intended to rest and get strong enough for their eagerly anticipated final journey home to Russia. They wanted to visit Lydia, who had previously moved to Oxford in 1935 and married the British psychiatrist Eliot Slater, whom she had met in Munich. She was expecting her first child. Leonid and Rosalia were followed to England by Josephine and Frederick, along with their children Charles and Helen. With the German invasion of Austria, Josephine and Frederick's Austrian passports no longer protected them and they had fled from Munich, abandoning their home. After a family reunion and period of recuperation, Leonid and Rosalia fully planned to move back to the country where their hearts lay: their homeland, Russia.

Rosalia's unexpected death, from a brain haemorrhage in her sleep, on 22 August 1939, left the family reeling and desolate. Boris wrote to his siblings on 10 October from Moscow: 'this is the first letter that I have been able to write to you, for various reasons, after Mama's death. It has turned my life upside down, devastated it and made it meaningless; and in an instant, as though drawing me after it, it has brought me closer to my own grave. It aged me in an hour. A cloud of unkindness and chaos has settled over my whole existence; I'm permanently distracted, downcast and dazed from grief, astonishment, tiredness and pain.'

A week after Rosalia's death, world war broke out. Leonid lived the rest of his life in Oxford, surrounded by his daughters and grandchildren. He would never see his sons, Boris or Alexander, again.

During the war, Pasternak was actively involved and served as a firewatcher on Volkhonka Street. Several times he dealt with the incendiary bombs that fell on the family apartment's roof. With others, he spent time on drill, fire-watching and shooting practice, delighted to discover that he had skill as a marksman. In spite of the war, Boris enjoyed moments of happiness, feeling that he was collaborating in the interest of Mother Russia and national survival. Yet amidst the camaraderie, there was the constant 'acuteness of pain' of the 'excessive intolerable separation' from his family.

Leonid Pasternak died on 31 May 1945, weeks after Russia's final victory in the war. 'When Mother died it was as if harmony had abandoned the world,' said Josephine. 'When Father died it seemed that truth had left it.' Boris shed 'an ocean of tears', on Leonid's death (he had often addressed him as 'my wonder papa' in his letters). It troubled the writer greatly that he had never been able to replicate the rare depth and quality of enduring, harmonious marital love that his parents had experienced. In most of his correspondence with his father, he rails against his own emotional shortcomings, endlessly verbally flagellating himself – 'I'm like someone bewitched, as if I'd cast a spell on myself. I've destroyed the lives of my family' – and relentlessly exposing his acute sense of guilt, which runs like a continuous fever through him.

Given how profoundly he revered his parents and loved his siblings, his choice to stay in Soviet Russia and to live apart from them was surprising. Despite the unbearable oppression of Stalin's censorship of the 1920s and '30s, he did not consider leaving Russia. On 2 February 1932 he had written to his parents about his calling to his beloved 'Mother land': 'This fate of not belonging to oneself, of living in a prison cell warmed from all sides – it transforms you, it makes you a prisoner of time. For herein too lies the primeval cruelty of poor Russia; once she bestows her love upon someone, her beloved is caught forever within her sights. It is as if he stands before her in the Roman arena, forced to provide her with a spectacle in return for her love.'

He continuously made it plain that he did not want to live the life of an exile. Yet, after the Revolution he was in emotional exile from his family. However successful he became, there is a sense that he was rudderless without them. Always searching, in many ways, he was lost. It was a constant source of shame and self-reproach that he was not able to emulate his parents' stable and happy union. He may have fallen in love easily, but his inability to sustain a happy marriage was one of his greatest torments.

# 3

# The Cloud Dweller

It was at a party in Moscow in 1921 that the thirty-one-year-old Boris met the painter Evgenia Vladimirovna Lure. Petite and elegant, with blue eyes and soft brown hair, Evgenia came from a traditional Jewish intellectual family from Petrograd. She spoke French fluently and had a cultural finesse which Boris was drawn to. His attraction no doubt bolstered by the fact that Leonid knew Evgenia's family and heartily approved of the union. Boris, who always sought his father's approval, duly fell in love with her.

'One wanted to bathe in her face,' he said, but also pointed out that 'she always needed this illumination in order to be beautiful, she had to have happiness in order to be liked'. An insecure and vulnerable beauty, she was flattered by the famous writer's interest in her. By the spring of 1922, they were married. 'Zhenya' was twenty-one years old.

If relationships act as mirrors to our flaws and our needs, Boris learned much about himself during his first marriage. Evgenia also had a volatile, artistic streak and their clash of egos was not conducive to marital harmony. Boris's fame was impacting his ego; he did not consider Evgenia enough of an artist to merit her difficult, emotional behaviour. Of the two of them, he considered himself the greater artist and assumed Evgenia would lay aside her ambition to help foster his, just as he had witnessed his mother do for his father. While he was by nature active, preferring to run everywhere rather than walk – probably to help burn off his excess nervous energy – Evgenia was languid, preferring to sit around the house. Energetically, they did not seem compatible.

Boris travelled with his new wife to Berlin for a holiday in the summer of 1922. It was Evgenia's first time abroad and the newlyweds relished their time in the German capital, visiting bustling cafes and art galleries. While Evgenia liked to sightsee and enjoy the pulsating life of fashionable quarters, Boris, like Tolstoy, was more drawn to the 'real Germany': the misery of slums in the northern districts of the city.

Boris was paid in dollars for some of his translation work. He spent his money freely. Ashamed of having so much relative to the poverty of so many, his tips, like his brother-in-law Frederick's, were always blushingly generous. According to Josephine, who sometimes accompanied her brother on his walks around Berlin, he also 'showered hard cash upon pale urchins with outstretched hands'. Boris explained his and Tolstoy's attraction to the less privileged: 'people of an artistic nature will be attracted by the poor, by those with a difficult, modest lot in life. There everything is warmer and riper, and there is more soul and colour there than anywhere else.'

Once the first cloudless weeks of gallery visiting and seeing old friends were over, the writer began to get restless, and irritable. Evgenia suffered from gingivitis, an inflammation of the gums, which caused her to cry a lot. But Boris was indifferent to her suffering. 'We, the family, sided with her,' explained Josephine, 'but what could we do? Boris did not display any kind of callousness: he simply seemed fed up with the incongruity of the whole set-up – the boarding house, the lack of privacy, his wife's uncontrollable tearful moods.' The family raised eyebrows further when he decided to take a room of his own where he could work in peace. This they considered sheer extravagance. The last straw came when Evgenia discovered that she was pregnant. The quarrels became fiercer: 'A child! Slavery! It is your concern, after all,' Boris would say to his wife, 'you are the mother.'

'What?' Zhenya would cry out, 'mine? Mine? Oh! You, you – you forget that I am devoted to my art, you selfish creature!'

The main source of their tension was whether and when they should return to Moscow. Boris was keen to get back to Russia, while Evgenia preferred Berlin, 'Russia's second capital'. The vitality of Russian intellectual life reached its zenith in the early 1920s, then declined under the impact of widespread political unrest and soaring inflation. The bleakness of Germany's fate saddened Pasternak, who later wrote: 'Germany was cold and starving, deceived about nothing and deceiving no one, her hand stretched out to the age like a beggar (a gesture not her own at all) and the entire country on crutches.' Typically theatrical, he added that it took him 'a daily bottle of brandy and Charles Dickens to forget it'.

Back in Moscow the couple moved into the Pasternaks' old apartment on Volkhonka Street. Soon after returning, on 23 September 1923, their son, Evgeny Borisovich Pasternak, was born. 'He is so tiny – how could we give him a new, an unfamiliar name?' Boris wrote. 'So we chose what was closest to him: the name of his mother – Zhenya.'

Uncertain of his income, and unable to make ends meet with the advances from publishers for his own work and translations, Pasternak worked for a short time as a researcher for the Library of the People's Commissariat for Education in Moscow. Here he was responsible for reading through foreign papers and censoring – cutting out – all references to Lenin. He turned this mundane exercise to his advantage: scouring the foreign press enabled him to keep abreast of Western European literature. During intervals he read, amongst others, Proust, Conrad and Hemingway. He also joined the Left Front of Arts, whose journal, *LEF*, was edited by the poet and actor Vladimir Mayakovski, who had been two years below Boris at school. When Boris became part of the front it was more as a gesture of solidarity to his old associate than a genuine desire to become actively involved in the group and its revolutionary agenda, and he broke with them in 1928. That same year he sent the first part of his autobiographical prose offering *Safe Conduct* to a literary journal for publication.

In April 1930 Mayakovski suffered a mental breakdown, penned a suicide note and killed himself. His funeral, attended by around 150,000 people, was the third-largest event of public mourning in Soviet history, surpassed only by those of Lenin and Stalin. In 1936, Stalin proclaimed that he 'was and remains the best and most talented poet of the Soviet epoch'. Olga later wrote of Mayakovski: 'In many ways the antidote of Pasternak, he combined powerful poetic gifts with a romantic anguish which could find relief only in total service to the Revolution – at the cost of suppressing in himself the urgent personal emotions evident in his pre-revolutionary work'.

Increasingly frustrated that he did not have the freedom to write what his heart desired, Pasternak found his daily life almost intolerable. Working conditions – always of utmost importance to Boris – had become unbearable. The entire Volkhonka Street block had been requisitioned by the state and turned into one communal apartment housing six families: a total of twenty people, sharing one bathroom and kitchen. Boris and his family were granted permission to use his father's old art studio as their living space. It was incredibly noisy, so Pasternak moved his work to the area which served as a dining room. Hardly conducive to concentration: it was open house to the other families, their visitors and relatives. Pasternak was at this time working on an intricate translation into Russian of Rainer Maria Rilke's haunting 'Requiem for a Lady Friend', which the writer had penned as a tribute to his friend the painter Paula Modersohn-Becker, who suddenly died eighteen days after giving birth to her first child.

By 1930 Pasternak had become infatuated again – this time with Zinaida Neigaus. What is extraordinary is that for a man with such a fierce sense of morality, Pasternak failed to honour one of the most basic codes of life – he ran off with the wife of one of his best friends.

He admired the esteemed pianist Genrikh Neigaus almost to the point of obsession. In a letter to his mother on 6 March 1930 he had written: 'The only bright spot in our existence is the very varied performances by my latest friend (for the past year), Heinrich Neuhaus [Genrikh Neigaus].

We – a few of his friends – have got into the habit of spending the rest of the night after a concert at one another's homes. There's abundant drink, with very modest snacks which for technical reasons are almost impossible to get hold of.'

Boris was quickly enthralled by Zinaida. The daughter of a St Petersburg factory owner, from a Russian Orthodox family, with her black hair cut short and well-defined lips, she was a classic 'art nouveau' figure. She was also everything Evgenia was not. While Evgenia was highly emotional and yearned for the fulfilment of her own creative life, Zinaida Neigaus was happy to facilitate her husband's career. When Genrikh gave winter concerts in cold halls, Zinaida would organise the arrival of the grand piano and lug the firewood in herself to stoke the fire. While her husband remained with his head in the artistic clouds – he was proud of telling friends that his practical skills were limited to fastening a safety pin – Zinaida raised their two sons, Adrian and Stanislav. She was endlessly energetic, robust, domestic and practical, unlike the elegant but languid Evgenia. Boris's nephew Charles, who met both women, remembered: 'Despite Boris's ardent description of Zinaida, I found her (admittedly more than twenty-five years later in 1961) one of the ugliest women I have ever met. Evgenia was softer, more sensitive and far more attractive than the harsh, raven-haired, chain-smoking Zinaida.'

Pasternak's interest in Zinaida grew during the summer of 1930 when he and Evgenia holidayed in Irpen near their friends, the historian Valentin Asmus, and his wife, Irina. Zinaida, Genrikh and their sons, then aged two and three, made up the party, along with Boris's brother Alexander (called Shura by the family), his wife Irina and their son Fedia. Irpen was beautiful: languorous heat, oxen grazing in the fields, meadows filled with wild flowers and in the far distance, the shaded banks of the River Irpen: summer at its fullest and finest. Boris and Evgenia's dacha stood in its own grounds surrounded by woods. Evgenia spent part of the summer painting an oil of a gigantic spreading oak tree which filled their plot of land. Long evenings were spent eating outside, watching fireflies and candles flicker in the dusk, discussing philosophy or literature, reciting poetry and listening to Genrikh play.

Zinaida had arranged for a grand piano to be delivered from Kiev so that her husband could practise for a recital that he was giving on the open-air stage of Kiev's Kupechesky Gardens on 15 August. The whole group from Irpen attended the concert. As the humid night progressed, thunderclouds gathered. Genrikh played the Chopin Concerto in E minor to great acclaim. By the end of the performance, a violent storm had broken out, with flashing lightening and thunderous noise. While the pianist and orchestra were sheltered under a platform canopy, the audience became drenched. Yet they all remained, happily entranced by the music. This evening and Genrikh's playing of Chopin's E-minor Concerto formed the subject of Pasternak's poem 'Ballade', which he dedicated to Genrikh.

While the summer proved to be the perfect tonic for Boris, Zinaida and Evgenia had taken against each other – perhaps intuitive to the fact that they were soon to become rivals. Initially, Zinaida tried to avoid the Pasternaks. She was not only alarmed by Boris's excessive praise of her domestic prowess – he would take any chance to help or gather firewood, bring in water from the well or hang around her to sniff her freshly scented ironing – but because she disliked Evgenia. Zinaida, rigorous to the point of military standards in her domesticity, found the elegant, ethereal Evgenia spoilt, lethargic and indulgent. Meanwhile Evgenia dismissed the stocky Italianate-looking woman as unsophisticated and coarse. Boris blithely ignored the mounting tensions between them.

The group broke up in September and by the end of the month, only Boris and Zinaida's families were left. They were all due to leave early next morning. The night before, Zinaida, having already packed, went to Boris's dacha to see if they were ready. She found Evgenia assembling the canvases that she had painted all summer, while Boris was busy putting things in suitcases with the painstaking care he had learned as a child. As there was little time left, Zinaida swept in and efficiently finished all their packing. Boris was lost in admiration. Zinaida, with her proprietorial and bossy nature, must, however, have been wholly unwelcome to poor Evgenia. Later, Boris expressed his veneration for Zinaida in the opening lines of the first poem in the collection *Second Birth*.

Would I have found the strength to act,
without the dream I dreamed in Irpen?
Which showed me what largesse a life could hold,
the night we packed our things to go.

The following evening the two families boarded the Moscow-bound train from Kiev. Genrikh and his two sons were asleep when Zinaida stepped out into the corridor to smoke. Boris left Evgenia and their son sleeping too, to follow Zinaida. For three hours they stood in the corridor talking as the train rattled on. Boris, who could contain himself no longer, confessed his love for Zinaida.

In an almost comical attempt to dampen his ardour, Zinaida recounted an episode from her childhood. She told Boris that from the age of fifteen she had been the mistress of her cousin, Nicolai Melitinsky, who was then forty-five. Her father, a military engineer, who had married her eighteen-year-old half-Italian mother when he was fifty, had died when Zinaida was ten. Finances had been tight for her mother, who scraped to send her to the Smolny Institute for girls. Meanwhile she and her middle-aged cousin met for trysts in a flat rented for that purpose. The guilt of these years was later to torment and appal her.

Naively, she had not bargained for the fact that the burgeoning novelist in Pasternak would be more engaged by her tale of humiliation than dispirited or disgusted. Shortly afterwards, Boris described her as a 'beauty of the Mary Queen of Scots type, judging by her fate'. Zinaida's teenage affair was to become Lara's 'backstory' in *Doctor Zhivago*: she is seduced by the much older lawyer Victor Ippolitovich Komarovsky: 'Her hands astonished him like a sublime idea. Her shadow on the wall of the hotel room had seemed to him the outline of innocence. Her vest was stretched over her breast, as firmly and simply as linen on an embroidery frame … Her dark hair was scattered and its beauty stung his eyes like smoke and ate into his heart.' When Lara talks of how damaged she is by her affair with Komarovksy, you can almost hear Zinaida on the train trying to discourage Boris. 'There is something broken in me, there is something broken in my whole life,' Lara says to Yury Zhivago. 'I discovered life much too early, I was made to discover it, and I was made to see it from the very worst side – a cheap, distorted version of it – through the eyes of an elderly roué. One of those useless, self-satisfied egoists of the old days who took advantage of everything and allowed themselves whatever they fancied.'

The seeds for Lara's character were sown by his meeting Zinaida, but when Boris later fell for Olga Ivinskaya, it was she who fully embodied as a living archetype his Lara.

Soon after his return from Irpen, Boris caused mayhem. Selfishly putting his own desires first, he confessed his love for Zinaida to Evgenia, then went to Genrikh and declared his devotion to the pianist's wife. In typical Boris style, the meeting was emotional and highly charged, with both men weeping. Boris spoke of his deep admiration and affection for Genrikh, and in an act of gauche insensitivity presented him with a copy of 'Ballade'. He then insisted that he was incapable of spending his life without Zinaida.

Boris's confidante, the poet Marina Tsvetaeva, thought her friend was falling headlong into disaster. 'I fear for Boris,' she wrote. 'In Russia poets die as an epidemic – a whole list of deaths in ten years. A catastrophe is unavoidable; first, the husband. Second, Boris has a wife and son; third, she is beautiful (Boris will be jealous) and fourth and chiefly, Boris is incapable of a happy love. For him to love means to be tortured.'

If Pasternak was tortured, so too were the women he loved. For months Zinaida would be torn by overwhelming guilt at breaking up her marriage. Boris was similarly racked over his treatment of Evgenia, writing to his parents in March 1931 that he had caused Evgenia 'undiminished suffering'. He concluded that his wife loved him because she did not understand him and deluded himself that she needed rest and freedom – 'complete freedom' to realise herself professionally. He appeared to be projecting – *he* needed freedom from his unhappy marriage to Evgenia, while the melodrama he thrived on was exactly the creative fuel he required.

On New Year's Day 1931, when Genrikh left for a concert tour of Siberia, Boris began obsessively calling on Zinaida, as often as three times a day, and temporarily moved out of the family's apartment. Unable to withstand Zinaida's vacillation any longer, after five months of ardent pursuit, he turned up at the Neigauses' Moscow home. Genrikh opened the door to Boris and addressed him in German as '*Der spätkommende Gast*' (the belated guest) and left to go to play at a concert.

Boris begged Zinaida once more to leave Genrikh. When Zinaida refused, he grabbed a bottle of iodine from the bathroom cupboard and in some sort of weak suicide bid, swallowed it all. His gullet burned and he started making involuntary chewing movements. When Zinaida realised what he had done she poured milk down Boris's throat to induce vomiting – he was sick twelve times – probably saving his life. A doctor came and 'rinsed out his insides' as a precaution against internal burns. The doctor insisted that the exhausted Pasternak must have complete bed rest for two days and that for the first night he must not move. So he stayed at the Neigauses, in a 'state of utter bliss' as Zinaida tended to him, moving noiselessly and efficiently around him.

Extraordinarily, such was his reverence for the melodramatic poet, that when Genrikh returned home at two o'clock that morning and learned of what had happened, it was to his wife that he turned and said: 'Well, are you satisfied? Has he now *proved* his love for you?' Genrikh then agreed to hand Zinaida over to Boris.

'I've fallen in love with Z[inaida] N[ikolaevna], the wife of my best friend, N[euhaus],' Pasternak wrote to his parents 8 March 1931. 'On January 1st he left for a concert tour of Siberia. I had feared this trip and tried to talk him out of it. In his absence, the thing that was inevitable and would have come about in any event, has acquired the stain of dishonesty. I've shown myself unworthy of N[euhaus] whom I still love and always will; I've caused prolonged, terrible and as yet undiminished suffering to Zhenia – and yet I am purer and more innocent than before I entered this life.'

Although Genrikh was shaken and hurt by Boris and Zinaida's affair – he had to stop playing in the middle of one concert during his Siberian tour and left the stage in tears – he was by no means an innocent party. Zinaida's eventual break with him was eased by Genrikh's own infidelities.

In 1929 he had sired a daughter by his former fiancée, Militsa Borodkina, and he married her in the mid-1930s.

In November 1932 Boris wrote to his parents and sisters from Moscow that Genrikh 'is a very contradictory person, and although everything settled down last autumn he still has moods in which he tells Zina that one day in an attack of misery he'll kill her and me. And yet he continues to meet us almost every other day, not only because he can't forget her, but because he can't part from me either. This creates some touching and curious situations.' However, Sir Isaiah Berlin, a great friend of Boris and Josephine, remembered that for years after Zinaida left him, Genrikh was a frequent visitor at the couple's dacha in Peredelkino, where Boris and Zinaida lived from 1936. After one typical Sunday lunch, Isaiah Berlin and Genrikh travelled back to Moscow together on the train. Sir Isaiah was somewhat taken aback when Genrikh turned to him and said, by way of explanation for why he had let his wife go: 'You know, Boris is really a saint.'

Sadly though, Boris was all too human. One of the things that plagued him most during his marriage to Zinaida was his fixation with Zinaida's teenage affair with Melitinsky. As mental torture is largely irrational, Zinaida was powerless to quell her husband's jealous anxieties. He often became paranoid staying in hotels because the 'semi-debauched set-up' reminded him of Zinaida's teenage trysts with Melitinksy. The story of Zinaida's youthful liaison became an obsession which triggered sleeplessness and mental depression. Boris once destroyed a photograph of Melitinksy which his daughter had bought to Zinaida as a gift following her cousin's death.

On 5 May 1931, when it was clear that Boris was not going to return to Evgenia, she and her son left Russia. They travelled to Germany, where Boris's family – Josephine, Frederick, Lydia, Rosalia and Leonid – greeted them with open arms, intent on cocooning them with familial love. 'Look after her,' Boris instructed his family. 'And we did,' said Josephine. Frederick organised and paid for Evgenia, who had been ill with tuberculosis, to spend the summer at a sanatorium in the Black Forest while her son stayed with the family at a pension on the Starnberger See in Munich.

Understandably, Boris's family in Germany, who loved Evgenia and adored little Evgeny, were shocked by Boris's behaviour. They saw him as having discarded his first wife and son, and handing responsibility over to them. Leonid's censure weighed heavily on Boris, who was left in no doubt that his family were appalled by the way he had treated Evgenia and Evgeny. On 18 December 1931, when Boris was openly living with Zinaida, his father wrote to him from Berlin:

Dear Boria!
What a lot I ought to write to you on all sorts of subjects – the terrible thing is that I know in advance that it's a pointless waste of time, because you, and all of you, act without thinking out the consequences in advance; you're irresponsible. And of course one's sorry for you as well, we are especially so – what a mess you've got yourself into, you poor boy! And instead of doing all you can to disentangle everything and as far as possible reduce the suffering on both sides, you're dragging it out even more and making it worse!

In early February 1932, Boris wrote Josephine a letter running over twenty pages. It is part an emotional confession of the guilt he feels at his treatment of Evgenia, part justification of his love for Zinaida – who he at one stage describes unflatteringly: 'always comes back from the hairdresser looking terrible, like a freshly polished boot' – part a catalogue of his neurotic mental state, which seems to veer near to madness; and part grateful homage to his sister, who Evgenia said 'did more for her than anyone else in the world' during the previous summer in Germany.

All is far from rosy. He admits to Josephine that he struggles with Zinaida's oldest son, Adrian, 'a hot-headed, selfish boy and a brutal tyrant towards his mother'. Living with another young boy makes the absence of his own son, Evgeny, even more painful. Boris also explains why, on his father's insistence, he did not vacate the rooms in Volkhonka Street for Evgenia and her son. They had returned to Moscow on 22 December

1931 but had been forced to go and live with Evgenia's brother for some time because it was apparently difficult for Boris to move apartments or find new ones due to restrictions imposed by the authorities and the requirements of necessary permits. This was not helped by the fact that Pasternak was already encountering restrictions due to the content of his work. 'All this comes at a time when my work has been declared to be the spontaneous outpourings of a class enemy,' Boris confided, 'and I'm accused of regarding art as inconceivable in a socialist society, that is, in the absence of individualism. Verdicts like these are quite dangerous, when my books are banned from libraries.'

Probably Boris and Zinaida's happiest time was the period they spent together in Georgia. In the summer of 1933 Pasternak had been commissioned to translate some Georgian poetry, and in order to master the language properly, and familiarise himself with the native tongue and colloquialisms, he visited the country.

To many Russians, Georgia, with its 'abundance of sunshine, its strong emotions, its love of beauty and inborn grace of its princes and peasants alike', was a place of enchantment and inspiration. Georgians were considered earthier and more passionate than their strait-laced Russian cousins. Pasternak made great friends with the acclaimed Georgian poets Paolo Yashvili and Titsian Tabidze. Of Yashvili he wrote: 'Talent radiated from him. His eyes shone with an inner fire; the fire of passion had scorched his lips and the heat of experience had burnt and blackened his face, so that he looked older than his years; and as though he had been worn and tattered by life.' Pasternak's love affair with the Caucasus would continue throughout his life, and he referred to Georgia as his second home.

According to Max Hayward, the Oxford academic who would later be recruited to translate *Doctor Zhivago* into English, the poems Pasternak composed to describe his journey over the Georgian Military Highway to Tbilisi ('probably the most breath-taking mountain road in the world') have not been equalled in calibre since Pushkin and Lermontov wrote on the same theme. For Pasternak the Caucasian peaks, receding in an infinite panorama of unexampled grandeur, offered a simile for a vision of what a socialist future might look like. But even in this prodigious setting, Pasternak favoured images that were domestic and intimate: the rugged lower slopes, for instance, reminded him of a 'crumpled bed'.

Pasternak's translations of Georgian poetry would be greatly admired by Stalin – a fact that may have saved the writer's life. Over a decade later, in 1949, as the secret police became increasingly aware of the controversial, anti-Soviet nature of the novel Pasternak was writing, a senior investigator in the prosecutor's office claimed there were plans to arrest him. However, when Stalin was informed, the leader began to recite: 'Heavenly colour, colour blue,' one of the poems that Pasternak had translated. Stalin, who was born in Gori in Georgia, was moved by Pasternak's lyrical translations of Georgian poetry. Instead of having him imprisoned or killed, as was the fate of many of Pasternak's contemporaries, Stalin is supposed to have said: 'Leave him in peace, he's a cloud dweller.' And on Pasternak's KGB file the immortal words were stamped: 'Leave the cloud dweller alone.'

In the early flush of happiness at his newfound stability, and possibly because he had anticipated from the start that she would play that role, Boris saw Zinaida as the facilitator of his craft. He wanted and needed her to be indispensable to his functioning as an artist. 'You are the sister of my talent,' he told her. 'You give me the feeling of the uniqueness of my existence ... you are the wing that protects me ... you are that which I loved and saw, and what will happen to me.'

When Evgenia finally cleared her belongings from the Pasternak apartment on Volkhonka Street in September 1932, and Boris moved back in with Zinaida, they found the house in a dilapidated condition. The roof leaked, rats had gnawed and ripped the skirting boards, and many window panes were cracked and missing. A month later, when Boris returned from a three-day trip to Leningrad, Zinaida had wrought an amazing transformation. The windows were repaired. She had hung curtains, fixed herniated mattresses and fashioned a new sofa cover from one of the spare curtains. The floors were polished, the windows were washed and sealed for the winter. Zinaida had even added various rugs, two cupboards and an upright piano which, extraordinarily, came from her ex-in-laws, Neigaus's parents, who had moved to Moscow and were now living with the abandoned Genrikh.

In 1934, Boris married Zinaida in a civil ceremony. So caught up was he in his fantasy image of Zinaida that he failed to see her shortcomings. Zinaida may have been a dab hand in the house, but for a man as impassioned as Boris, she was not the champion and soul mate he yearned for. Not only did Zinaida not understand his poetry, she could not fathom her husband's creative courage. Worse, she increasingly feared his poetry's power to upset the equilibrium of her well-managed household by provoking official disfavour.

A considerable strain in their relationship was caused by the arrest of Boris's friend, the poet Osip Mandelstam. One evening in April 1934, Boris bumped into him on a Moscow boulevard. To his consternation – even 'the walls have ears' he warned – Mandelstam, a fearsome critic of the regime, proceded to recite an incredibly scathing poem he had written about Stalin. (Lines included: 'His fingers are fat as grubs,/And the words, final as lead weights, fall from his lips …/His cockroach whiskers leer,/And his boot tops gleam.')

'I didn't hear this; you didn't recite this to me,' Boris said to him, agitated. 'Because, you know, very dangerous things are happening now. They've begun to pick people up.' These were the early ominous beginnings of what would become the Great Terror, when hundreds of thousands of people accused of various political crimes – espionage, anti-Soviet agitation and conspiracies to prepare uprisings and coups – were quickly executed or sent to labour camps. Boris told Mandelstam that his poem was tantamount to suicide and implored him not to recite it to anyone else. Mandelstam did not listen and inevitably, was betrayed. On 17 May he was arrested by the NKVD.

When he found out, Pasternak valiantly tried to help his friend. He appealed to the politician and writer Nikolai Bukharin, recently appointed editor of *Izvestiya* newspaper, who had commissioned some of Pasternak's Georgian translations. In June, Bukharin sent Stalin a message with the postscript: 'I'm also writing about Mandelstam because B. Pasternak is half crazy about Mandelstam's arrest, and nobody knows anything …'

Pasternak's entreaties paid off. Instead of being sent to almost certain death in a forced labour camp, Mandelstam was sentenced to three years' internal exile in the town of Cherdyn, in the north-east Urals – Stalin having issued a chilling command that was passed down the chain: 'Isolate but preserve'. Boris was astonished to be called to the communal telephone in the hallway at Volkhonka Street and told that it was Stalin on the line. According to Mandelstam's wife, Nadezhda:

Stalin said that Mandelstam's case was being reconsidered and that everything would be all right with him. An unexpected reproach followed – why didn't Pasternak turn to writer's organisations or 'to me' to plead for Mandelstam? Pasternak's answer was 'writer's organisations haven't been dealing with this since 1927, and if I hadn't pleaded, you might not have got to know about it'.

Stalin stopped him with a question: 'But he is an expert, a master, isn't he?'

Pasternak answered, 'That's not the point.'

'Then what is the point?' Stalin asked.

Pasternak said that he would like to meet and speak with him.

'What about?'

'About life and death.'

Stalin hung up the phone.

When word of the telephone conversation with Stalin got out, Pasternak's critics claimed he should have defended his friend's talent more vigorously. But others, including Nadezhda and Osip Mandelstam, felt happy with Boris's response. They understood his caution and thought he had done well not to be lured into the trap of admitting that he had, indeed, heard Osip's 'Stalin Epigram'. 'He was quite right to say that whether I am a master or not is beside the point,' Osip declared. 'Why is Stalin so afraid of a master? It's like a superstition with him. He thinks we might put a spell on him like shamans.'

In 1934, Pasternak was invited to the First Congress of the Soviet Writers' Union. He was disquieted by the official praise and by efforts to turn him into a literary public hero who had not been politically compromised. His work was increasingly being recognised by the West and he felt uncomfortable with this attention. Ironically, his writing was becoming more difficult to publish, so he concentrated on translation work. In 1935 he wrote to his Czech translator: 'All this time, beginning with the Writers' Congress in Moscow, I have had a feeling that, for purposes unknown to me, my importance is being deliberately inflated … all this by somebody else's hands without asking my consent. And I shun nothing in this whole world more than fanfare, sensationalism, and so-called cheap "celebrity" in the press.'

Pasternak and his family now accepted accommodation in the Writers' Union apartment block on Lavrushinsky Lane in Moscow and a dacha in Peredelkino. Pasternak acquired the rights to one of the properties, shaded by tall fir trees and pine trees, with the money he had received from his Georgian translations. In 1936 he still held high hopes that his parents would return to Russia and live with him there. This writers' colony, built on the former estate of a Russian nobleman outside Moscow, had been created to reward the Soviet Union's most prominent authors with a retreat that provided bucolic escape from their city apartments. Apparently, when Stalin heard that the colony was to be called Peredelkino, from the Russian verb *peredelat*, which means to re-do, he suggested it would be better to call is Perepiskino, from the verb to rewrite. Kornei Chukovsky, the Soviet Union's best-loved children's author, described the system of the writers' colony as 'entrapping writers with a cocoon of comforts, surrounding them with a network of spies'.

Such state controls did not sit comfortably with Pasternak. Nikolai Bukharin once said that Pasternak was 'one of the most remarkable masters of verse of our time, who has not only strung a whole row of lyrical pearls on to the necklace of his talent, but has produced a whole number of revolutionary works marked by deep sincerity'. But Pasternak pleaded: 'Do not make heroes of my generation. We were not: there were times when we were afraid and acted from fear, times when we were betrayed.'

At a writers' meeting in Minsk, Pasternak told his colleagues that he fundamentally agreed with their view of literature as something that could be produced like water from a pump. He then put forward the view for artistic independence, before announcing that he would not be part of the group. Almost an act of literary suicide, the audience were stunned. No one risked so public a speech as this until after Stalin's death. After this, there were no more efforts to draw Pasternak into the literary establishment. For the main part he was left alone, while the purges on writers continued with terrifying frequency and force. In October 1937, his great friend Titsian Tabidze was expelled from the Union of Georgian Writers and arrested. Paolo Yashvili, rather than be forced into denouncing Tabidze, shot himself dead at the offices of the Writers' Union.

When in 1937 Osip Mandelstam was allowed to return from exile, Zinaida feared having any contact with him and his wife, in case it threatened her family's safety. Boris abhorred what he saw as such moral cowardice. On several occasions, Zinaida prevented him from receiving friends and colleagues at Peredelkino for fear of contagion by association. Once, when Osip and Nadezhda turned up at the Peredelkino dacha, Zinaida refused to receive them. She forced her husband back onto the verandah to tell his friends lamely and with considerable embarrassment: 'Zinaida seems to be baking pies.' According to Olga Ivinskaya, Zinaida always 'loathed' the Mandelstams, who she considered were compromising her 'loyal' husband. Olga claimed that Zinaida was famous 'for her immortal phrase: "My sons love Stalin most of all – and then their Mummy."'

Zinaida's antipathy towards the Mandelstams would have incensed Boris and caused further rifts between them. Boris's belief in his destiny at this time gave him a certain fearlessness that Zinaida could not begin to match. She later admitted: 'no one could know on whose head the rock would fall and yet he showed not an ounce of fear'.

On 28 October 1937, Boris's friend and neighbour at Peredelkino, Boris Pilnyak, was arrested by the secret police. His typewriter and the manuscript of his new novel were confiscated and his wife arrested. The NKVD report implicated Boris too: 'Pasternak and Pilnyak held secret meetings with [the French author André] Gide, and supplied him with information about the situation in the USSR. There is no doubt that Gide used this information in his book attacking the USSR.' In April, after a trial lasting just fifteen minutes, Pilnyak was condemned to death and executed. His final words to the court after months of imprisonment were: 'I have so much work to do. A long period of seclusion has made me a different person; I now see the world through new eyes. I want to live, to work, to see in front of me paper on which to write a work that will be of use to the Soviet people.'

Another of Pasternak's friends, the playwright A. N. Afinogenov, who had been expelled from the Communist Party and from the Writers' Union for daring to criticise the dictatorship through his work, was abandoned by all his friends except Boris. On 15 November he wrote: 'Pasternak is going through a hard time now; he has constant quarrels with his wife. She tries to make him attend all the meetings; she says he doesn't think about his children, and his reserved behaviour seems suspicious and he will be arrested if he continues to be aloof.'

Pasternak confided to the literary scholar and critic Anatoly Tarasenkov in 1939: 'In those horrendous, blood-stained years anyone might have been arrested. We were shuffled like a pack of cards. I have no wish to give thanks, in a philistine way, for remaining alive while others did not. There is a need for someone to show grief, to go proudly into mourning, to react tragically – for someone to be tragedy's standard bearer.'

In spite of unimaginable pressures, Pasternak stayed true to himself in his professional life. His loyalty to his friends was unwavering. Osip Mandelstam was again arrested in 1938 and eventually died in the gulag. The only person to visit Mandelstam's widow after his death was Boris. 'Apart from him no one had dared to come and see me,' said Nadezhda.

It is almost miraculous that Pasternak was not exiled or killed during these years. Why did Stalin save his 'cloud dweller'? Another quirk that may have saved the writer's life was that Stalin believed the poet had prescient powers, some sort of second sight.

In the early hours of 9 November 1932, Stalin's wife, Nadya Alliluyeva, committed suicide. At a party the previous evening, a drunken Stalin had flirted in front of the long-suffering Nadya and had publicly diminished her. That night, when she heard rumours that her husband was with a lover, she shot herself in the heart.

The death certificate, signed by compliant doctors, said that the cause of death was appendicitis (as suicide could not be acknowledged). Soviet ritual required collective letters of grief from different professions. Almost the whole of the literary establishment – thirty-three writers – signed a formal letter of sympathy to Stalin. Pasternak refused to add his name to it. Instead, he wrote his own letter in which he hinted that he shared some mythical communion with Stalin, empathising with his motives, emotions and presumed sense of guilt.

In his letter, Boris wrote: 'I share the feelings of my comrades. On the evening before, I found myself thinking deeply and continually about Stalin for the first time from the point of view of an artist. In the morning I read the news, and I was shaken just as if I had been present, and as though I had lived through it, as though I had seen it all.' It appears that Stalin may well have believed that Pasternak was a 'poet-seer' who had prophetic powers. According to the émigré scholar Mikhail Koryakov, writing in the American Russian-language newspaper *Novy Zhurnal*: 'from that moment onwards ... it seems to me, Pasternak, without realising it, entered the personal life of Stalin and became some part of his inner world'.

As neither Pasternak nor an increasingly nervous Zinaida could have known about this golden protection from on high, that he continued to work on *Doctor Zhivago*, drafting the structure throughout the mid-thirties, seems almost to be a further act of literary suicide. Looking back, he explained to the Czech poet Vitezslav Nezval: 'Following the October Revolution things were very bad for me. I wanted to write about this. A book in prose about how bad things were. A straightforward and simple narrative. You understand, sometimes a man must force himself to stand on his head.'

Pasternak forced himself to stand on his head yet again in 1937 when the Writers' Union asked him to sign a joint letter endorsing the death sentence of a high-ranking official plus several other prominent military figures on charges of espionage. Pasternak refused. Incensed, he told the union: 'the lives of people are disposed of by the government, not by private individuals. I know nothing about them [the accused]. How can I wish their death? I did not give them life. I can't be their judge. I prefer to perish together with the crowd, with the people. This is not like signing complimentary tickets to the theatre.' Pasternak then penned a letter to Stalin: 'I wrote that I had grown up in a family where Tolstoyan convictions were very strong. I had imbibed them with my mother's milk, and he could dispose of my life. But I did not consider I was entitled to sit in judgement over the life and death of others.'

Tensions now erupted with Zinaida, who argued with Boris and urged him to sign the Writers' Union letter, fearing the consequences for their family if he did not. His adherence to his beliefs made him seem selfish in her eyes. Zinaida was pregnant, which sadly did not seem cause for great celebration at the time. Their marriage was struggling due to their extreme ideological differences and to the political pressures of the times. When Boris first learned of Zinaida's pregnancy, he wrote to his parents that her 'present condition is entirely unexpected, and if abortion weren't illegal, we'd have been dismayed by her insufficiently joyful response to the event, and she'd have had the pregnancy terminated.' Zinaida later wrote that she very much wanted, 'Boria's child', but her acute fear that Boris could be arrested at any moment made it hard to carry the pregnancy. So convinced was Zinaida that Boris was likely to be arrested at any moment that she had even packed a small suitcase for this emergency.

'My wife was pregnant. She cried and begged me to sign, but I couldn't,' wrote Boris. 'That day I examined the pros and cons of my own survival. I was convinced I would be arrested – my turn had come. I was prepared for it. I abhorred all this blood and I couldn't stand it any longer. But nothing happened. I was later told that my colleagues had saved me – at least indirectly. Quite simply no one dared to report to the hierarchy that I hadn't signed.'

It offers insight into his bullish mentality that, fully aware that he might be shot or seized that night, Pasternak wrote: 'We expected that I would be arrested that night. But, just imagine, I went to bed and at once fell into a blissful sleep. Not for a long time had I slept so well and peacefully. This always happens to me after I have taken some irrevocable step.'

On 15 June Pasternak saw his signature displayed on the front page of the *Literaturnaya Gazeta*, along with those of forty-three other writer colleagues. He rushed from Peredelkino to Moscow to protest to the secretariat of the Writers' Union about the unauthorised inclusion of his signature, but by then the heat had gone and no one took much notice. Again, against his better instincts, he had been saved.

Boris's dear friend Titsian Tabidze was not so lucky. After his early morning arrest on 11 October 1937, he had been charged with treason, sent to the gulag and tortured. He was executed two months later, though no announcement was made at the time. It was not until after Stalin's death in the mid-1950s that the truth emerged. Boris mourned his friend keenly, remaining loyal to Titsian's wife, Nina, and daughter Nita. All through the 1940s, when they all prayed that Titsian was alive somewhere in Siberia, Boris assisted the family financially, sending them all the royalties from his translations of Georgian poetry and regularly inviting them to stay at Peredelkino. Titsian's crime was similar to Pasternak's. He had written with conscience about Russia, and been openly defiant at a time when literary modernity was crushed by the Soviet state. After an attack on Titsian in the press, Boris had urged him in a letter: 'Rely only on yourself. Dig more deeply with your drill without fear or favour, but inside yourself, inside yourself. If you do not find the people, the earth and the heaven there, then give up your search, for then there is nowhere else.'

Pasternak's second son, Leonid, was born just into the new year, 1938. Boris wrote to his family in Berlin on New Year's Day: 'The boy was born lovely and healthy and seems very nice. He managed to appear on New Year's night with the last 12th strike of the clock. And he was mentioned in the statistics report of the maternity hospital as "the first baby, born at 0 o'clock of the 1st January 1938". I named him Leonid in your honour. Zina suffered a lot in childbirth, but she seems to be created for difficulties and bears them easily and almost silently. If you'd like to write to her and can do so without feeling obligated, please write.'

It is a mark of how far his marriage to Zinaida was unravelling that, eighteen months earlier, while Zinaida organised the house move to Peredelkino from Moscow all by herself – moving her sons and all the family's furniture – Boris went to stay with his former wife Evgenia, at her Tverskoi Boulevard home. 'He was very drawn to young Zhenya and to me. He lived a few days with us and entered our lives so naturally and easily, as though he had only been away by chance,' Evgenia later wrote to her friend Raisa Lomonosova of Boris's stay with her that summer; 'But despite the fact that, in his words, he is sick to death of that life, he will never have the courage to break with her [Zinaida]. And it is pointless him tormenting me and reviving old thoughts and habits.'

For Boris, Evgenia's artistic temperament suddenly seemed less stifling, compared with Zinaida's bland domesticity. It gave rise to a nostalgia in Boris for his first family and underlined his dour sense of duty to his second. He found Zinaida's personality 'challenging' and 'inflexible' and was by now aware that their characters were too different for them to reside together in any sort of harmony. Years later, Zinaida's daughter-in-law, Natasha (who married Boris and Zinaida's son, Leonid), said of her mother-in-law: 'She had a very rigid character. She was practical and disciplined. She would say "now we go to lunch" and everyone would sit down. She was the head of the table, like a captain running a ship.'

Pasternak's friend the poet Anna Akhmatova observed that at the beginning, being blindly in love, Boris failed to see what others perceived: that Zinaida was 'coarse and vulgar'. To Boris's literary friends, she did not share his desire for spiritual and aesthetic pursuits, preferring to play cards and chain-smoke into the early hours. But Akhmatova correctly predicted that Boris would never leave Zinaida because he 'belonged to the race of conscientious men who cannot divorce twice'. It was inevitable that his emotional journey was not yet over. He was about to meet Olga, the soul mate who would be his Lara, for whom he had longed all his life.

# 4

# Cables under High Tension

Six months after their first meeting at the *Novy Mir* offices, when Olga introduced Boris to her two young children, it was clear their love was incontrovertible. Both were obsessed by each other, consumed by an irresistible power of attraction. After Boris met Irina and Mitia that April evening in 1947, he was more forcefully drawn to Olga than ever. Yet this was further complicated by his heightened awareness of the pain and trauma he was awakening for them all in betraying Zinaida. 'Boris suffered immensely from the ramifications of his romantic decisions,' reflected Irina.

When the children were tucked up in bed that spring night, Boris sat with Olga in her tiny bedroom until midnight, the two of them alternating between elation at the strength of their passion and fevered despair at the practical reality of their situation.

Boris told Olga that he was tormented by his feelings for her and for his own family in Peredelkino. That every time he returned to Zinaida after walking with Olga in Moscow, when he saw his 'no longer young' wife waiting for him, he was reminded of Little Red Riding Hood abandoned in the forest. He just could not get out the words that he had rehearsed over and over about how he wished to leave her. Boris tried to break free of his deep emotional and ardent attraction to Olga that night in her apartment, confessing his relentless guilt towards Zinaida. He explained to Olga that she had nothing to do with his indifferent feelings towards his wife. He had lived unhappily with Zinaida for the previous ten years. He admitted that he had known within the first year of marriage to Zinaida that he had made a fearful mistake. Astonishingly, he confessed that it was not really her he liked but her husband, Genrikh, whose talents he revered. 'I was so captivated by the way he played the piano,' Boris said. 'At first he wanted to kill me, the strange fellow, after she left him. But later on he was very grateful to me!'

Boris spoke with such anguish to Olga about the drama of the break-up of his first marriage and the 'hell' of his domestic set-up with Zinaida, that there was no question of Olga doubting him and his motives towards her. Of course he wanted more than anything to pursue a great love affair with her, but he could not envisage how he could disentangle himself from yet another marriage. As he stood at the door to leave her, the night folding in behind him, he told Olga that he felt that he had no right to love. The good things in life were not for him. He was a man of duty and she must not deflect him from his set way of life – and his work. He added that he would look after Olga for the rest of his life. An honourable promise, considering they had not yet consummated their relationship.

After Boris left, Olga could not sleep. Restless, she kept going to the balcony, listening to the sounds of daybreak, watching the street lamps grow dim under the young lime trees of Potapov Street. At six in the morning the doorbell rang. Boris was standing there. He had gone to his dacha at Peredelkino by train – unlike Yury Zhivago, who galloped to and from his true love – then come straight back and walked the streets of Moscow until dawn. Olga was wearing her favourite Japanese dressing gown, decorated with little houses. She pulled him towards her and they embraced in silence. Both knew that regardless of the complexity of the situation and the potential destruction caused by their ardour, they could not live without each other.

The next day Olga's mother took the family on a trip to Pokrovskoye-Streshnevo on the outskirts of Moscow, where there was an eighteenth-century house surrounded by sweeping parkland. Boris and Olga were left to spend their first night and day together 'like newlyweds'. Olga took great pleasure in ironing Boris's crumpled trousers for him: not the most romantic of acts, but Boris being Boris, he was 'jubilant' that they could live like a married couple for this twenty-four-hour period. To mark the happy occasion, he inscribed a small red volume of his verse for Olga: 'My life, my angel, I love you truly. April 4th, 1947.'

From the moment that they became lovers, Boris and Olga were inseparable. He would come to her apartment every day at six or seven in the morning. Spring that year turned into a hot summer: the lime trees were laden with blossom, the boulevards seemed to have the fragrance of molten honey. They were completely in love, able to exist on little sleep, fuelled by the adrenalin of desire, excitement and yearning. Boris wrote a poem called 'Summer in Town', about this time. It became one of Yury Zhivago's poems in *Doctor Zhivago*.

Conversation in a half tone.
With a flurry of haste
The whole sheaf of hair
Is gathered up from the nape of the neck.

From under the heavy comb
A helmeted woman looks out,
Her head thrown back
With all its plaited hair.

Outside, the hot night
Promises a storm,
The passers-by scatter,
Shuffling home.

Brief thunder
Echoes sharply,
And the wind stirs
The curtain at the window.

Sultry
Silence.
Fingers of lightning
Search the sky.

And when the dawn-filled,
Heated morning
Has dried the puddles in the streets
After the night rain

The centuries-old, scented,
Blossoming lime-trees
Frown
For lack of sleep.

As the affair between the besotted writer and Olga intensified, tensions escalated between Olga and her mother, Maria Kostko. For while Olga and even little Irina were excited that a poet of Boris's calibre had entered their lives, Maria was vehemently against the union. All she wanted was for her daughter to find the emotional and financial security of a suitable third husband. 'It is impossible, unthinkable, unjustifiable to have a relationship with a married man,' Maria repeatedly reproached Olga. 'We even have the same age, him and I.' It must have been doubly alarming for Maria that her daughter was not only embarking on a relationship with a married man but such a famous and controversial figure. In her eyes this would have been akin to Olga signing her death warrant, given the frequency and ferocity of arrests. She had good reason to fear, for Maria had direct experience of Stalinist repression, having spent three years in the gulag during the war. Worse, the betrayal had originated close to home: it was believed that her second son-in-law, Alexander Vinogradov, had tipped off the authorities, saying Maria had 'slandered the leader' in a private conversation about Stalin in their home. It is thought that part of his motive was to get his mother-in-law out of their crowded apartment. A lawyer revealed to Olga that there was indeed a letter of denunciation from Vinogradov towards her mother in Maria's police files, a revelation that caused fearful rows between Vinogradov and Olga before he died in 1942. Subsequently Olga learned that the camp where her mother was being kept had suffered enemy bombing; prison order had broken down and prisoners were dying of hunger.

Around early 1944, Olga bravely set out for the camp, travelling to the Sukho-Bezrodnaya station, 1,500 kilometres east of the Volga. This was the station for the forced-labour camp complex known as Unzhlag. Without a ticket, Olga had to lie down under the seats of a cattle train, where, wrapped in a greatcoat, soldiers helped hide her behind their bags and boots. Amazingly, Olga made it to her destination, where she found her mother 'more dead than alive'. She gave Maria the special ration that Olga had received as an official state blood donor and managed to get her out of Unzhlag, persuading the authorities that her mother was a liability, an ageing invalid incapable of any useful work. She brought her back to Moscow, illegally – along with many stories of the soldiers' bravery in helping her, which she later shared with her children. This would not be the last time that Olga 'would travel in a cattle train', and 'it would not be the last time that she would meet soldiers, but their kindness would become rarer'.

Olga's courage set sharply against Zinaida's apathy and caution; it was something that Boris applauded and was drawn to. Yet while he himself was fearless professionally, as a writer, his personal courage became sorely tested as his affair with Olga developed.

Before long their moments of bliss became punctuated with rows and demands. Olga recalled a particular pattern to their conflict: 'No, no, Olia, it's all over,' Boris kept repeating, during one of his attempts to 'break free'. 'Of course I love you, but I must stop seeing you because I cannot go through with all the horrors of leaving my family. Unless you can accept that we must exist in a kind of higher world and wait for some still unknown force to bring us together, it would be better not to see each other again. We cannot live a life together on the ruins of somebody else's.'

Pasternak later recreated this exact inner struggle in *Doctor Zhivago*. Yury is torn between his fervent longing to be with Lara and his guilty self-disgust at deceiving Tonya. In his head, he wants to break off relations with Lara, but it becomes clear to him that more than flighty romance which could be jettisoned, their union draws on some mythical spiritual connection which his heart cannot overrule:

He had decided to cut the knot and he was going home with a solution. He would confess everything to Tonya, beg her to forgive him and never see Lara again.

Not that everything was quite as it should be. He felt now that he had not made it clear enough to Lara that he was breaking with her for good, for ever. He had announced to her that morning that he intended to confess everything and that they must stop seeing one another; but now he had the feeling that he had softened it all down and not made it sufficiently definite.

Lara had realised how unhappy he felt and had no wish to upset him further by a painful scene. She tried to listen to him as calmly as she could. They were talking in one of the empty front rooms. Tears were running down her cheeks, but she was no more conscious of them than the stone statues on the house across the road felt the rain running down their faces. She kept saying softly: 'Do as you think best, don't worry about me. I'll get over it.' She was saying it sincerely without any false generosity, and she did not know that she was crying, she did not wipe away her tears.

At the thought that Lara might have misunderstood him, and that he had left her with the wrong impression and false hopes, he nearly turned and galloped straight back to her, to say what he had left unsaid and, above all, to take leave of her much more warmly, more tenderly, in a manner more suitable to a last farewell. Controlling himself with difficulty, he continued on his way …

In the distance, where the sun was refusing to go down, a nightingale began to sing.

'Wake up! Wake up!' it called entreatingly; it sounded almost like the summons on the eve of Easter Sunday: 'Awake, O my soul, why dost thou slumber.'

Suddenly Yury was struck by a very simple thought. What was the hurry? He would not go back on the promise he had given himself, the confession would be made, but who said that it must be made that day? He had not said anything to Tonya yet, it was not too late to put it off till after he had been to town once again. He would finish his conversation with Lara, with such warmth and depth of feeling that it would make up for all their suffering. How splendid, how wonderful! How strange that this had not occurred to him before!

At the thought of seeing Lara once more his heart leapt for joy.

By now, according to Olga, she and Boris were 'simply powerless to leave each other'. Boris's son Evgeny saw how 'an awareness of the sinfulness and obvious doomed nature of their relations imparted a particular glow to them at that time. Pangs of conscience on the one hand, and light-hearted egoism on the other, often faced them with the need to part, but pity and a thirst for emotional warmth drew him towards her again.' In his poem 'Explanation', Boris described the torment and contortions wrought by their love, likening the couple to 'cables under high tension':

… Again I rehearse my excuses,
Or again grow weary of it all,
Once more a woman from next door
Skirts the courtyard wall, not to disturb us.

Don't cry, don't purse your swollen lips,
Don't draw them together like that –
You'll make them just as sore and cracked
As they were from last spring's fever.

Take your hand from my breast:
We are cables under high tension
Watch out – or once again
We shall again be thrown together

...

But strongly as I may be bound
By the aching shackles of our nights,
The pull away is stronger still,
And I'm beckoned by the passion to break free.

The sense of pressure mounting on Boris was heightened by egregious oppression and political pressure. He was under constant surveillance from the authorities due to the anti-Soviet nature of his work, while his contemporaries who were not seen to serve the interests of the new Soviet system were executed, exiled to prison camps or tortured. He had already received news that his dear friend Osip Mandelstam had perished somewhere in the gulag, while his confidante Marina Tsvetaeva had hanged herself in 1941, soon after her return from exile.

Personal disappointments caused volatility, pressure and rifts too. According to Olga, 'by this time Zinaida Nikolayevna had heard about me, and was also beginning to make his life a misery'. As Zinaida was practised in fending off young admirers who threatened her husband's matrimonial and artistic equilibrium, it is likely that initially she did not take rumours of his liaison with Olga that seriously. A rational, robust character, she would not have let a mere infatuation dent her cast-iron sense of self.

Although Boris had consistently warned Olga that he could not leave Zinaida for her, as their affair continued Olga began to make more demands on him. Maria did not help matters by constantly nagging her daughter, saying that Boris should make a clean break from his family, posing the age-old question: if he loves you so much, why doesn't he leave his wife for you? She became interfering, ringing Boris and berating him for making Olga ill, or for not being dutiful enough to her.

Due to the terrors of the political climate, Maria had been transformed from ex-prison camp inmate into an overseer who made it her business to uphold Soviet petty-mindedness. Given that she had been sent to the gulag once, it was hardly surprising that she was afraid that Olga's affair with Boris would lead to another prison sentence. This resulted in hysterical rows between Olga and her mother, amid a general atmosphere of fetid secrecy, typical of Soviet society of the day. Boris stood his ground. 'I love your daughter more than my life, Maria Nikolayevna,' he told her, 'But don't expect our life to change outwardly all at once.'

'Our household was bubbling with hidden passion,' Irina remembered of this time. 'I was ten years old and confused as I could feel the undercurrent. A year went by and there were many uproars and sputters.' She recalls Olga crying in her bedroom or throwing bowls and spoons at her mother's husband, who did not care for Boris nor his poetry. Irina felt sorry for him: 'My poor grandfather, whom my brother and I loved so much.'

Olga and Boris continued to tramp the streets together, rowing in doorways of strange houses, before making up again. Irina watched as her mother returned from meeting after meeting with Boris, and if they'd had a row, she would take his photograph down from the wall. Inevitably, it would soon be put back up. 'Where's your pride, Mama?' Irina once asked her. Far from blaming Boris for putting her mother in a precarious position by not instantly leaving Zinaida for her, Irina felt acute sympathy for the writer's domestic plight. 'This genius, this sensitive, troubled soul, created exactly the same scene with his second wife that he did with his first,' she said. 'He was incapable of divorcing twice and because of that, he suffered a lot.'

As with Boris, Olga put her heart before her young family. Her parenting took a back seat to her love affair. She was impassioned, neurotic and undoubtedly selfish in pursuit of her love of Boris, as their relationship brought her family into a dangerous spotlight. She was however grateful for and touched by Boris's affection for her children. 'I thought of Boris as more than a husband,' Olga admitted. 'He had entered my life and seized possession of it entirely, leaving no corner untouched. I was overjoyed by his tender, loving treatment of my two children, particularly Irina, now rapidly growing up.'

It must have been incredibly painful for Boris's sons, Evgeny and Leonid, from his first and second marriages, as Boris developed a closeness to Irina, the daughter he never had. There was definitely the feeling from the Pasternak family that Boris mistreated his first family at the expense of the second. Equally, there were similar feelings of injustice from Zinaida and her son, Leonid, as Boris spent more and more time with Olga, Irina and Mitia. Charles Pasternak, Boris's nephew, vividly remembers as a young boy the 'long arguments' in the family over Boris's favourable treatment of his second son Leonid over his first-born, Evgeny. Natasha Pasternak, who married Boris's son Leonid, said that Boris had 'little time for Evgeny' and that his son visited Peredelkino 'infrequently, and when he came, he came as a guest, not a family member'.

Irina believes it was impossible for Boris to forsake his love for Olga, despite the pain and trouble he caused. 'Although Boris went through immensely hard times and was often at the end of his tether, he had the capacity to rebound very quickly. My mother had a very optimistic nature and she always cheered him up and soothed him. He appreciated those qualities very much and so he needed her. She became indispensable to his work, his life and his happiness.'

Boris, true to form, was working extremely hard during this time, channelling his personal angst into his writing. As the Soviet authorities had passed a resolution on 9 September 1946, denouncing him as 'an author lacking in ideology and remote from Soviet reality', and as attacks on him continued into 1947, his paid translation work was drying up. *Novy Mir* even rejected some of his poems. He fuelled his ire and frustrations into *Zhivago*, which he knew, under the existing political conditions, would bring him no income at all. 'I started to work again on my novel when I saw that all our rosy expectations of the changes the end of the war was supposed to bring Russia were not being fulfilled,' he told his friend, the playwright Alexander Gladkov. 'The war itself was like a cleansing storm, like a breeze blowing through an unventilated room. Its sorrows and hardships were not as bad as the inhuman lie – they shook to its core the power of everything specious and unorganic to the nature of man and society, which has gained such a hold over us. But the dead weight of the past was too strong. The novel is absolutely essential to me as a way of expressing my feelings.'

Daily he wrote about Yury Zhivago's passion for Lara interlaced with guilt over his infidelity to his dutiful wife, Tonya. 'Life became converted into art and art was born of life and experience,' he said at that time. He was living the same double life with Zinaida in Peredelkino, while Olga waited for him in Moscow. In *Doctor Zhivago* he wrote:

The nearer he was drawn to Lara and her daughter, the less he ventured to take domesticity for granted and the stricter was the control imposed on his thoughts by his duty to his family and the pain of his broken faith. There was nothing offensive to Lara or Katya in this limitation. On the contrary, this attitude on his part contained a world of deference which precluded vulgar familiarity.

But the division in him was a sorrow and a torment and he became accustomed to it only as one gets used to an unhealed and frequently reopened wound.

It seems foolishly naïve or wantonly brazen, given the authorities' surveillance of Pasternak, that as he wrote *Doctor Zhivago*, he gave regular readings of his work in progress. As word grew of these illustrious readings, his literary fans coveted an invitation. On 6 February 1947 the pianist Maria Yudina held a reading at her home, which she and her friends were looking forward to 'as a feast'.

The day before, when Boris was walking Olga home from her *Novy Mir* offices, he had invited her to join him: 'Let me take you to see a woman pianist I know. She will play the piano and I have promised to read her a little from a new prose work of mine,' he urged her. 'It won't be a novel as the word is generally understood. I shall skim through years and decades, perhaps dwelling on trivialities. I think I may call this new thing "Boys and Girls" or "Pictures from Fifty Years of Daily Life!" I have a feeling that you will write your page in it as well!'

The event was packed, in spite of a raging blizzard outside. Boris had worried that he might not make the reading, as the snowdrifts made it difficult for him to reach Yudina's apartment. He was driven with Olga in a friend's car and they got lost. Olga sat in the back of the car, admiring

Boris's profile as he turned to talk to the driver. Boris, wearing felt boots that were 'grotesquely oversize for him', kept jumping out of the car, trying to work out where they were. Suddenly, among the houses whitened with snow, they saw the flickering light of a lamp shaped like a candle in the window. This drew them to the right apartment and was to become a familiar leitmotif in *Doctor Zhivago*; the flickering candle behind the frozen window pane: 'As they drove through Kamerger Street, Yura noticed that a candle had melted a patch in the icy crust on one of the windows. Its light seemed to fall into the street as deliberately as a glance, as if the flame were keeping a watch on the passing carriages and waiting for someone.'

The image of a burning candle also inspired a poem, which would become Yury Zhivago's 'A Winter Night'. Boris wrote this poem the following morning and brought it to Olga at her office later that day.

The evening was a resounding success. Maria Yudina, dressed in her best black velvet dress, played Chopin. According to Olga, 'BL was particularly affected by the music and his eyes shone. I was beside myself with happiness.' Boris then read from chapter three of his draft novel. He delighted the packed room with the passage about the young student Zhivago dancing with his fiancée, Tonya, and the Christmas tree lights at the Sventitskys' house: 'Yura was standing absent-mindedly in the middle of the ballroom, watching Tonya as she danced with a stranger,' Boris read out. 'She swept up to him, flounced her short satin train like a fish, and vanished':

She was very excited. During the interval, she had refused tea and had slaked her thirst with innumerable tangerines, peeling them and wiping her fingers and the corners of her mouth on a handkerchief the size of a fruit blossom. Laughing and talking incessantly, she kept taking her handkerchief out and putting it back inside her sash or her sleeve or the frilled neck of her dress.

Now, as she brushed past him, spinning with her unknown partner, she caught and pressed Yura's hand and smiled. The handkerchief she had been holding stayed in her fingers. He pressed it to his lips and closed his eyes. The handkerchief smelled equally enchantingly of tangerines and of Tonya's hand. This was something new in Yura's life, something he had never felt before, something sharp and piercing that went through his whole being from top to toe. This naively childish smell was like a friendly, sensible word whispered in the dark. He pressed the handkerchief to his eyes and lips, lost in its kindly smell. At that moment a shot rang out inside the house.

Everyone turned and looked at the curtain which hung between the ballroom and the sitting-room. There was a moment's silence. Then uproar broke out. Some people rushed about screaming, others ran after Koka into the sitting-room from which the sound of the shot had come, and from which still other people were emerging, weeping, arguing and all talking at once.

'What has she done, what has she done?' Komarovsky kept saying in despair.'

Inside Maria Yudina's stiflingly hot house, wiping perspiration from his face, Boris answered endless questions from his rapt audience about how the story would unfold. The passage continues to describe Yury's realisation that it is Lara who has fired the shot at the lawyer Komarovsky. As she faints, the keen young doctor attends to her, instantly drawn to and mystified by her character and circumstance. Tonya's innocence is in contrast to an otherworldliness of the intriguing Lara.

When Josephine Pasternak was in her late teens, she and Boris had an impassioned conversation, sitting on her brother's bed in their Moscow apartment, about female beauty. 'He said that there are two very different kinds of beauty. One – a beauty that was there for everybody to see, more tangible, so to speak, easier to grasp, to understand, and another one – a noble one, retiring, and in fact much more impressive, though one had to be up to the standard of such beauty in order to appreciate it.' Boris cited his first love, Ida Vysotskaya, as an example of the 'noble' type of beauty, and her sister Lena Vysotskaya's beauty as more accessible and open to understanding. 'It also seems to me that Lara "the girl from a different world" also belonged to this other, albeit perfect in its own way, more accessible type of beauty,' said Josephine.

Tonya in *Doctor Zhivago* would definitely have been considered the more noble kind of beauty, yet it was the other kind of allure that fascinated Boris. A beauty that reflected emotional suffering. As he writes in *Zhivago*: 'I don't like people who have never fallen or stumbled. Their virtue is lifeless and it isn't of much value. Life hasn't revealed its beauty to them.'

Irina's description of her mother's 'tired beauty' explains Boris's instant attraction to Olga. 'It wasn't the beauty of a brilliant victor,' said Irina, 'it was almost the beauty of a defeated victim. It was the beauty of suffering. When Boris looked into my mother's beautiful eyes, he could probably see many, many things in them ...' When Yury Zhivago first sets eyes on Lara, he is instantly bewitched: 'Here was the very thing which he, Tonya and Misha had endlessly discussed and had dismissed as "vulgar", the force which so frightened and attracted them and which they controlled so easily from a safe distance by words. And now here it was, this force, in front of Yura's very eyes, concrete, real, and yet confused and veiled as in a dream, pitilessly destructive, and complaining and helpless – and where was Yura's childish philosophy now and what was he to do?'

After the reading at Marina Yudina's house, as Boris was seeing Olga home, he told her that a candle seen from the outside in the cold, leaving the mark of its breath on a frosty pane of glass, had been a much-needed symbol in his poetry. And now there had been this window gleaming in the night, like a portent of what was to come. Boris had felt, he confided in Olga, exactly the same about it as the young Zhivago; beyond this window with its candle there was a life certain to be linked in the future with his own life, though for the time being it was only beckoning. But he clearly had a vivid sense that Olga was to become his destiny.

As he made progress with *Doctor Zhivago*, he continued to read drafts to small gatherings at apartments in Moscow, and at Peredelkino, noting comments from the guests which would lead him to make adjustments to the text. At a reading in May 1947, the audience included Genrikh Neigaus, with whom he had rekindled his friendship. Boris embraced and firmly kissed Genrikh before starting the reading, to an elite group which included Leo Tolstoy's granddaughter. Pasternak's protégé, the poet Andrei Voznesensky, attended many of the readings at Peredelkino. They 'took place in his semi-circular beacon-like study on the upper floor. We'd gather together. Chairs would be brought up from downstairs. There were usually about twenty present. We'd fall silent. Pasternak sat down at his table. He wore a light silvery service-type jacket. As he read, Pasternak stared at something above our heads, visible to him alone. His face became longer, thinner. The readings usually lasted about two hours. He was considerate of his audience. Afterwards, he would ask each person in turn which poem they'd liked best. Most would answer "all of them". And the evasiveness of the reply would annoy him.'

Guests would then be invited to the dining room downstairs, the pale pinkish walls of which were covered by Leonid Pasternak's paintings and some of his sketches for *Resurrection*. On the window sills were rows of geranium plants, kept inside during the winter, giving the dining room the light feeling of a conservatory. 'Oh those Peredelkino meals!' Voznesensky recalled fondly. 'There were never enough chairs. Stools were pulled up. Pasternak would preside, Georgian fashion, relishing the ritual. He was a kind host. A departing guest would be reduced to confusion, he always handed everyone their coat himself. At our first meeting, this astonished me. And awestruck, I tore my coat from his grasp.'

Unfortunately, these literary soirees were also attracting unwelcome attention. The deputy editor of *Novy Mir* described them as the 'underground readings of a counter-revolutionary novel'. The secret police were also monitoring the literary gatherings, noting the book's contents for the moment when they would strike.

While Olga was able to attend some of the Moscow readings, she was not present at the Peredelkino soirees, as the dacha was Zinaida's domain. Zinaida, who didn't understand or particularly like her husband's work and constantly counselled him against attracting further controversy with his prose, would not have been upstairs, listening, as Olga would. She was downstairs, chain-smoking. It must have been a considerable comfort for Boris when Olga, a champion of his work, was among his devoted audience, radiating support.

The young poet Evgeny Yevtushenko remembers seeing Olga at Boris's public reading of his translation of Faust: 'in the auditorium, wearing a white stole over her shoulders, sat the beauty Olga Ivinskaya'. The literary historian Emma Gerstein was less generous. Present at Maria Yudina's gathering for Boris, she damningly described Olga as a 'pretty but fading blonde' who, during an interval in the reading, 'hurriedly powdered her nose, hiding behind a cupboard' – hardly a sin, considering how hot it was in Maria Yudina's packed apartment. Straight after the evening Gerstein wrote to Boris's friend Anna Akhmatova, informing her in slightly caustic terms, perhaps even with a touch of envy, of 'Pasternak's new love story' – an allusion to his relationship with Olga as well as a reference to the novel he was writing.

If Zinaida had her suspicions about her husband's new love story the previous year, they were painfully confirmed in April 1948.

Every morning, before Boris climbed the stairs for his working day, Zinaida would enter his study to vigorously dust and clean. Although she rarely read her husband's prose or poetry, she understood how essential his daily writing routine was to him, jealously guarding him from contact with boisterous family life. Her two sons by Genrikh were disciplined by her to live in the dacha 'almost noiselessly' so as not to disturb their stepfather's creativity. She allowed no one upstairs into his study, which, Boris told his parents, she 'personally polishes with a foot-cloth every morning'. Pasternak's working space was atypical of many writers. 'I personally do not keep heirlooms, archives, collections of any kind, including books and furniture. I do not save letters or draft copies of my work. Nothing piles up in my room; it is easier to clean than a hotel room. My life resembles a student's.'

Unlike a student's, his working routine never varied. Over that he exercised cast-iron discipline. His personal regime was similarly rigid. He rose early and washed outside at the pump in the garden. On bitter winter days, his torso bare, he would crack the ice and push his head into the frozen water. After his writing day, he would take a long, brisk walk, his pockets bursting with sweets to proffer to children he might meet in the village. Andrei Voznesensky said of him: 'Nothing was allowed to interfere with his daily routine of work, lunch, rest. By his evening stroll, as by the sun, the people of Peredelkino checked the time.'

It would have been in the early morning as he completed his outdoor ablutions (the lavatory was in its own small shed in the garden at Peredelkino), when Zinaida was tidying her husband's desk in readiness for the day's writing that lay ahead, that she found a love letter to him from Olga. Given Boris's minimalist approach and clutter-free desk, along with his admission that he did not keep letters, it seems even more extraordinary that his billet-doux from Olga was found there. Whether Zinaida moved a book to dust and discovered it, or whether it was exposed, lying wantonly open before her, she stood there and read it.

Regardless of her previous suspicions, the truth of the situation must have come as a biting shock. It was inevitable that from Moscow circles, abuzz with chatter about Boris and Olga, word had filtered back to Zinaida. However, on reading this passionate letter, Zinaida realised once and for all that she had wholly underestimated the strength of the union. Zinaida was forced to see the relationship for what it was – the first genuine threat to her familial and domestic stability. She 'understood immediately that this was a great love'.

Boris knew that Zinaida was fastidious in her cleaning, so it seems a textbook case of a man wanting to be caught. Had he subconsciously left the letter to be found, hoping it would force a solution? Boris may have been courageous in his art, but in his personal life he was disappointingly weak. He desperately sought a resolution to his situation, but found he did not possess the strength to make the necessary break with either Zinaida or Olga. When he was with Olga, he was drawn to her sensitivity, emotional intelligence and femininity. When he was back at Peredelkino, working, he appreciated Zinaida's lack of emotionalism and her robust practicality. He told his family: with Zinaida 'words and moods play almost no part in her make-up, being replaced by actions and real situations'. In *Doctor Zhivago* he wrote:

At home he felt like a criminal. His family's ignorance of the truth, their unchanged affection, were a mortal torment to him. In the middle of a conversation he would suddenly be numbed by the recollection of his guilt and cease hearing a word of what was being said.

If this happened during a meal, his food stuck in his throat and he put down his spoon and pushed away his plate. 'What is wrong with you?' Tonya would ask, puzzled. 'You must have had some bad news when you were in town. Has anyone been arrested? Or shot? Tell me. Don't be frightened of upsetting me. You'll feel better when you've told me.'

Had he been unfaithful to her because he preferred another woman? No, he had made no comparison, no choice. He did not believe in 'free love' or in the 'right' to be carried away by his senses. To think or speak in such terms seemed to him degrading. He had never 'sown wild oats', nor did he regard himself as a superman with special rights and privileges. Now he was crushed by the weight of his guilty conscience.

'What next?' he sometimes asked himself, and hoped wretchedly for some impossible, unexpected circumstance to solve his problem for him.

A misplaced letter left to be found, perhaps?

Boris's heart-breaking indecision was taking its toll on Olga. Until one day, at the family apartment, 'all the screams and scenes came to an end', recalled Irina. Olga's nerves could no longer bear Boris's endless vacillations and it appears that she made some sort of weak suicide bid. The details around it are extremely shaky. Irina claims that shortly afterwards her grandmother arranged for Olga to be committed to a psychiatric institution. 'All we could see was my grandparents whispering and looking guilty,' says Irina.

The days went by and Olga did not reappear. The children listened at the door to their grandparents talking in hushed tones and learned that

Maria had had their mother committed. 'Mum's empty bedroom became our playroom,' and the children's grandparents took on the role of parents. Irina's independence had been fostered early. She learned not to rely on her mother for emotional support. More, it was the other way around. Irina knew too young that Olga's romantic life took priority. No wonder she felt much closer to her grandmother and to her grandfather, whom she and her brother 'loved so much'.

Whether Olga had in fact attempted suicide or was just having an extreme episode, is unclear. It is quite likely that Maria thought that life for everyone would be a lot safer and a lot more peaceful if Olga was securely kept away from the family home. It was certainly more tranquil. 'The house was calm again,' remembers Irina.

But just as the family had 'got used to the idea of not having her around anymore', Olga reappeared out of the blue. 'She looked pale and was wearing a headscarf as you did in hospital,' Irina recalled. 'She appeared very calm and much smaller. She remained motionless in the house for a long time until one day things got back to normal.'

Boris's reaction to news of his lover's 'cry for help' was to send Zinaida to tell her that their affair was over. This seems extraordinarily heartless and cowardly. Boris had of course attempted a similarly theatrical 'suicide bid' in front of Zinaida eighteen years earlier. But given Boris's narcissistic nature, there was only room for one drama queen: him.

Zinaida quickly swung into action, her mind focused by the fact that their son, Leonid, was seriously ill with pneumonia. She had already suffered a terrible loss a few years earlier when her eldest son, Adrian, died from tuberculosis meningitis, aged just twenty. The illness had kept him in hospital throughout the war and caused him to have a leg amputated as doctors battled to save him. 'That's life,' wrote Boris to his sisters, of this time. 'His mother, who adored him, knowing he was at death's door and that every minute counted, tore herself in half between Sokolniki (the hospital) and Peredelkino (us and the dacha) and on the day before he breathed his last, she came to us to dig up the potato beds so as not to miss the harvesting season.' Practical to the last, Zinaida displayed an obdurate rationality and practicality that Boris admired, feared and possibly also secretly abhorred. Boris wrote to Olga Freidenberg: 'Yesterday Zina and I bought the ashes of her elder son from Moscow and buried them under the currant bush he had planted as a little boy in our garden.'

Zinaida had always protected her sons with a ferocity that alarmed Boris. 'When it's a question of her children, she'll bare her teeth like a she-wolf, even when there's no need,' he once told his parents. Three years later, as Zinaida and Boris stood by Leonid's sickbed, Zinaida extracted a promise from her husband that he would never see Olga Ivinskaya again. Determined to keep her family together, staunch Zinaida went to personally see off her rival.

She found Olga at the house of her friend Liusia Popova, a former actress who had studied at the Moscow Institute of Drama, whom Olga had been introduced to through Boris. Pretty and petite, Liusia had first seen Pasternak at one of his poetry recitals, waited for him at the exit and introduced herself. They later struck up a friendship and it was to Liusia that Boris had first confided his love for Olga. Both women were astounded when Zinaida appeared at the house on Furmanov Street, Moscow. Presumably Boris had told Zinaida of his mistress's whereabouts.

'Zinaida didn't make a scene. She was very dignified and composed,' says Irina. She stood there and delivered a short speech: 'You are young,' Zinaida told Olga. 'You should get married. I am old. I am at the end of my life. You have everything to live for. This is the end of my life.' Zinaida was fifty-four years old. Yet she presented herself to Olga, twenty years her junior, as decrepit, almost finished. Olga later described the encounter with the 'heavily-built, strong-minded woman' to her family. She said that she 'didn't give a damn' for Olga and Boris's love and although she no longer loved Boris herself, she would not allow the family to be broken up.

Zinaida later described meeting Olga in equally unflattering terms. 'I found her appearance very attractive but her manner of speaking quite the opposite,' she said. 'Despite all the coquettishness there was a certain hysteria about her.'

The encounter was cut short by more high drama: Olga suddenly became so 'ill through loss of blood' that Liusia and Zinaida had to rush her to hospital, the bleeding apparently caused by medication Olga had been prescribed by the psychiatric clinic.

When Olga was discharged from hospital Boris came to visit her 'as though nothing had happened'. He made his peace with Maria, and he and Olga carried on their affair as before. Zinaida's visit appeared to have had the opposite effect. It merely drove the lovers back into each other's arms.

As spring turned to summer Boris was once again a frequent visitor to Olga's home, allowing Irina to grow even closer to him and fonder of him. Irina's nickname for him was '*Classoosha*', an affectionate take on the word classic, as Pasternak was considered one of the great Russian classic writers.

One day, Boris arrived to take ten-year-old Irina out. 'It was the first time that I was alone with this man who remained an enigma to me and who had turned our life upside down,' said Irina, who remembers feeling 'intimidated' by him. As Boris had been paid for some translation work, he wanted to take her to buy her a present. The snow was thawing, creating streams of running water in their street, and Irina felt self-conscious in a coat cut from her grandmother's old fur-lined coat. 'I am soaking wet, the snow is melting and we are likely to get our feet wet,' Irina said to him, awkwardly.

'Do you feel that you always need to say something?' Boris boomed. 'That you cannot stay without saying a word and that you must entertain me? I so understand that, I know this feeling so well.'

Irina was struck by the blatant honesty of his retort. It was as if he had 'removed her armour'. She was touched that everything she did, however gauche, seemed to make sense to him. They took a taxi to a bookshop where Boris greeted everyone loudly and introduced Irina. 'He filled the already cramped shop with his voice and his movements.' She felt reassured that he seemed well loved in the shop and that nobody considered him an eccentric, as she did. They bought the works of other classic writers – 'Goncharov, Ostrovsky, Turgenev and Chekhov'. When they returned home, Irina heard Boris exclaim to Olga: 'Isn't it wonderful, Olioucha, she asked for some Chekhov!'

On 25 May 1948, Boris sent Irina a copy of Chekhov, adapted for children. On the flyleaf, in his big flowing hand, he had written: 'Dear Irochka, my treasure, please forgive me for not coming to see you on your birthday yesterday. I wish you happiness for the rest of your life. Keep up with your studies and hard work. That's all that matters in life. Your B.L.'

Boris was certainly working hard on his novel. On 12 December he wrote to Frederick, Josephine and Lydia from Moscow, addressing them as: 'My dear Fedia and girls!' In the letter he makes it clear that he is doing everything he can to get the first half of *Doctor Zhivago*, already in manuscript form, to them. Did they know of a good Russian copy-typist? he asks. And if he is owed any money in England from translation work, could they pay the typist to make three copies and check them? He wanted the manuscript to be sent to Maurice Bowra (the eminent English literary historian), Stefan Schimanski (an English critic and translator of Pasternak's works in Russian) and their friend, the English historian and philosopher, Isaiah Berlin.

'Printing it – I mean, publishing it in print – is absolutely out of the question, whether in the original or in translation – you must make this absolutely clear to the literary people whom I should like to show it to,' he continued, updating them about his work in progress: 'Firstly, it isn't completed, this is only half of it, needing a continuation. Secondly, publication abroad would expose me to the most catastrophic, not to say fatal, dangers. Both the spirit of the work itself, and my situation as it has developed here, mean that the novel can't appear in public: and the only Russian works allowed to circulate abroad are translations of those published here.' Fearing criticism from his sisters, he wrote: 'You won't like the novel because it lacks cohesion, and was written in such haste. One reason is that I couldn't drag it out, I'm not young any more, and anyway, anything could happen from one day to the next, and there were a number of things I wanted to get written down. And I was writing it in my own time, unpaid and in a hurry so as not to overstretch my budget, but to try and make time to get down to some paid work.'

In spite of his self-deprecation with his family, praise was mounting from literary friends to whom he had managed to send the first type-script. On 29 November 1948 he received the following letter from his cousin Olga Freidenberg, from St Petersburg, who was a distinguished scholar and later a university professor:

Your book is above any judgement. Everything that you say of history as the second universe can be referred to in your book ... It is a special variation of Genesis. It makes my skin tingle to read the philosophical discourses in it. I am just afraid that I am on the verge of discovering the final mystery that one hides inside himself and all his life he wishes to express it and waiting for its expression in art or science and is frightened to death of this because it must remain an eternal mystery.

Pasternak felt intense pressure to get his work read by those he respected, as he was inordinately proud of his book. It was his answer to a lifelong dream to produce a long prose work about his generation and its histor-ical fate. All writers are prone to frustrations and fears that their work will not get published, let alone stand the test of time. Pasternak, who had already been working on the novel for thirteen years, knew that he was taking monumental risks in privately distributing the politically controversial material. At first, he had been optimistic about the Bolshevik revolution, believing it would liberate the masses, but when he saw the reality of the war it created, he became a fierce opponent of the Soviet regime. He blamed collectivisation for ruining the rural economy and destroying the lives of millions. Pasternak could not have made his scorn for the political elite any clearer. As Yury Zhivago states: 'Ordinarily, people are anxious to test their theories in practice, to learn from experience, but those who wield power are so anxious to establish the myth of their own infallibility that they turn their back on truth as squarely as they can. Politics mean nothing to me. I don't like people who are indifferent to the truth.' As Pasternak had no idea that Stalin had issued orders to protect him, and ordinary citizens were killed or sent to the gulag for expressing anti-Stalinist views in their own homes, to be circulating his trenchant views in his novel was literally flirting with death.

Pasternak recognised the dangers, describing them in what would be his last letter to his family for almost a decade. (Due to the 'era of suspicion', he was forced to halt all correspondence with his sisters; he resumed contact with them in the summer of 1956, during the Khrushchev 'thaw'.) 'Even if you should hear one day that I've been hung, drawn and quartered,' he told them, 'you must know that I've lived a most happy life, better than I could ever have imagined, and my most solid and stable state of happiness is right now, and in all the recent past, because I have finally learned the art of expressing my thoughts – I possess this skill to the degree that I need it, which was never the case before.' He wrote this letter at the zenith of his affair with Olga. As his son Evgeny explained: 'The impact of their happy relations during the first three years was revealed in Lara's image, her appearance and the lyric warmth of the chapters devoted to her. My father always believed that it was the awakening of "an acute and happy personal impression" that gave him the strength to cope with the difficulties of the work on the novel.'

Little did Olga know that due to widespread knowledge of her affair with Boris, and her unflinching support of the book that he was writing, it was not Boris who would be 'hung, drawn and quartered' but she herself who would shortly receive unwelcome visitors.

On the evening of 6 October 1949, the secret police arrived at Olga's home with a summons that held terrifying ramifications. The authorities had hatched a plan that would strike right to the heart of the 'cloud dweller'. They would send his mistress and muse to a prison camp, and torture her instead.

# 5

## Marguerite in the Dungeon

Earlier that day, 6 October, Boris and Olga had met at the editorial offices of Goslitizdat, the state publishing house for literature, where Boris was due to collect some money. Afterwards, he had sat down with his beloved on a bench in the nearby public gardens. Enjoying the autumnal beauty, Boris asked Olga to come to Peredelkino that evening: they could be alone there, he told her, and he wished to read her another chapter of his book. 'By this time our relations had settled into an extraordinary phase of tenderness, love and understanding,' said Olga. 'He was now wholly absorbed by the novel, by the need to complete *Doctor Zhivago* as his main life's work – a design summed up in one sentence in a letter to a correspondent in Georgia: "One must write in a way never known before, make discoveries, so that unheard-of things happen to you – that is life and the rest matters nothing."'

As they were idly chatting in the gardens Olga became aware that a man in a leather coat had sat down near them and seemed to be closely monitoring their conversation. She leaned in closer to Boris to whisper that she had heard that morning that the authorities had arrested Irina's lovely, elderly English teacher at school, due to his wife's shady dealings with money. As Boris and Olga walked together to the Metro station, they noticed the man in the leather coat following them. Olga had a premonition that she did not want to leave Boris that day. However, she was in the middle of translating a volume of Korean lyrics and the author was coming to see her later that evening with his corrections. She had also promised Boris that she would type out one of her own poems for him.

Early in 1948, Olga had told Boris that she was unhappy at *Novy Mir*, as she was receiving unwanted comments about her unprofessional relationship with the famous writer. He encouraged her to leave her job, telling her he would support her and would help her to become proficient in the art of literary translation in her own right. Olga, who adored poetry and had written her own poems since she was a young girl, was only too happy to agree. In her small room on Potapov Street, Boris tutored her in the basic principles. At first, Olga, clumsy in the art, would pad out a dozen lines into at least double, and Boris would laugh affectionately at her for taking such liberties. He taught her how to 'preserve the sense by discarding words – how to strip an idea bare and clothe it in new words, as concisely as possible, without striving to prettify it'. Olga could have had no better guide than Pasternak, a dedicated and patient teacher, who showed her how to pick her way gingerly along the delicate boundary between translation in the strict sense and improvisation on the essence of the material. As Olga began to master her translations, she entered into a working partnership with Pasternak. He used to refer to the Potapov apartment as 'our shop'. Often he would start a translation, before Olga would take over and finish it, freeing him up to work on his novel. As well as loving the sense of collaboration, she was also making 'a good living' out of her translations. Like Boris, she began to hold literary soirees at home, evenings of poetry and discourse among writer friends.

'The work of our "shop" had its moments of comedy,' Olga wrote. 'When editors began to accept and recognise my work and I was receiving, with pride, my first payments for it, BL one day put a translation done by himself among some of mine and submitted it under my name with the rest. He was as happy as a small boy when the publisher turned down this particular one and sent it back to me for revision!' Boris was generous in his praise of Olga's abilities. She was constantly astounded and touched that a poet of his genius behaved towards her – a mere beginner in the art of translating – as though they were professional equals. 'Everything seemed just then to be going very well for us, and I was enjoying the peculiar feeling of freedom which came from the closeness that had grown up between us,' she remembered. 'He had just dedicated his translation of *Faust* to me, and I had said I would give him a poem by me in return.'

As soon as she returned to her apartment in Potapov Street, she sat down at the typewriter. As she was typing out her poem for Boris, she was overcome by a feeling of deep anxiety very much at odds with her earlier exuberant happiness.

At around eight, the door burst open and a dozen uniformed police entered. These were Stalin's state security men – the MGB (later renamed the KGB). They proceeded to ransack Olga's apartment. She was so stunned and terrified that she was initially unable to swallow due to a pain in her throat. She could not grasp what was happening. In her confusion, she wondered if they were there in connection with the corrupt wife of Irina's English teacher. Then the 'quite preposterous' thought dawned on her – could they be there 'on account of Boria?' The officers, smoking heavily, rifled through her books and private papers, throwing her belongings around, setting aside for seizure any book, letter, document or scrap of paper that mentioned Boris Pasternak. She looked on in disbelief as her son Mitia, with his sweet mop of curly hair, arrived home from school and proceeded to feed his pet hedgehog, which he kept on the balcony. One of the MGB men approached him, put his hand on Mitia's head and said 'good boy'. Olga noted how Mitia, in an unchildlike gesture, pushed his hand away.

Olga was now in no doubt that they were there due to her association with Pasternak. 'The many books that Boria had given me, with the unstinting, generous dedications in his hand, often covering all the blank pages were now being pawed by these strangers. They also seized all my letters and notes.' She could only watch, helpless, as they seized the red volume of verse that Boris had sent her after they consummated their relationship, the one he had inscribed: 'My Life, my angel, I love you truly'. They also took the confessional notebook in which she had written out her life history to Boris, which he had returned to her for safekeeping. While some of the men continued to search the apartment, others grabbed Olga. She was told that they had a warrant for her arrest for 'expressing anti-Soviet opinions of a terrorist nature'. Their warrant also declared: 'it is proven that her father fought alongside the Whites in 1918 and that her mother was convicted in 1941', the words barely registering as terror pounded in her ears. Impotent to defend herself, she was taken away.

'At that moment, they broke the thread of my life,' she wrote. She looked around the room and the last thing she remembered was seeing her poem to Boris, unfinished, in the typewriter.

On hearing of Olga's arrest, Boris immediately contacted Liusia Popova, who went to meet him on Gogol Boulevard. She found him sitting on a bench near the Metro station. He began to cry. 'Everything is finished now,' he said. 'They've taken her away from me and I'll never see her again. It's like a death, even worse.'

Irina was still at school on the second shift (in the postwar years, because of severe overcrowding, Soviet schools worked in two shifts), so Olga had no way of saying goodbye to her daughter. As Olga was dragged down the stairs, her stepfather, who had lived through the terrible business of his wife's arrest, stood weeping on the staircase, calling after Olga: 'You'll soon be back, you haven't robbed or killed anyone.'

When Irina came home from school on that dark October night, trudging through the frozen streets, she glanced up as she neared the family apartment. She knew something was not right: the ceiling light had been switched on in her mother's bedroom. As this rarely happened, it was with mounting dread that she rang the doorbell. Her worst fears were confirmed when the door was flung open by a policeman in military uniform. Irina looked past him to the row of elegant greatcoats with epaulettes and matching military caps hanging on the coat stand in the hall. The schoolgirl diligently hung up her own modest coat and peered into the sitting room. Through the fog of cigarette smoke from the chain-smoking guards, she saw her grandmother sitting, ashen, her face swollen from crying. She saw her Aunt Nadia and her stricken grandfather. The room seemed packed. As well as family, she realised that other people connected to her mother had been summoned by the authorities as 'witnesses'. They too were stunned by the shock of it all. Their kindly caretaker with his large bushy moustache still had his apron on over his quilted jacket. He remained with his head bowed low. A friend of Olga's, Alexei Kruchenykh, a futurist poet who attended her literary soirees, perched on a nearby sofa, also visibly frightened. Irina's great-uncle, Uncle Fonia, had been innocently paying the family a visit, only to be caught up in the drama. He sat 'with his light-blue eyes almost starting out of their sockets with terror'.

Irina went to her bedroom where Mitia was being comforted by their great-aunt, Milia. Aunt Milia explained to Irina that her mother had been taken away to the Lubyanka prison an hour before. In a bid to quell her fears, or merely to detach herself from the unfolding horror, Irina picked up a book, lay down on her bed and started to read. She shrugged at Aunt Milia: what else do you expect me to do? She then became agitated, as she started to think about her pet fish. She worried that they might die if she didn't go into the kitchen and change their water. Haunted by the image of the huge fish dying alone in the tank, Irina got up and went to remonstrate with the guards, who refused her entry to the kitchen and sent her back to her room.

She lay back on her bed, straining to listen as the tension mounted in the sitting room. When Uncle Fonia was asked for his official papers, he was thrown into confusion. At that time he was working as a night-watchman at the Cocktail Hall on Gorki Street. This was an institution frequented by foreigners and members of the Soviet elite, which served as a useful listening post for the secret police. Uncle Fonia used to bring Irina and Mitia cocktail straws and paper napkins from the bar as little gifts. In his blind panic he assumed that the police were investigating him for stealing from work; when asked for his papers, he pulled reams of paper napkins out of his pockets, to the officers' great derision.

Similarly tragic-comic was Alexei Kruchenykh. As the poet's writing day was divided up according to a rigidly strict timetable, which Irina remembered as being 'simply a mania with him', he boldly announced that he must go home at all cost to take his sleeping pills. It was essential to his work, he added, that he spent the night in his own bed. When the officers prevented him, he became obstreperous. The rest of the group watched, anxious that Kruchenykh should not escalate matters. They tried to calm him down in urgent whispers. Eventually, he took a sleeping tablet and agreed to lie down on the sofa, folding his frame awkwardly onto his side, to everyone's relief. Doors continued to bang and hearts leapt as officials came and went late into the night.

After a few hours, the officers began to leak slivers of news. Irina's grandfather heard that Olga had had a 'bad journey' across Moscow to the Lubyanka, and had cried hysterically all the way there. By four in the morning, the official business seemed to be over and the guests in the sitting room were released. Irina and Mitia were tucked into their beds by their grandparents, who did their best to soothe them. The children lay back in the dark, silent yet united in one thought. Would they ever see their mother again?

As dawn broke, Irina listened to her grandparents negotiating with the police. Under Soviet law, the officers explained, Irina and Mitia would have to be put in a children's home because they had no resident mother or father. The officers tried to persuade them that the children would be better off in a home because they could not all live off their grandfather's cobbler's wage. Maria could not tell them the truth. That Boris Pasternak was already helping them financially. She was quite sure that Pasternak would come to their rescue and would not let the children be sent to an orphanage. To Irina's relief, the following morning she found that her grandparents had signed papers saying they would look after the children and that they would not be taken away.

Across Moscow, at the MGB's yellow-brick headquarters on Lubyanka Square, Olga found herself in an isolation unit. The Lubyanka was only five storeys high, but – so ran the Russian joke – it was the tallest building in Moscow because 'you could see Siberia from its basement'. Olga had been placed in solitary confinement while the authorities processed her. She was then strip-searched by female guards and subjected to a 'humiliating examination'. Further indignities continued as everything she valued, her ring, her wristwatch, even her bra, was taken away from her. They later explained that they had confiscated her bra in case she tried to hang herself with it.

Sitting in her tiny, dark cell, she was consumed with thoughts only of Boris: 'What if I don't see Boria?' she fretted. 'How terrible it will be for him, that first moment when he learns I'm gone! And then the thought flashed through my mind that he too must surely have been arrested – they would have picked him up on the way home after we parted!' Astonishingly, all Olga could think about at this time was her lover. Not her children. It didn't seem to occur to her that if anything happened to her, they would be orphaned.

Olga was kept in solitary confinement for three days, during which time she 'crossed the fateful boundary, the Rubicon which divides ordinary humans from prisoners'. She was finally moved after she ripped off the hem of her dress, put it around her neck and began to try to pull the fabric up towards her ears. The fact that two guards instantly burst into her cell and hauled her down a long corridor before pushing her into a larger cell proves that she was under constant surveillance. For now, the authorities wanted her alive.

Her new cell – Cell No 7 – contained fourteen other women. As she looked around, she saw that the beds were screwed to the parquet floor and had 'good' mattresses on them. The women lying on them had covered their eyes with pieces of white fabric, to protect themselves from the blindingly bright light of the lamps overhead. Olga soon understood that this was part of a refined method of torture by sleep deprivation. Interrogations always took place at night. Sleeping was 'not allowed' in the daytime when a dazzling light was shone onto the prisoners' faces continuously. The effect of this sleep deprivation was that 'the prisoners began to feel that time had come to a halt and their world had collapsed about them. They ceased to be sure of their innocence, of what they had confessed to, and which other persons they had compromised apart from themselves. In consequence they signed any raving nonsense put before them, and named the names needed by their tormentors to fulfil some fiendish plan for the liquidation of "enemies of the people".

After the oppressive experience of solitary confinement, with no light, air or comradely spirit, the new cell seemed to have certain advantages. Luxuries, even. Olga was struck by the sight of a table, a teapot and a set of chess pieces. The other women clamoured around her, bombarding her with questions. Olga told them naively that she couldn't imagine why she had been arrested, that it must be some mistake and that she would surely be released in a day or two when the authorities realised this. Unfortunately, her optimism was severely misguided as the long, monotonous days of waiting dragged on. Day after day passed and still she was not summoned for interview or interrogation. Almost unnervingly, it seemed as if nobody was in the least concerned with her.

One of the cellmates, an odd woman with a waxen complexion called Lidochka, tried to reassure her, telling her: 'You'll certainly be released if they haven't yet called you out for an interrogation after all this time. It must mean they have nothing on you.' Olga was later to discover that not all inmates could be trusted. Lidochka was in fact a stool pigeon who worked for the prison authorities and whose job it was to report everything that the women said in the cell. (Olga learned much later that this same strange woman, who dreamed of earning a pardon by spying in the cell and who got cigarettes from the interrogators as a reward, was brutally killed in a labour camp by fellow prisoners. When they discovered her true loyalties, they ducked her head in a cesspool and held it there until she drowned.)

Fortunately, there were other women who could be trusted in the cell. Olga quickly made a friend in an elderly fellow prisoner, Vera Sergeyevna Mezentseva. A former doctor in the Kremlin Hospital, she had been present at a New Year's Eve party when a group of doctors had proposed a toast to the 'immortal Stalin'. Another doctor remarked that the 'immortal' one was very ill, supposedly from cancer of the lip through smoking a pipe, and that his days were numbered. A third doctor then claimed that he had once treated Stalin's double. After being denounced by an informer present at the gathering (in those days there tended to be one present at any gathering), the whole group of doctors had been thrown into the cells. Vera Sergeyevna, who had played no part in the conversation, faced a minimum of ten years in jail.

Also among the cellmates to whom Olga became close was Trotsky's twenty-six-year-old granddaughter, Alexandra. She had just finished her studies at the Institute of Geology. She had been arrested for copying out into her notebook some verses of an illicit poem supporting Jewry. One day, when Alexandra was called out of the cell 'with belongings', she clung to Olga, terrified. Afterwards, Olga was haunted by the sound of her wails as the guards pulled her away. They were later told that Alexandra had been sent off for five years 'somewhere in the Far North', with her mother, who was in the next cell. Mother and daughter were both considered 'socially dangerous elements'.

Olga later wrote: 'Nowhere do you come closer to a person than in prison. Nobody listens and speaks to you like the cellmates who see their own fate reflected in your own, and from nobody else do you get such sympathy.'

While Olga lived in perpetual fear, her heart quickening every time the cell door opened, Boris waited anxiously to hear news in Peredelkino. He felt increasingly isolated and alone without his soul mate. Tormented by Olga's arrest, he fully expected to be taken into custody himself at any moment. And he knew that it was due to him that Olga had been arrested in the first place. This heightened his guilt that he had tried to break off relations with her earlier that year. On 9 August 1949, two months before Olga's arrest, he had written to his cousin, Olga Freidenberg, of his conflicted feelings for his lover:

I struggle with my need to talk out all my troubles to you because this thought can't be executed. I've had a new big attachment, but as my life with Zina is real, I had to sacrifice the former sooner or later and, strange to say, while everything was full of torment, pangs of conscience, a broken heart, and even horrors, I could easily tolerate it and sometimes seemed happy. But now, I feel inconsolably despondent, my loneliness, my dangerous position at the edge of a literary criticism, the final purposelessness of my efforts as a writer, the strange duality of my fate 'here' and 'there' and so on and so forth.

But once Olga was incarcerated, he pined for her, each day the familiar ache of longing becoming more intense. Less than a week after Olga's arrest, he wrote to his friend Nina Tabidze of his despair:

Life literally repeated the last scene of Faust – Marguerite in the Dungeon. My poor O. followed our dear Titsian. It happened a week ago on October 9th. Probably the rivalry of no man could seem so threatening and dangerous as to evoke jealousy in its most acute, sucking form. But I often, since my green days, had been jealous of a woman's past, of her disease, the threat of death or departure, of the forces far away and insurmountable. Thus I am jealous now of the power and bondage and uncertainty instead of my touch and voice ... Suffering will make my work deeper, including still sharper features in all my being and all my consciousness. But it's no fault of hers, poor soul, is it?

As he had predicted to Nina Tabidze, Boris's writing did indeed become 'deeper'. He channelled the anguish, guilt and pain caused by his separation from Olga into his prose. Like his hero Yury, who only develops his poetic and philosophical gifts as he is separated from his wife, children and his mistress, Lara, so Boris's writing is heightened as he lives on the edge of a political and emotional abyss. Acute jealousy is a strong theme in *Doctor Zhivago*. He writes of his passionate love for Lara and the grisly side-effect of such intimacy: his tormented possessiveness. 'I am jealous of your hairbrush, of the drops of sweat on your skin, of the germs in the air you breathe which could get into your blood and poison you,' Yury says to Lara. 'And in exactly the same way as though he were an infectious illness, I am jealous of Komarovsky who will take you away from me some day, just as certainly as death will some day separate us. I know this sounds like a lot of confused nonsense, but I can't say it more clearly. I love you beyond mind or memory or measure.'

As the weeks passed and Boris was left alone by the authorities, free to continue writing, he became increasingly convinced that he was not being arrested thanks to Olga's valiant conduct in the Lubyanka. And he was right. A fortnight after her arrest, her interrogations finally began.

Olga had just eaten her supper (potatoes and salted herring) and lain down on her cell bed to sleep, when the duty guard rushed in to demand: 'What are your initials? Get dressed for interrogation!'

Agitated, she put on her dark-blue crepe de chine dress with large white polka dots, which her mother had handed in to the prison. It was Boris's favourite dress. As she put it on, Olga felt a fantastical surge of expectation that she would shortly be released. She even envisaged walking home through the streets of Moscow, and Boris's elation when he came to her apartment the following morning and found her there.

The guards took her out of the cell and led her down long corridors, past closed, mysterious-looking doors from which echoed occasional terrifying cries and wails of distress. They stopped outside a door numbered 271. Olga was not led into a room but what looked like a cupboard. Suddenly, the cupboard 'revolved' and she found herself rotated into a large room with soldiers standing chatting. They fell silent as she passed by. She was ushered into a vast, smart, brightly lit office. Sitting behind a desk was a 'handsome, portly figure with brown eyes, sleek, steeply-arching eyebrows, dressed in a long military tunic with small buttons up to the neck'.

Olga was not yet to know that this was Viktor Abakumov, Stalin's Minister of State Security, and one of the leader's most violent henchmen. During the war Abakumov had led the military counter-intelligence unit, SMERSH, an acronym for 'Death to Spies', which set up blocking positions immediately behind the front lines and executed Red Army soldiers who attempted to retreat. The unit also hunted down deserters and brutally interrogated German prisoners of war. Before torturing his victims, it was said that Abakumov would unroll a bloodstained carpet to protect the sheen on his office floor.

Abakumov motioned for Olga to sit down on a chair some way from him. On his desk was piled a haul of books and correspondence that had been taken from her apartment during the police raid, including one of her favourites, Pasternak's *Collected Prose Works*, which a colleague had brought back for her from a trip abroad. The title page was covered by a dedication to her in Boris's flowing hand, which to Olga 'always looked like a flock of cranes sailing across the sky'. Boris had written: 'To you as a memento – even if imperilled by all these pictures of my ugly mug.' The first printed page of the book showed a sketch of Boris, aged seven, sitting writing at a table, one leg dangling from a chair, drawn by his father, Leonid. It was followed by the artist's self-portrait, showing Leonid as a 'handsome, grey-haired man in a soft-brimmed hat'.

Olga could also see the small red volume of verse in which Boris had written those 'blissful words': 'My life, my angel, I love you dearly.' Dated April 4th, 1947, it was, to Olga, 'the year when our closeness had begun to seem to him like some stupendous victory or gift'.

Among the stash on his desk there were other signed books of Boris's verse and translations; her personal diary; bundles of letters (157 in total); various photographs of Olga; many books in English; and some of Olga's own poems. She sat there in her chair, ready to meet her fate. Telling herself to cast all hopes aside, she thought to herself that she must await the end and not lose her dignity.

'Tell me now, is *Boris* anti-Soviet, or not, do you think?' Abakumov asked sternly. Before she could reply, he continued: 'Why are you so bitter? You've been worrying about him for some reason! Admit it now – we know everything.'

As Olga did not know the identity of her interrogator, she fearlessly responded with none of the caution that an encounter with a dangerous figure such as Abakumov would normally demand.

'You always worry about a person you love,' she replied. 'If he goes out on the street, you worry in case a brick falls on his head. As regards whether Boris Leonidovich is anti-Soviet or not – there are too few colours on your palette – only black and white. There is a tragic lack of half-tones.'

Abakumov arched his eyebrows and gestured to the pile of Olga's confiscated books. 'How did you come by these?' he asked. 'You no doubt realise why you are here at this moment?'

'No, I don't. I am not aware of having done anything.'

'Then why did you plan to get out of the country? We know all about it.'

Olga replied indignantly that she had never in all her life thought of leaving Russia.

Abakumov brushed this aside, impatiently: 'Now listen here, I would suggest that you think very carefully about this novel Pasternak is passing round to people at the moment – at a time when we have quite enough malcontents and enemies as it is. You are aware of the anti-Soviet nature of the novel?'

Olga contradicted him 'hotly' and tried in a rather disjointed way to describe the contents of the part of the novel already completed.

Abakumov cut her short: 'You will have plenty of time to think about these questions and how to answer them. But personally, I would like you to appreciate that we know everything, and that your own as well as Pasternak's fate will depend on how truthful you are. I hope that next time we meet, you will have nothing to conceal about Pasternak's anti-Soviet views. They are clear enough from what he says himself.'

'Take her away,' he said imperiously, looking at the guard.

As Olga was led back along the corridors to her cell, the Lubyanka clock showed that it was three in the morning.

Olga spent fitful hours trying to sleep under the blinding lights. She began to understand the effect of the sleep deprivation as she was becoming confused in her mind and feeling exhausted. Just as she was allowed to go to bed and had covered her face with a handkerchief in a bid to shield her eyes from the powerful blaze of the lights, the door opened with a clang.

Again she was led down a long corridor, this time to a simpler office occupied by a man in a military tunic whom she had not encountered before. He explained that he was Anatoli Sergeyevich Semionov (a junior official). He then explained that her interrogator the day before had been Minister Abakumov himself.

Semionov urged Olga to confess that she and Pasternak had been planning to escape abroad and to declare Pasternak's novel anti-Soviet. When Olga protested once more that she was not aware of having done anything wrong, Semionov smiled ironically: 'Ah, but it will take six or eight months for us to establish whether you've done anything wrong or not.' Olga felt herself go cold. This was the crossing of another boundary. 'The door had slammed shut and there was no question of going home.'

Semionov asked Olga about her family. 'Talk to us about your father.'

'As far as I know my mother left him in 1913. According to my Uncle Vladimir, he died from typhoid in 1914,' Olga replied.

'Please don't make things up,' Semionov demanded. 'We know for sure that he joined forces with the Whites in 1918. And what about your mother, wasn't she condemned of anti-Soviet activities?'

'My mother has never been involved in anti-Soviet activities.'

'Tell us how you met Pasternak?'

'We met in October 1946 at *Novy Mir*, where I was working at the time.'

'When did you become intimate?'

'April 1947 ...'

Olga's interrogation sessions with Semionov became a nightly ordeal. He was not particularly rough with her, and thankfully never physically violent. She appreciated this as she had learned from her cellmates that some of their interrogators became aggressive, slapping them across the face and verbally abusing them. Semionov spoke instead in a mocking tone, endlessly repeating the same stereotyped phrase about how 'Pasternak sat down at a table with the British and Americans but ate Russian bacon.' Olga found this phrase increasingly irritating, hearing it over and over again. In the end, Semionov declared that Pasternak was a British spy. The fact that he had family in England and had held several meetings with the British diplomat Isaiah Berlin was, for his inquisitors, evidence enough of his disloyalty.

Semionov's interrogations of Olga went on for weeks. The conversations were always along the same lines. 'It became a matter of ordinary routine for me during my stay in the Lubyanka,' she later recalled, 'even in hell, it thus appeared, life could be quite humdrum.' A classic interrogation followed these lines:

*Semionov*: Speak to us about Pasternak's political opinions. What do you know about his undermining activities, his pro-Britain opinions and his betraying intentions?

*Olga*: Pasternak does not belong to this category of people, he has no anti-Soviet views. He has no intention to betray his country. He has always loved his homeland.

*Semionov*: So how do you explain that we found in your house a publication written in English dedicated to his work? How did you get hold of it?

*Olga*: The truth is that Pasternak gave it to me. It is about his father, who was a painter and it was published in London.

*Semionov*: How did Pasternak get it?

*Olga*: Simonov [the editor of *Novy Mir*] brought it back from one of his trips abroad.

*Semionov*: What more do you know of Pasternak's ties with England?

*Olga*: I think that he once got a parcel from his sisters who are living there.

*Semionov*: How do you explain your relationship with Pasternak? He is, after all, a lot older than you?

*Olga*: Love.

*Semionov*: I don't believe that. No, you were joined together by your shared political views and treasonous intentions.

*Olga*: We did not have any such plans. What I loved about him and still love is the man he is.

*Semionov*: After questioning witnesses, it was concluded that you have continually praised Pasternak's work and that you have presented them as a contrast to work from patriotic writers such as Sourikov or Simonov, whereas the artistic methods of Pasternak in depicting Soviet reality are wrong.

*Olga*: That is right, I have praised his work as a model to Soviet writers. His work is very precious for Soviet literature. His artistic methods are not wrong but just subjective.

*Semionov*: Let's get back to your statement about Pasternak's anti-Soviet views.

*Olga*: It is true that he was shocked by the living conditions in the USSR. I think this was because he felt that he had been deprived unfairly of his audience but he has never admitted to any slander about soviet reality and nothing in his opinions leads us to believe that he was capable of treason.

*Semionov*: Talk to me about his pro-British feelings.

*Olga*: It is true that he likes Britain as he is always very keen on translating British literary work.

And so on. After one of these relentless sessions, Olga was asked to write a summary of *Doctor Zhivago*. She was given a few sheets of paper, so she leaned forwards, resting the paper on the desk in front of her and began to write. She described the burgeoning novel as the story of an intellectual, a doctor, who had found life difficult in the years between the revolutions of 1905 and 1917. He was a man of artistic temperament, a poet. Zhivago himself would not survive the present day, but some of his friends would. There would be, she explained in her barely legible handwriting, nothing discreditable to the Soviet system in the novel. What was to be written was the truth. It was an account of the whole era written by a genuine writer, who, instead of retreating into his own personal world, decided to bear witness to the times.

Semionov picked up her pages of handwritten scrawl, glanced across them and scoffed: 'It is no good, what you are writing. You must simply say that you have actually read this work and that it constitutes a slander on Soviet life ...'

Later, Semionov focused on Pasternak's poem 'Mary Magdalene' and the possibility that it might refer to Olga. The poem begins:

As soon as night falls my tempter is beside me.
He is the debt I pay to my past.
Memories of debauchery
Come and suck at my heart,
Memories of myself, a slave to men's whims,
A fool, out of my mind,
To whom the street was shelter.

'What era does it refer to?' he asked Olga. 'And why have you never told Pasternak that you're a Soviet woman, not a Mary Magdalene, and that it is simply not right to give such a title to a poem about a woman he loves?'

'What makes you think it's about me?' Olga asked.

'But it's obvious – and we know all about it, so there's no point in denying it! You must speak the truth: this is the only thing that might make things easier for both you and Pasternak.'

Another time, confusing Mary Magdalene with the Madonna, Semionov asked Olga: 'Why are you trying to make yourself out to be a Magdalene? You've been the death of two husbands, both of them honest communists, and now you turn pale at the very mention of this scoundrel who eats Russian bacon but sits at the table with the British ...' So sick and tired was Olga of hearing about the wretched 'Russian bacon' that she angrily retorted that the Russian bacon had actually been paid for by Pasternak's translations of Shakespeare and Goethe.

Semionov often returned to ridiculing the romance itself. 'But what have you got in common?' he jeered. 'I can't believe that a Russian woman like you could ever really be in love with this old Jew – there must be some ulterior motive here! I've seen him myself. You can't love him. He's just mesmerised you, or something. You can almost hear his bones creak. A fine specimen! You must have some ulterior motive.'

During one interrogation, when a loud banging was suddenly heard on the iron gates of the Lubyanka, Semionov said with a mocking smile: 'Hear that? It's Pasternak trying to get in here! Don't worry, he'll make it before long ...'

It was true, Boris would indeed soon be summoned to the Lubyanka, but for reasons Olga could never have guessed.

Ironically, while Olga was vigorously defending her lover and his novel during her nightly interrogations at the State Security headquarters, Boris was left alone in Peredelkino, free to continue writing. By the autumn of 1949 he had completed five chapters. His writing was subject to long periods of suspension, when he worked on his poetry and translations in order to earn necessary funds. In Soviet literary circles, attacks were mounting and he had begun to realise how serious and precarious his situation was. If he wasn't allowed to write, how could he earn a living? And how soon would it be before the authorities came for him? It was inconceivable to Boris, refusing to toe the party line by writing pro-Soviet original material, that he would not be arrested. He found this an incredibly challenging and unstable period, always living as if on borrowed time.

In March 1947 a critique by the poet A. Surkov had appeared in the newspaper *Culture and Life*, 'violently denouncing' Boris's work. Pasternak's poetry, said Surkov, 'clearly shows that scant spiritual resources are not capable of creating real poetry, that reactionary ideology will not let the poet's voice become a voice of the epoch ... Soviet literature cannot put up with his poetry'. Surkov was shortly to become the secretary general of the Soviet Writers' Union. Olga later described this as a case of a 'literary bureaucrat against a poet of genius in a shameful campaign'. Surkov, who Olga added 'hated Boris' due to bitter envy of his talent, alleged that Pasternak wished to undermine the existing political system. The following April, 25,000 entire copies of Pasternak's *Selected Works* of poetry, printed and ready for distribution, were pulped on 'orders from above', the day before publication day.

Pasternak knew that public appearances by him were regarded as undesirable and due to the restrictions under which he was placed, he could only be conceived of as a translator. He spent the latter part of 1948 putting *Doctor Zhivago* on hold to translate Johann Wolfgang von Goethe's *Faust*, Part 1 and 2, which he finished in February 1949. Translating *Faust* gave him as much a sense of spiritual freedom as *Hamlet* had earlier; he told the sculptor Zoya Maslennikova that it helped him 'to become bolder, freer, to break bonds of some sort, not just of political and moral prejudice, but in the sense of form'.

It is clear that working on Goethe's *Faust*, a tragic play about selling your soul to the devil, would have appealed to the tortured Boris; not least because here at least he could express himself creatively, without having to worry that he was antagonising the authorities. In Part 1, Faust does not seek power through knowledge, but access to transcendent knowledge denied through the rational mind. Goethe's themes of mysticism would have resonated with Pasternak, as would the blend of psychology, history and politics in Part 2: themes he was also wrestling with in *Doctor Zhivago*.

Pasternak saw Olga as his Marguerite – an enchanting, innocent maiden. In one of his letters to Josephine he writes that if she wants to know what Olga looks like, she should look at the illustration of

Marguerite in his translation of *Faust*. 'It's almost her likeness,' he said. Boris even used to correspond with his sisters, using the name 'Marguerite' to refer to Olga, to conceal her identity from Zinaida. Goethe's Marguerite was the embodiment of soft femininity and purity, as Olga was to Boris. He later dedicated his translation of *Faust* to his lover, writing: 'Olga get out of this book, take a seat and read it.'

If Pasternak thought that he was relatively safe in translating *Faust*, in that he could not be accused of antipathy towards the state, he was wrong. Almost predictably, in August 1950, his translation of the first part of *Faust* led him to be attacked in *Novy Mir*. 'The translator clearly distorts Goethe's ideas ... In order to defend the reactionary theory of "pure art" he introduces an aesthetic and individualist flavour into the text. He attributes a reactionary idea to Goethe and distorts the social and philosophical meaning.'

Pasternak wrote to Ariadna Efron, the exiled daughter of his dear late friend, the poet Marina Tsvetaeva: 'There has been much concern over an article in *Novy Mir* denouncing my *Faust* on the grounds that the gods, angels, witches, spirits, the madness of poor Gretchen, and everything "irrational" has been rendered much too well, while Goethe's "progressive" ideas (what are they?) have been glossed over. But I have a contract to do the second part as well! I don't know how it will all end. Fortunately, it seems that the article won't have any practical effect.' At least the work was bringing in some money: he wrote to his sisters in England that 'Zina is able to indulge Lyonia [their son, Leonid] and we're not suffering deprivation.'

When circumstances allowed he returned to *Zhivago*. The immense guilt he felt at Olga's incarceration – and his awareness that the Soviet authorities sought to manipulate and punish him through her suffering – seemed to revive him, producing in him tremendous bursts of creative energy. He could write fearlessly, convinced that the novel would never be published in Russia. So while Olga was defending his book, denying that it was anti-Soviet, Pasternak was channelling his fury against the political machinations and privations of the day into a brave and decidedly anti-Soviet book. Writing to his friend Zoya Maslennikova, he defended his position explaining that his novel could be seen as 'anti-Soviet' only if 'by Soviet one is to understand the desire not to see life as it is'. In *Doctor Zhivago* he writes:

> Such a new thing, too, was the revolution, not the one idealised in student fashion in 1905, but this new upheaval, today's born of the war, bloody, pitiless, elemental, the soldiers' revolution, led by the professionals, the bolsheviks.
>
> And among his new thoughts was Nurse Antipova [Lara], caught by the war at the back of beyond, with her completely unknown life, Antipova who never blamed anyone, yet whose very silence was almost a reproach, mysteriously reserved and so strong in her reserve. And here too was Yury's honest endeavour not to love her as whole hearted as his striving throughout his life until now to love not only his family or his friends, but everyone else as well.

What Pasternak did not yet know, as he wrote about Lara, was that reality was exceeding even *his* reaches for fiction. While in the Lubyanka, Olga discovered that she was pregnant. She was carrying Boris's child.

Olga was delighted by this discovery, not least because as soon as the pregnancy was confirmed, conditions for her eased. She was allowed to receive white bread, salads and puree instead of *kasha*, the daily gruel of porridge made from buckwheat. Her extra food rations were handed to her through the hatch in the cell door. She was also allowed to buy twice the usual amount of food rations from the prison store. She was able to take a daily twenty-minute walk. However, the chief and most tangible concession was that she was allowed to sleep during the day after interrogations. While her cellmates were not permitted any rest after nightly interrogations, and were forced to pace the cell or sit and brood, Olga was allowed to go back to sleep. The warder on duty would come in, prod her with his finger and say in a respectful tone: 'You are allowed to sleep. Lie down again.'

'And I would go back to sleep,' Olga recalled, 'a sleep without dreams, into which I fell as though into an abyss, interrupting in mid-sentence anyone who happened to be telling me about her interrogation during the night. My kind cell-mates talked in whispers so as not to disturb me, and I would wake up again only to eat the mid-day meal.'

After lunch, the prisoners whiled away the afternoon, their 'leisure hours'. 'These too exist in hell,' Olga noted wryly, sewing with a fishbone needle in which an eye had been made for the thread, or 'ironing' their dresses. This they did in preparation for the next interrogation by sprinkling them with water and sitting on them. Any time that remained they spent talking and reciting poetry.

Olga knew that some contact had been made with her mother, Maria, because she had received her parcel (containing the blue crepe de chine dress, plus money for food). What Olga cannot have known then was that her interrogator, Semionov, occasionally rang Maria to update her on her daughter's situation. Irina described Semionov's calls to her grandmother: 'He was extremely polite – of which grandmother was very glad indeed, since we were now social outcasts and such politeness seems like a gift or a favour. Because of it we went on hoping ...' He also permitted Olga to keep a rare book from the prison library – a one-volume edition of Pasternak's poetry.

One evening, a few months into Olga's imprisonment, Maria got a call from a woman called Lidia Petrovna, who had just been released from the Lubyanka. She said that she had been in the same cell as Olga and had some information. She asked to meet with Maria. The situation for Olga in the Lubyanka is becoming 'very bad', she told her; her daughter was pregnant and ill.

Olga was around six months pregnant when, during one of Semionov's interrogations, a new interrogator suddenly came into the the room. She noted that Semionov spoke more sharply to her in his presence. 'Well now,' the stranger said, 'you have so often asked for a meeting, and we are going to let you have one. Get ready for a meeting with Pasternak.'

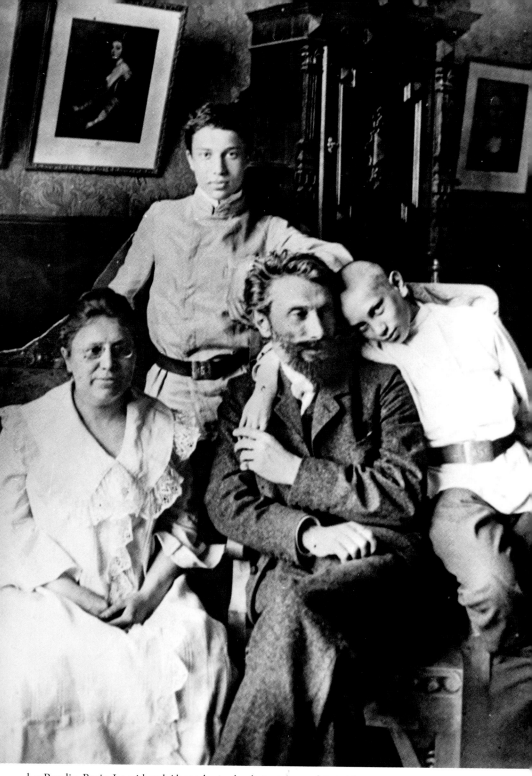

l-r: Rosalia, Boris, Leonid and Alexander in the dining room of their Moscow apartment, 1905

l-r: Boris, Leonid and Alexander, with Lydia and Josephine in front, 1906

l-r: Leonid, Lydia, Rosalia, Josephine, an unknown friend and Boris in 1916 at Molodi, the estate where they spent their summers before the Revolution

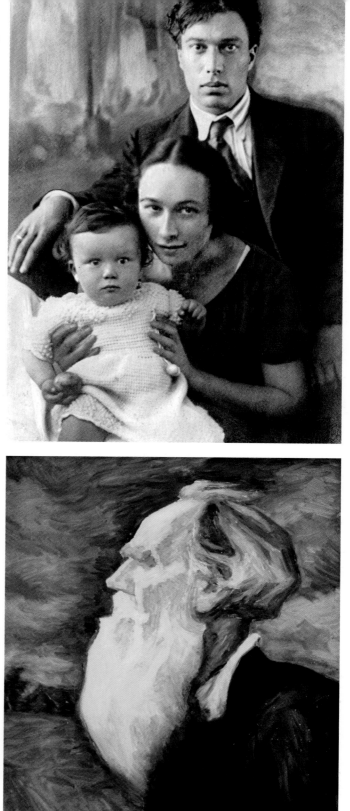

Boris with his first wife
Evgenia and their son
Evgeny. Moscow, 1924

Portrait, *Tolstoy against
a Stormy Sky*, painted
by Leonid. Yasnaya
Polyana, 1901

Frederick, Evgeny, Evgenia and Josephine on a lake near Munich, 1931

Leonid and Rosalia with (l-r) Charles and Helen Pasternak and Evgeny, at a picnic in the German countryside, 1931

Leonid's drawing of his grandson Charles, aged 2, Munich, 1932

Olga aged 25, Moscow, 1937

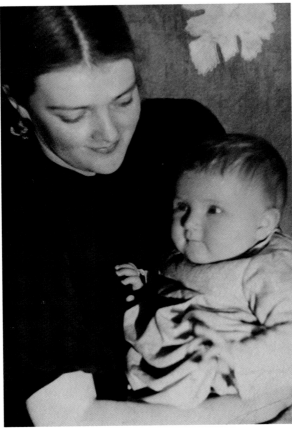

Olga and her baby daughter
Irina, Moscow, 1939

Olga aged 30,
Moscow, 1942

Irina with her
grandmother Maria and
grandfather Dimitri
Kostko on the day
Maria was sent to the
gulag. Moscow, 1943

СССР

МИНИСТЕРСТВО
ВНУТРЕННИХ ДЕЛ

ИТЛ

"АК"

4 мая 1953 г.

7-АЧ 5/XI 53 Y 001954

# СПРАВКА

Выдана гражданину (ке) Ивинской Ольге Всеволодовне 1912 года рождения, уроженцу (ке) г. Тамбов гражданство (подданство) СССР национальность русская осужденному (ой) по делу Управления МГБ. СССР

«29» Июля 1950 г. по ст.ст. 58-10ч. УК РСФСР к лишению свободы на пять лет с поражением в правах на _____ года, имеющему (ей) в прошлом судимость не судима

в том, что он (она) отбывал (ла) наказание в местах заключения МВД по «4» мая 1953 г. и по с. 1 Указа президиума Верховного Совета СССР о 27/III 53. со снятием судимости

С применением

Освобожден а (на) «4» мая 1953 г. и следует к избранному месту жительства гор. Москва
(город, село, дер., район, область)

до ст. Москва Моск. Рязан. жел. дороги.

Начальник лагеря (ИТЛ) "АК"
полковник б/сл. _____
Нач. Отдела (части) _____

Печать

Olga's release papers from the gulag, 4 May 1953

Olga was absolutely 'overcome with joy at the thought of being able to embrace him, of being able to say a few tender words of encouragement'. Both her interrogators signed a piece of paper, wrote out a pass and handed it to a guard. Olga, 'giddy with happiness', followed her escort out of the Lubyanka. She was put in a prison van with blacked-out windows and driven through the city to another government building. There she was led along endless long corridors, with many staircases leading upwards, yet she was always taken downstairs. Deeper and deeper down she was marched, until she reached a poorly lit basement. Feverish, exhausted and disorientated, she could go on no longer. Suddenly, she was pushed through a metal door that clanged shut loudly behind her. She looked back in terror but no one was there.

It was difficult to see through the gloom and there was a sickly strange smell. When Olga's eyes adjusted to the semi-darkness, she could just make out a whitewashed floor with pools of water, zinc-topped tables and what appeared to be cadavers partly covered by tarpaulins. Suddenly she realised that the smell was 'the unmistakeable sweetish smell of a morgue'. Semionov had promised her she would see Boris. She had spent every day of her long incarceration worrying that he was being mistreated in some other cell, convinced that he had been arrested. 'Could it be that one of those corpses was the man I loved?' she wondered.

After being locked inside the morgue for some time, Olga's legs gave out and she collapsed onto the floor, her feet in one of the icy pools of water. Oddly enough, her sense of terror then passed. 'I suddenly felt completely calm. For some reason, as though God had put it in my mind, it dawned on me that the whole thing was a monstrous hoax, and that Boria could not possibly be here.'

Eventually, the metal door clanged open again and Olga was dragged to her feet and led back along a series of corridors and stairs. Her belly ached and she could not shake off the interminable inner chill or the sickly sweet smell. The authorities' attempts to reduce her to flailing despair may have failed, but in other ways, far more sinister, Olga would soon discover that they had succeeded in their aim.

\*   \*   \*

Her next destination was a room containing Semionov. 'Please forgive us,' he said, with a smile playing over his face, 'we made a mistake and took you to the wrong place altogether. It was the fault of the escort guards. But now prepare yourself: we are waiting for you.'

Olga was astonished when a door opened and it was not Boris who entered, as she was still naively expecting, but an elderly man who after a few moments she recognised: Sergei Nikolayevich Nikiforov, Irina's English teacher. Olga was aghast – so this was it – another sick joke. This was her 'meeting' with her beloved.

Nikiforov was being interrogated by a glib and brazen young officer with a pimply face. Olga was about to be subjected to a ritual of Soviet interrogation: a staged confrontation with a witness who had been primed, almost certainly after torture, to offer evidence of her treachery. Olga was astonished by his appearance. Usually neat and tidy, he was unkempt, he had a straggly beard, his trousers were unbuttoned and his shoes had no laces.

'Do you confirm the evidence you gave yesterday that you were present at anti-Soviet conversations between Pasternak and Ivinskaya?' asked Semionov. Olga, who shouted out in astonishment – as Nikiforov had never even seen her together with Boris – was immediately reprimanded not to speak out of turn.

'Now you told us that Ivinskaya informed you of her plan to escape abroad together with Pasternak, and that they tried to persuade an airman to take them out of the country on a plane. Do you confirm this?'

'Yes, that is so,' said Nikiforov.

Olga could not contain herself, she was so outraged by this complete fiction. 'Aren't you ashamed Sergei Nikolayevich?' Semionov motioned for her to be silent by putting his finger to his lips.

'But you confirmed it yourself, Olga Vsevolodovna,' he mumbled.

It was then that Olga understood. The old man had been induced to give false information after he was told that Olga had already confessed to crimes that had never even occurred to her, let alone actually happened.

'Tell us how you listened to anti-Soviet broadcasts at the home of

Ivinskaya's friend Nikolai Stepanovich Rumiantsev,' continued the bullish young interrogator.

Nikiforov became confused and began to shift his ground. 'That's not actually so, I think ...' he stammered.

'So you were lying to us?' his interrogator snapped at him.

Poor Nikiforov began to whine and prevaricate. It was unbearable for Olga to witness the old man's distress; her family had all been so fond of him. Olga tried to come to both their defences, stating that he had seen Pasternak in the flesh only twice, and that was only at the public poetry readings which Olga had arranged for him to attend.

Nikiforov was ushered out of the room with his interrogator. Semionov turned to Olga and said smugly: 'You see, not all interrogators are like yours.' Then added: 'Let's go home. There's no place like home ...'

Years later, Nikiforov the school teacher wrote to Olga, 'I have pondered for a long time whether to write to you. In the end, the conscience of an honest man ... prompts me to account for the situation in which I put you – believe me, against my will, given the conditions then existing.'

I know that these conditions were familiar to you and that to some extent they were experienced by you as well. But they were of course applied to us men more forcefully and severely than to women. Before our meeting at that time, I had repudiated two documents, even though I had signed up to them. But how many people are able to go boldly, and uprightly, to the scaffold. Unfortunately, I do not belong to their number, because I am not alone. I had to think of my wife and shield her.

To put it more clearly, the times were then such that by virtue of the situation, as it were, one person dragged another after him into the same abyss. In repudiating and disowning the two documents signed by me, I did so in the firm knowledge that they were false and had not been drafted by me. But as I have said, I was compelled, if only for a time, to save myself from the scaffold with which I was threatened.

Touched by Nikiforov's honesty and his confession, Olga recalled: 'When I think of my terror in the morgue, I understand very well indeed that a prisoner is only to be condemned if he bears false witness simply to please his jailers, or to save his own skin. But he cannot really be blamed for losing his head or giving way to terror. Nikiforov was not the only one. All too many others, during the first few days of their imprisonment, were turned into informers, witnesses for the prosecution and, in general, servants of the inquisition.'

That so many prisoners weakened under terrible pressures makes Olga's bravery in the face of persistent interrogation, and while pregnant with her lover's child, even more impressive. She did not use anyone else to save her, least of all Pasternak, the man she was protecting. Irina proudly agreed: 'It is clear that my mother came out of her questioning victorious. If their aim was to build a case against Pasternak, none of her statements could be used against him.'

Hours after being returned to her 'home cell' in the Lubyanka, Olga felt searing pains in her abdomen. She was taken to the prison hospital. A doctor's note in an official document stated that Olga was in the clinic 'due to bleeding from the womb' and that 'the arrested person said that she was pregnant'. She had lost the baby. 'Here Boria's and my child perished before it was even born,' Olga later pitifully recalled.

'I am not convinced it was a natural miscarriage,' said Irina, looking back. 'My mother was six months pregnant. I think that she was deliberately sent to the morgue and left in the freezing cold to induce a miscarriage ... Boris Pasternak was known all over the world. They did not want the circumstances of a baby's birth or death to be known ... This was the authorities' way of closing the whole story down. If news of the baby had got out, people would begin to talk about Pasternak again. This was their way of silencing talk on Pasternak and getting rid of potential embarrassment. It was a truly horrible, sickening regime.'

Olga's case – No 3038 – which had been opened on 12 October 1949, was closed on 5 July 1950. A troika – a three-man tribunal – issued a 'mild' sentence. Under Article 58 of the Soviet Criminal Code, which dealt with political crimes, Olga was to spend five years in a re-education labour camp 'for close contact with persons suspected of espionage'. The Accusation Act for her case read: 'The witnesses' statements have enabled us to uncover your actions: you have continued to denigrate our regime and the Soviet Union. You have listened to the "voice of America". You have slandered Soviet writers who had patriotic views and you have praised to the skies Pasternak's work, a writer with anti-establishment opinions.'

It marked the beginning of a new and terrible ordeal for Olga, who was destined for the labour camps of Potma, over 800 kilometres away from Moscow, in the 'Autonomous Soviet Socialist Republic of Mordovia'. If they couldn't touch Boris, Olga would serve in his place.

# 6

## Cranes Over Potma

Whilst Olga was still in the Lubyanka, word reached Boris, via Maria, that his lover was pregnant. Boris proceeded to rush around Moscow, telling friends and even the slightest acquaintances that Olga would soon be having their baby in prison, enlisting their sympathy, and fixating on the idea of being a father again. He had no way of knowing of the unborn child's death.

When an official summoned him to go to the Lubyanka prison it confirmed to him that he was to be handed the baby in person. He was going to a 'terrible place' he told Liusia Popova, where he had been instructed that 'they want to hand something over to me'. He broke the news of Olga's pregnancy to Zinaida, who 'made a terrible scene'. However, for once he stood his ground, announcing to his furious wife that they must take the child in and care for it until Olga was released. When Liusia asked how Zinaida had taken the news of Olga's pregnancy, his response was resigned: 'I just had to put up with it; it's only right that I should suffer too in some way … what kind of life can the child have in there? Of course, they want me to go and pick it up. But in case I don't come back, I just wanted you to know where I am going.'

At the Lubyanka, Boris was met by Semionov, Olga's interrogator. Semionov took him to a side room and instead of handing him a baby, gave him a large bundle of letters and books: the love letters that he had written to Olga and the books with their precious inscriptions.

Utterly confused and bewildered, Boris became agitated. He argued with Semionov, repeatedly demanding to know what was going on. During the meeting, the door kept opening and shutting as a number of officials peeked in; they had heard that the famous poet was in the building and wanted to see Pasternak with their own eyes. When Boris was not given the answers he sought, he asked for a pencil and paper so he could write a letter to the Minister of State Security, Abakumov.

Later Semionov used the letter in his interrogations of Olga. Covering most of the page with his hand, he said to her: 'You see, even Pasternak himself admits you could have done something wrong from the point of view of the State.' When Olga saw the 'soaring cranes' of Boris's handwriting, she felt elated: it was proof that he had not been killed. It was the first concrete evidence she had had of his existence for over ten agonising months.

In his letter to Abakumov, Pasternak had written that if the authorities believed that Olga had done something wrong, then he was willing to accept this. But if that was the case, then he too was guilty of the same crimes. And if his standing as a writer counted for anything, they should take him at his word and put him in prison instead of Olga. 'In this totally sincere letter to the Minister,' Olga reflected later, 'there was of course also a certain characteristic element of playing the innocent, but whatever he did was dear to my heart and came only as further proof of his love.'

Boris left the Lubyanka wholly dejected. 'They didn't give me the child but asked me to take away some of my letters,' he told Liusia Popova. 'I said they were addressed to her [Olga] and should be given back to her. But in the end I had to take a whole bundle of them, and some books with dedications as well.' 'So instead of the child, you'll take home some love letters and other such things – which will be just as bad,' came Liusia's pragmatic response. She advised him not to take the whole bundle back with him to Peredelkino and risk Zinaida's wrath but to read them through and sort them out beforehand.

Boris took her advice: he went to see Olga's family. According to Irina: 'The minute he came back to us, he tore every single page out of the books he had written on. Books he had given her during their love affair all signed with dedications full of love and affection. Was that because he thought they had been read at the Lubyanka?' she wondered. Or maybe out of guilt?

Pasternak was acutely aware that Olga's continued incarceration was a blow levelled at him. Due to Stalin's instructions and because of a mounting awareness that the arrest of a writer of his stature – he was an international celebrity and Nobel Prize candidate – would have unfavourable repercussions abroad, he remained untouched. Pasternak also worried for other friends who benefitted from no protection. He was still waiting to hear news of Titsian Tabidze, while the brother of another good friend, Alexander Gladkov, was in a camp in Kolyma. Alexander sent his brother the 'precious gift' of a volume of Boris's poetry. When he eventually returned from his years in the gulag, his brother told Boris that he used to wake early every day in the barracks, to read his verses. 'If ever something prevented me from doing so, I always felt as if I had not washed.' Boris replied: 'Oh if only I had known this then, in those black years, life would have been so much more bearable to think that I was *out there* too.'

That month Olga was taken to the transit camp of Butyrki, which she described as 'a veritable paradise compared with the Lubyanka'. She, too, knew that the past months of interrogation had been aimed at only one person – Boris. 'Just as a dossier was kept on Pushkin in the Third Section in the days of Nicholas I,' Olga later observed,

so during the whole of his active life there was a file at the Lubyanka on Pasternak in which not only everything he wrote was entered, but also every word ever uttered by him in the presence of innumerable informers. Now we had 'progress' of a kind: Pasternak was not merely a subversive poet, but a British spy, no less. There was a kind of logic here: his father had lived and died in England, and his two sisters were still there. In other words: a British spy. From this it followed that if not Pasternak himself, then at least I must be packed off to a camp.

Many years later, Boris wrote to the German poet Renate Schweitzer: '[Olga] was put in jail on my account, as the person considered by the secret police to be closest to me, and they hoped that by means of a gruelling interrogation and threats they could extract enough evidence from her to put me on trial. I owe my life and the fact that they did not touch me in those years to her heroism and endurance.'

Olga's family soon learned the devastating news that she had been transferred out of the Lubyanka en route for the gulag. Of these uncertain, distressing times Irina said: '1949, 1950, 1951 … those terrible years went by like hearses, and each one of them was worse than the previous one.' Irina was thirteen years old when she 'lost' her mother to the camps. Fortunately, much of her emotional stability and sense of security came from her grandparents. 'But it was a difficult age not to have my mother.' However, their 'true guardian was Pasternak.' After Olga was arrested, Maria decided to give their 'unrealistic love affair' her blessing, and from that point on she fully welcomed Pasternak into her home. Boris already helped with the children's school fees, but when Maria's husband died in 1950, he took complete financial responsibility for the family. 'It is thanks to him that we were able to ignore the misery and difficulties that were surrounding us, enabling us to enjoy a reasonably normal childhood like anybody else,' said Irina. 'My memories are not just about dresses mended a thousand times, nor about split pea soup either. I can also remember Christmas trees, presents, books and trips to the theatre. Thanks to Pasternak, we were able to live.'

Boris regularly visited Olga's family, bringing them money as often as he could. 'He was always in a rush as he had a lot to do,' Irina remembered, 'but most likely he wanted to run away from the pity we made him feel. He felt responsible for our tragic fate, for our orphan status, for my mother's arrest and therefore for our adored grandfather dying of a broken heart. He was devastated by my mother's sentence. It killed him.

'*Irochka*, I know you don't want me to go but I need to,' Boris would say. 'He would always kiss me goodbye really loudly, slam the door and run down the stairs … My grandmother put the money in her bag. She would pay the rent and would then buy us all kinds of nice things with whatever was left over.'

During this time, the family had no concrete information about Olga's fate. It was only later that they discovered that after the short 'vacation' in the less harrowing transit prison, she had been sent with other 'harmful elements' to the Potma rehabilitation camp.

From Butyrki, Olga and the other prisoners were crammed into a passenger coach. The stench was suffocating. Olga was fortunate enough to get a 'berth' on the luggage rack at the top of the compartment, from where she could see the sky. 'Sick at heart, as I gazed out at the moon, I mentally composed a poem about separation.' The last part of their journey was a forced march across open country. Olga walked next to a kind old army general, who tried to comfort her by saying, reassuringly: 'Everything will soon be over.'

Olga was completely unprepared for how gruelling life at Potma would be. The blazing summers proved worse than the arctic winters. For thirteen hours a day she had to work in the parched Mordovian fields, turning over the bone-dry, unyielding earth. Her nemesis and main tormentor was a sadistic female brigade leader called Buinaya. An agricultural expert and prisoner, she was a 'small, scrawny woman with a sharp nose, and looked just like a bird of prey'. Buinaya was serving a ten-year sentence for getting into trouble on a collective farm. Her two sons were in camps for criminals in the north. She enjoyed the confidence of the prison authorities, maintaining her privileged status by showing the escort guards how to bully and intimidate women like Olga.

Olga's five-year sentence was considered short; most were decades longer. The lighter sentences were a cause of resentment amongst the prisoners. One of Olga's fellow inmates, an old peasant woman from Western Ukraine, had received a twenty-five-year sentence just for giving milk to a stranger. Buinaya reserved her most intense hatred for privileged Moscow women, whom she saw as pampered and ineffectual at hard labour. She preferred the hefty Ukrainian peasant women who had worked in the fields all their lives, and who displayed considerably more stamina. Equally, the peasants resented the Muscovites with their 'ridiculously short prison sentences', considering them barely any better than their jailers as they enjoyed, in their eyes, relative leniency.

The only emotional sustenance for the homesick and lonely prisoners, who never knew their exact fate, was a letter from home. A home they were all too painfully aware that they might never see again. The Muscovite women would do anything for the chance of a letter – being prepared to work on Sundays for the chance of earning even the slightest privilege – which made the peasant women hate them all the more.

But it was a group of nuns who were singled out for the most appalling cruelties. They refused to report for work in the fields, preferring to go to the punishment block with its stifling cells, crawling with bugs. And so they were dragged out like sacks and flung in the dust next to the guard house, where they lay under the broiling sun exactly as they had fallen. Impassively, the soldiers then kicked and tossed them over towards the guard-house walls; pretty young women, older, weaker nuns – all were treated with the same rough contempt. The nuns in turn 'openly scorned their tormentors and just went on chanting their prayers, whether in the barracks or in the fields, on the occasions when they were dragged out there by force.' Unlike the rest of the prisoners, they could do without letters, which made them more resilient. 'The camp authorities hated them and were quite baffled by the firmness of their spirit shown by these women they were so mistreating.' They 'even refused to take the meagre sugar ration we were given, and the camp officials simply couldn't understand what kept them alive. In fact, they were kept alive by their faith', wrote Olga.

Olga remembered the summer of 1952 as being the worst. 'This was hell on earth. This was surely what it must be like to live in hell?' The day started at seven in the morning, when Olga had to work a few cubic metres of hard-baked soil. To earn her food rations she had to turn it over, hoeing with unpractised hands, finding it difficult to even lift up the achingly heavy pick. Buinaya would shriek at the women all day. She regularly grabbed Olga violently by the arm, thrusting the pick back into her hands when she dropped it. 'The only thing was to sweat it out to the end of the day, cursing the sun, which was now flaming white-hot in the June sky and took such a very long time to go down. Oh for a breath of wind! But even the wind, when it blew, was hot and brought no relief.' Even though there was no question of the workers making their impossible quota, or even half of it, they were frequently punished by having their mail – letters and parcels – stopped.

The Mordovian summer seemed never-ending and without mercy. Olga felt utter despair: 'Oh for the slush of autumn – how much better to wade through the mud of these Mordovian roads. Let me soak in a rain-sodden quilted jacket, anything rather than swelter in a smock of "Devil's skin".' The prisoners' grey smocks, with numbers marked on the back and the hems weighted with chloride of lime, were made of a cheap shiny material known as 'Devil's skin', which did not let the air through. Sweat poured off the prisoners, flies crawled all over them. There was no shade. Not a moment's respite. Added to this, Olga's shoes of imitation leather were ten sizes too big for her petite size thirty-four feet. She had to tie them onto her feet with tape. They seemed to get glued into the ground and often she literally couldn't move.

Some of the women, including Olga, wore strange-looking hats made of gauze stretched over pieces of wire, to prevent them from passing out in the heat or their skin from blistering. Buinaya 'despised' them for this attempt to save their complexion, ridiculing them as precious. She had never shaded her face from the sun, so her skin was leathery, wrinkled and aged, even though she was only forty.

As she worked, Olga's head was alive with Boris. For over two years she had received no word of him, so had no idea if he was alive or dead. He was injected 'like dye' into her nervous system; so consumed was she with thoughts of him. To keep her mind agile – and to ward off insanity, or a complete mental breakdown – she memorised his poems, along with poems that she composed all day in her mind. There was no point in trying to write the verses down, as the prisoners were searched every evening. Even innocent scraps of paper were taken away and destroyed.

At last, the interminable working day would end and the prisoners crawled slowly home, raising the dust as they shuffled wearily by in lines. Olga remembered the wooden camp gates as usually being silhouetted by a dark red sunset. Far from a sign of beauty and hope, this merely threatened another blisteringly hot day to come. Women guards hurried out to frisk the prisoners, ensuring that they brought nothing inside. Every night, Olga lay awake wondering how she could escape work the following day. When she first arrived she was still plagued by stomach pains and haemorrhages after losing the baby. Her health and weakening state worsened in the heat, and she dreaded toiling in the fields.

One night, Olga finally decided that she would not go out the following day. She dreamed of being able to rest in the shade of the barracks. Summoning her most rebellious spirit, she put her Devil's skin dress to soak in a basin of water next to her bunk. Her mother had sent her a dressing gown of pale blue, light-weight fabric. She yearned to put it on; to feel the soft respite of the cool material against her parched skin. But she had been forced to hand the dressing gown in to officials when a tightening of regulations led to the confiscation of all prisoners' personal belongings.

As dawn broke, she lay in her slip, suddenly gripped with fear at what she had done. The roll call was going on outside and, her nerve wavering, she realised that she had nothing to put on, as her spare smock was being mended by the nuns. When her brigade was called out and Olga was not present, a triumphant Buinaya reported her. The guards stormed into Olga's barracks, dragged her outside, bruising her arms they gripped her so tight, and threatening her with every conceivable punishment.

She had hastily wrung out her dress, and now stood in it, soaking wet and clinging to her body, in front of the entire prison camp. Instantly it was covered by a fine, grey dust, and then began to turn stiff in the morning sun. Olga was then forced to file past the camp officers on the steps of the guard house, humiliated by their mocking stares, as they waved through the brigades on the way to their day's labour in the fields.

That evening, as Olga came to the perimeter gates at the end of another broiling day, she hardly had the strength to wait for the blissful words of command: 'Stop work! Stand in formation!' The tongues of the guards' sheepdogs were hanging out, she noticed – for they too were spent with dehydration and heat exhaustion. Clouds of dust swirled in the air. 'There was one more agonising procedure: the body search. You pressed forward eagerly to the hands waiting to feel you up and down – anything to get into the compound as fast as possible, splash water on your face, and collapse on your bunk, without bothering to go for the evening meal.'

Olga dropped down onto her mattress, too shattered to remove her ill-fitting shoes and dress. Her feet throbbed, her body pounded. She had only one wish: to sleep. All the prisoners prayed for sleep, to escape from the horrors of the day. And to dream of birds. This was considered a sign that you were to be released. Suddenly she felt a heavy hand on her shoulder. It was the security officer's female orderly, sent to bring her to him. Olga felt the derisive gaze of the peasant women hot on her. Being called to an officer would mean that they would consider her a 'squealer'. She left her bunk, studiously avoiding eye contact with her cellmates. Unlike in the Lubyanka, there was no camaraderie among the inmates, few friends to be made. If there was a potential kindred spirit, the women were always too tired to cross the compound and seek each other out. Instead each inmate retreated into her own personal hell.

Outside was a beautiful Mordovian night. The moon was low and large in the sky, while the air smelled fragrant as Olga walked past the incongruous, freshly watered flower beds that lined the barracks. From the outside, seeing the white-painted buildings and well-tended borders, you could not envisage the abominations inside. The suffocating stench, the groans of the wretched, lonely and sick crammed into filthy cells.

Olga was led to a cosy-looking house with a green-shaded lamp in the window. The warm domestic scene was, of course, misleading. This turned out to be the lair of the camp's 'Godfather' – a security office whose duty it was to organise surveillance of the prisoners and recruit informers among them. Olga could not have known as she walked inside what fate awaited her; was she to be interrogated, tormented or shot?

Surely, her failed bid to avoid a day's work in the fields would not escape severe punishment.

She was met by a thickset, corpulent man with boils erupting on his face. The last thing that she expected, panic thrumming, was to be handed a parcel. 'Here is a letter for you, and a notebook. Some poems or other,' the officer said, his tone surly. 'It is not allowed for you to take them away. You must sit and read them here. Sign afterwards to say you've read them.' He busied himself reading a file, while Olga sat down and opened the package. When she saw 'Boria's cranes' flying over the pages, her lover's free-flowing hand looping over, tears began to well in her eyes. He had written her a poem – about the miracle of their reunion:

When the snow covers over the roads
And lies heavily on the rooftops
I'll go outside to take a walk
– And find you standing at the door ...

Accompanying it was a twelve-page letter, and a little green notebook full of more poems.

... Trees and fences retreat,
Into the distant murk,
Alone among the snowdrifts,
You're standing at the corner.

Olga devoured each precious word, 'all those twelve pages full of love, longing, hopes and promises', and her heart began to flood. All the fears she had harboured over the previous two years – Did he still love her? Would he fight for her? Stand by her? – melted away. 'So he missed me, and loved me – just as I was now, in my smock with its convict's number, my size 44 shoes, and my sun-scorched nose.'

In his letter Boris told her: 'We are doing everything we can and will go on doing it. I am telling them that if we have done something wrong, then the guilt is mine, not yours. They should let you go and take me instead. I have some literary standing after all …' She begged the camp guard to let her keep the letter and the poems. 'There are no instructions to let you have them,' he muttered in reply. 'You must leave them here.'

As she read and reread the letter and poems into the early hours, under the guard's watch, Olga was bolstered by the thought that the all-powerful Minister of State Security, Abakumov, must be making some kind of exception for her. Although there had been 'no instructions' to hand the letter and poems over to her, there had been orders to let her read them: to attest that she had seen them. Somebody was concerned with her case. Why else would she have to sign for them? Proof to some-one – Boris? the Moscow authorities? – that she was still alive.

The first weak light of dawn pushed through as Olga walked back to the barracks. Instead of lying down, she obsessively studied her face in a small piece of tarnished mirror. Her eyes, she conceded, had not lost their cornflower-blue intensity, but her skin had coarsened and her nose had peeled too many times. One of her teeth had chipped at the side. It occurred to her as she scrutinised her face in the semi-light that her beloved Boris was writing to her as he had known her, over two years before. Vivacious and radiant. One more year in the labour camp and she worried that she would be unrecognisable to him; a decrepit, worn-out old woman.

She clung on to his words – 'I write to you, my joy and wait for you …' – repeating them endlessly on a loop in her head. It didn't matter now that she would face another torturous day in the fields after a sleepless night. 'Boria's "cranes" had flown over Potma!' Despite the withering stares she'd get from the Ukrainian women, who would now consider her an informer, she would sail through the day ahead. And she would pray to dream of soaring cranes that night.

Pasternak had, in fact, written many letters to Olga during the previous two years, but these had been confiscated by the camp authorities, as it was 'not permitted to write to persons who are not close relatives'. As soon as Boris realised he began to send postcards masquerading as Olga's mother.

After Olga received the package that unexpected night in the labour camp, she began receiving the postcards. Olga was charmed by their humour and passion. She found them 'very funny; it was hard to imagine someone like my mother ever writing things which were so poetic and involved'. All of them were sent from Potapov Street and carried her mother's signature at the bottom: Maria Nikolayevna Kostko.

'The small republic of Mordovia came into our life never to leave it again with all the postal correspondence that came with it,' remembered Irina. 'Pasternak also sent letters to this "happy" land, actually postcards, and driven by a sweet conspiratorial spirit, he was signing them with my grandmother's name … Did he really think he was fooling them? Who would have been stupid enough to think that our grandma with her serious and reasonable nature could write on postcards such fanciful and fantastic poems as well as those inspired remarks that would leave them both feeling exaltation and dereliction?'

On 31 May 1951, Boris penned the following postcard:

My dear Olia, my joy! You are quite right to be cross at us. Our letters to you should pour straight from the heart in floods of tenderness and sorrow. But it is not always possible to give way to this most natural impulse. Everything must be tempered with caution and concern. B.[oris] saw you in a dream the other day dressed in something long and white. He kept getting into all kinds of awkward situations, but every time you appeared at his right side, light-hearted and encouraging. He has decided it must mean he is going to get better – his neck is still giving him trouble. He sent you a long letter and some poems, and I sent you a few books. But it has all gone astray, it seems. God be with you, my darling. It is all like a dream. I kiss you endless times,

Your Mama.

And on 7 July:

My darling! Yesterday, the 6th, I wrote you a postcard, but it dropped out of my pocket somewhere on the street. I am going to play a guessing game; if it does not get lost, but reaches you by some miracle, then it means you will soon come back and all will be well. I wrote you in that postcard that I will never understand BL and am against your friendship with him. He says that if he were to speak his mind, he would say that you are the most supreme expression of his own being he could ever dream of. The whole of his past life, the whole of his future no longer exist for him. He lives in a fantastic world which he says consists entirely of you – yet he imagines this need not mean any upheaval in his family life – or in anything else. Then what does he think it means? I hug you, my purest dear, my pride, I long for you,

    Your Mama.

Back in Peredelkino, Boris was consumed with writing the latter part of *Doctor Zhivago* which he conceived of as a monument to Olga: his Lara. The scenes of Lara's departure and their separation at the end of the book directly reflect Boris's heartbreak. He had already written the poem 'Parting', which appears as one of Yury Zhivago's poems at the end of the book, and which Pasternak wrote immediately after Olga's arrest:

From the threshold a man looks in
He cannot recognise his house.
Her departure was like a flight
And everywhere are signs of havoc.

All the rooms are in chaos;
Tears and an aching head
Prevent him from seeing
The measure of his ruin.

Since morning there has been a roaring in his ears.
Is he awake or dreaming?
Why does the thought of the sea
Keep pushing into his mind?

When the great wide world
Is hidden by the frost on the window,
The hopelessness of sorrow
Is even more like the desert of the sea.

She was as near and dear to him
In every feature
As the shores are close to the sea
In every breaker.

As after a storm
The surf floods over the reeds,
So in his heart
Her image is submerged.

In the years of trial,
When life was inconceivable,
From the bottom of the sea the tide of destiny
Washed her up to him.

The obstacles were countless,
But she was carried by the tide
Narrowly past the hazards
To the shore.

Now she has gone away;
Unwillingly perhaps.
This parting will eat them up,
Misery will gnaw them, bones and all.

He looks around him.
At the moment of leaving
She turned everything upside down,
Flung everything out of the chest of drawers.

Till dusk he roams about
Putting back into the drawers
The scattered scraps of stuff,
The patterns used for cutting out,

And pricking himself on a needle
Still stuck in a piece of sewing,
Suddenly he sees her
And cries quietly.

Alone in his study, Boris retreated into an unhappy solitude. His insomnia, which plagued him intermittently all his life, was worsening; while increasingly he felt the isolation and ambivalence of his place in literature. Without Olga he had lost his greatest champion and supporter. She played a decisive part in his writing life, not just in providing the creative fuel for the love affair central to the plot, but as she was a generation younger than Boris, she helped to give the novel a more contemporary – more 'Soviet' – flavour. In the novel, he writes of his anguish at his separation from Olga/Lara:

So dark and sad was it in Yury's heart that, although it was early in the afternoon and full daylight, he felt as if he were standing late at night in some dark forest of his life, and the new moon, shining almost at eye level, was an omen of separation and an image of solitude.

He was so tired that he could hardly stand. He threw the logs out of the doorway on to the sledge in smaller armfuls than usual; the touch of the icy wood sticky with snow hurt him through his gloves. The work did not make him feel any warmer. Something within him had broken and come to a standstill. He cursed his luckless fate and prayed for Lara, that God might spare the life of the lovely, sad, humble and simple-hearted woman he loved. And the new moon stood over the barn blazing without warmth and shining without giving light.

The strain Pasternak was under personally and professionally was having a dangerous impact. Irina recalled an incident in 1950: 'A few months later we were hit by another blow. Grandmother climbed the stairs to our apartment four steps at a time to tell us that it was all over: Pasternak had suffered a heart attack.'

Boris's heart problems had first flared after Olga's arrest and his visit to the Lubyanka. Although he was a relatively robust and fit sixty-year-old, the heart attack, which had been caused by a thrombosis, was a warning. Typical Boris, he expressed his anxieties about his health in his novel, giving Yury Zhivago similar cardiac problems: 'It's the disease of our time. I think its causes are of a moral order,' he wrote. 'A constant, systematic dissembling is required of the vast majority of us. It's impossible, without its affecting your health, to show yourself day after day contrary to what you feel, to lay yourself out for what you don't love, to rejoice over what brings you misfortune ... Our soul takes up room in space and sits inside us like the teeth in our mouth. It cannot be endlessly violated with impunity.'

Boris recovered, aided by Zinaida's attentive ministrations at Peredelkino. For the next two years he continued to work on the novel, and his *Faust* translations, as none of his original works were published. He was desperate to finish *Faust* in order to turn back to *Zhivago* – 'a completely unselfish and unprofitable undertaking, since the novel is not destined for publication under current conditions'. What is more, he wrote, 'I am not writing it as a work of art, although it is a fiction in a larger sense than my earlier things were. But I do not know whether there is any art left in the world and what meaning that might have. There are people who love me very much (there are very few of them), and my heart is in debt to them. For them I write this novel, I'm writing it as a long letter to them, in two books.'

The scenes of Yury's heartache for Lara reflect the unbearable nature of Boris's longing for Olga: 'Something other than himself wept and complained in him and shone with gentle words in his darkness. His soul sorrowed for him and he too grieved for himself ...' On the spiritual union of their love, he wrote: 'You and I, it's as though we had been taught to love in heaven and sent down to earth together to see if we had learned what we were taught. What we have together is a supreme harmony – no limits, no degrees, everything is of equal value, everything gives joy, everything has become spirit. But in this wild tenderness which lies in wait for us at every moment there is something childishly untamed, forbidden. It's a destructive wilfulness hostile to domestic peace. It's my duty to be afraid of it and to distrust it.'

In October 1952, after Olga had endured the worst summer of her life in the labour camp, Boris suffered a second, far more serious heart attack. He had spent the previous months plagued by toothache and boils on his gums. A heart condition was confirmed when he fainted coming home from the dentist. He was rushed to Moscow's Botkin Hospital, where the head ward doctor, Professor B. E. Votchal, was seriously concerned about Pasternak's chances of survival. Boris spent his first night, as he described it, 'with a miscellany of mortals at death's door'. The rest of the week he was lodged in a common ward because the hospital was overcrowded. When he improved a little, Zinaida agitated to have him transferred to the Kremlin Hospital, where the renowned Jewish professor, one of Moscow's finest cardiologists, Miron Vovsi was in charge. (Months later, after Pasternak's discharge from the hospital, Vovsi, who had been the head doctor with the Red Army during the war, was arrested as an alleged member of the Zionist terrorist group known as the 'doctor-wreckers'.)

During that first night, as he drifted in and out of consciousness on a gurney in the hospital corridor, Pasternak had contemplated his proximity to and fear of death. On 6 January 1953 he was back at Peredelkino. 'Ninochka! I am alive, I am at home ...,' he wrote to Nina Tabidze:

When it all happened I was taken to hospital and for some five evening hours I was lying in the casualty ward and then in the corridor of a common overcrowded municipal hospital. Between swoons and attacks of vomiting and nausea I was seized with such a feeling of peace and bliss! And by my side everything was going on in such a familiar course, things were grouped so distinctly and prominently, and shadows were falling so abruptly. A verst-long corridor with sleeping bodies, all dark and silent, with a window at the end looking on the garden lost in an ink-like turbidity of a rainy night, and behind the trees the gleam of the Moscow glow was seen.

And this corridor and a green globe of the lampshade on the table and the nurse on duty, and silence and the shadows of nurses and the proximity of death behind the window and behind one's back. In its concentration it was such a bottomless, such a super-human poem.

At that moment, which seemed the last in my life, more than ever did I wish to speak to God, glorify everything one sees, grasp and imprint it.

'Dear God,' thus I was whispering. 'Thank you for your language which is majesty and music, for making me an artist, for your school of creative power, for all my life being a preparation for this night.' And I exulted and cried with happiness.'

It was just like Boris to be erudite and lyrical in the face of death. Yet he was practical too. 'Was it culpability he felt towards us when he scribbled a note on a message for his secretary, Marina Baranovich, while waiting on a stretcher in one of Botkin's hospital corridors asking her to find a way to raise a thousand roubles and have the money delivered to our address?' asked Irina. 'The money was handed over to us and this is how we were able to survive. Pasternak survived too.'

In his two-and-half-month stay in the Kremlin ward, Boris also underwent dental surgery. His long equine teeth were replaced with a gleaming set of American dentures, giving him a more distinguished appearance.

At Peredelkino, Zinaida once again nursed and nurtured Boris back to health, which only increased his feelings of guilt and despair. Now he owed *both* women his life.

On 2 January, as soon as Boris was physically able, he wrote Olga's mother a long, detailed letter about how he had arranged authorisation of payment for his translation work at Goslitizdat to come straight to her. Thoughtfully, yet aware of his duplicity, he urged Maria to ring the editor 'so he can arrange payment and speed things up, and find out … how much will be paid, and when. Tell both of them *not to phone me at home* about these earnings, say I have a friend (a man) who has been in trouble and has been away for four years, his children are still at school and on their own, you are their grandmother and this money has been earmarked by me especially for them.' Towards the end of the letter he added rather insensitively: 'Z. N. [Zinaida Nikolayevna] saved me. I owe my life to her. All this, and everything else as well – everything I have seen and gone through – is so good and simple. How great are life and death, and how insignificant the man who does not know it!'

His letter to Maria was full of love and gratitude, however: 'Dear Maria Nikolayevna! I took the liberty of asking Marina Kazimirovna [Baranovich] to open your letter and read it to me over the telephone. How I recognised and felt you in it!' he wrote. 'How much of your warm-hearted self there was in it, how much feeling and life! I send lots and lots of kisses for it! I could hardly refrain from phoning you right away – I am still trying to keep myself in hand now, because I am not supposed to get worked up. Thank you, thank you! Irochka, my darling girl, thank you, and thank you as well, Mitia, for all your concern and tears. I owe part of my recovery to both of you, dear children and to your hopes and prayers, Ira.'

On 5 March 1953, Josef Stalin died of a cerebral haemorrhage. When the leader's death was announced, Boris declared to Zinaida that 'a terrible man died, a man who drenched Russia in blood'.

'On the day of Stalin's death, Boria and I were still separated from each other,' Olga wrote. 'I was in the Potma camp, and he was in Moscow. In both places – in Potma as well as in the capital city, and in the country at large – there were waves of panic. The vast majority, millions of people, wept for Stalin and asked each other through sobs: what will happen now? Others rejoiced – but in silence, furtively, and looking over their shoulders. Only very few were bold enough to give open expression to their joy. BL had been right to say: "men who are not free always idealise their bondage".

A report, based on the testimonies of two Polish women prisoners who were released after Stalin's death, describes Olga's behaviour in Potma. They believed Olga to be Boris Pasternak's wife. The report reads: 'Ivinskaya impressed them by her unwavering patriotism, and surprised them by improvising literary readings after work time for intellectuals in the camp, at which she usually recited Pasternak's poems.'

When news broke that amnesty was to be given to some gulag prisoners after Stalin's death, Boris was hopeful that Olga would be released. He quickly sent another postcard to her from 'Mama':

April 10, 1953. Olia, my little girl, my darling! How close we are now, after the decree they've just published, to the end of this long and terrible time! What a joy that we have lived to see the day when it is behind us! You will be here with the children and with us, and your life will stretch out before you again like a broad highway. That's the main thing I wanted to say and share our delight in. The rest is so unimportant! Your poor BL has been very ill – I have written to you about this before. In the autumn he had a heart attack and spent three months in hospital. After that he stayed in a sanatorium for two more months. Now, more than ever, he is possessed by only one thought: to finish his novel, so that nothing is left undone, in case the unforeseen happens. We just met him on Chistye Prudy [Metro station]. This was the first time after a long while that he has seen Irochka. She has grown a lot, and become very pretty.

...

April 12, 1953. Olia my angel, my baby girl! I am finishing the card I began the day before yesterday. Yesterday Ira and I sat with BL on the boulevard. We read your letter, wondering when we may expect you here, and going over our memories. How marvellously you write, as usual, and what a sad, sad letter! But when you wrote it, the decree on the amnesty had not yet come out, and you did not know the joy awaiting us all. Our only concern now is that this longed-for happiness should not cause us to pine away with impatience, that the deliverance about to come should not overwhelm us by the very fact of being so near at hand and momentous. So arm yourself with patience and remain calm. At last we are nearly at the end of the way. From now on everything will be so wonderful. I am feeling fine and am glad to see BL looking well. He thinks Irochka's eyes, which used to turn up at the corners, have evened out now. She has become very pretty. Forgive me for writing such silly things.

Your Mama.

The day before, Boris had arranged to meet Irina on a bench in a Moscow boulevard, as he was not able, after his illness, to climb the five flights of stairs to their apartment. It was an emotional rendezvous, heightened by the ecstatic news that Olga would indeed be included in the prisoner amnesty. Irina had also been terrified that she would never see Boris again, that he would succumb to a heart attack. '[I] saw a dark silhouette sitting on a bench, wearing a familiar hat, his sergeant cap,' she said of their meeting. 'I ran towards this individual for whom, for the first time, I felt a really vibrant and burning sense of family connection, closeness, tenderness and joy ... I will never forget the black compacted snow of the boulevard, his brand-new face (he had lost some weight since his illness and had had his teeth fixed ) the bells of the tramways, our kisses and a bit later on my neighbour's exclamations who had seen everything: "But who were you kissing so passionately?"'

Rather unexpectedly, their conversation took an unpleasant and almost farcical turn. With his peculiar brand of insensitivity, Boris told Irina that, while he would never abandon her mother, his relationship with Olga could not continue in the same vein. Completely inappropriately, he asked the sixteen-year-old to tell Olga that the couple could no longer be together. He implored Irina that she needed to make her mother see and accept this new reality. That so much time had gone by, during which they had both suffered so much, that she would undoubtedly understand that going back to where they had broken off would only be a 'pointless constraint'. With breath-taking tactlessness, Boris continued to explain to Irina that Olga must free herself from him and only count on his devotion and faithful friendship. He just did not see how he could leave Zinaida, who had worked so hard to nurture him back to health after his two heart attacks. He must therefore sacrifice his personal feelings to her on the 'altar of devotion and gratitude'.

Irina might reasonably have asked where his devotion and gratitude were to her mother, who had just risked three precious years of her life in hell, due to him. But, having experienced so many of Boris's histrionics, Irina refused to take his 'strange mission' too seriously. She found his request 'a typical blend of candour, splendid naivety and downright cruelty', and perceptively decided to dismiss it. It was a mark of her loyalty to both Boris and to her mother that she only told Olga about the bench conversation many years after Pasternak's death. Of the future of their relationship, Irina shrugged pragmatically: 'They would just have to deal with it themselves. And that's what they did.'

Equally accommodating of Boris, and intuitive to his anxieties, Olga continued to worry that he might find her altered. She knew that he had a horror of changes in people who were dear to him. He had been reluctant to see his sister, Lydia, who wanted to come and visit him in Russia, as he almost preferred to preserve her in his memory as the beautiful young girl he grew up with. 'How terrible,' he had once said to Olga, 'if she turns out to be an awful old woman, someone completely foreign to us.'

Olga anticipated that Boris expected her to return from the camp like that. 'But then he saw that I was just the same – though a little thinner perhaps. And my love for him and closeness to him somehow always brought me back to life in an astonishing way. In short, our life, after being torn apart by sudden separation, now bestowed an unexpected gift on him – so once more nothing mattered except the "living sorcery of hot embraces", the triumph of two people alone in the bacchanalia of the world'. As Irina predicted, when Olga returned to Moscow that April, passion, loneliness, and guilt, drove Boris straight back into her mother's outstretched arms.

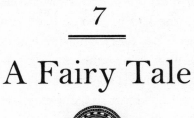

# 7

# A Fairy Tale

Reunited after three and a half years apart Olga and Boris were both 'seized by a kind of desperate tenderness', and a resolve to stay together for the rest of their lives. 'It is impossible for me to reproduce all that he said to me during those extraordinary first minutes after my return from the camp,' Olga recalled. 'Or to convey the manner in which he spoke. He was ready to "turn the earth upside down", and we were to "kiss like two worlds".'

Boris was only just strong enough to slowly climb the stairs to her Moscow apartment, where, in her bedroom, they could finally be alone to reclaim each other. In the safety of his embrace, Olga pressed her head against her lover's chest and without saying a word, listened to his heart beating. Every time they subsequently met after being apart, she would carry out this affectionate ritual. 'While I was with him, it was not given to him to grow old.' Their renewed attraction, after such a long separation, seemed urgent and more potent. They simply could not, and would not, exist without the other.

A report written by Pasternak's future publishers, Collins Harvill, in 1961 gives an insight into Olga's situation on her release:

The position of persons who returned under these conditions to normal life, after their prison camp experiences, is not generally understood in the West. The authorities which had tormented them and disrupted their family life immediately became their assiduous benefactors. They provide them with the means of recuperations in sanatoria, they secure living quarters for them when necessary, even in the centre of Moscow, they see to it that they obtain adequately paid employment, and they sometimes, as in the case of Mme Ivinskaya, provide them with domestic help. In exchange they expect from the ex-detainee a certain amount of co-operation, on the one hand by refraining from recrimination, complaints and the publishing of their experiences, and on the other, a cheerful, positive and creative attitude to Soviet reality and occasionally a little assistance to the security organs in the performance of their delicate tasks.

Mme Ivinskaya accepted this situation, as did so many others, for the sake of her union with the children and with Pasternak. Her return to life meant for Pasternak a return to creative work, and at last the great saga on which he had been working for most of his life, started taking definitive shape.

Olga's reappearance in Boris's life inspired and lifted him. He returned to writing *Zhivago* with a passion and gusto that he had not experienced since the traumatic first few months of Olga's incarceration. Having spent almost eight years writing the first half of the novel, he drafted the second half (ten parts) in a speedy twelve months and completed the final draft of the whole novel two years later. Of Yury Zhivago's reunion with Lara, he wrote:

Even more than by what they had in common, they were united by what separated them from the rest of the world. They were both equally repelled by what was tragically typical of modern man, his shrill textbook admirations, his forced enthusiasm, and the deadly dullness conscientiously preached and practised by countless workers in the field of art and science in order that genius should remain extremely rare.

They loved each other greatly. Most people experience love, without noticing that there is anything remarkable about it.

To them – and this made them unusual – the moments when passion visited their doomed human existence like a breath of time-lessness were moments of revelation, of ever greater understanding of life and of themselves.

He goes on to describe the intense emotions of reunion, as Lara and Yury are holed up together in Varykino: 'that wilderness in winter, without food, without strength or hope – it's utter madness. Let's be mad if there is nothing but madness left to us.' So they 'burst in like robbers' to the empty, icy house. Aware that their days together are numbered as 'death is really knocking at our door', they prepare to be alone together for the last time. 'We'll speak to one another once again the secret words we speak at night, great and peaceful like the name of the eastern ocean,' Yury tells Lara. The sense of their doomed passion is heightened that night. As the wolves bay outside, Yury gets up before dawn and sits amid the stillness at a bare desk, inspired to write his poetry. 'At such moments Yury felt that the main part of his work was not being done by him but by something which was above him and controlling him.'

Boris always liked to see himself in a heroic light; after all, his arche-type, Yury Zhivago, is a noble man: a poet and a doctor. He believed that it was in some way due to the influence of his name that Olga was released from the gulag two years early. 'It was I who unwittingly brought it on you, Olia,' he told her, 'yet as you say yourself, they were afraid of going too far – five years is nothing, after all, by their standards, when they measure sentences in tens of years! They wanted to punish me through you …' Far from reproaching him for all she had suffered, Olga was 'over-joyed' to feel that Boris now thought of her as part of his family.

To commemorate his lover's liberation, Pasternak penned the allegor-ical poem 'A Fairy-Tale', and included it as one of Yury's poems at the end of Zhivago. In the novel, Pasternak describes how Yury bases the poem on the legend of Saint George and the Dragon; the gruesome dragon presiding over a dark forest represents Stalin and his labour camps: 'Last night he had tried to convey, by means so simple as to be almost flattering and bordering on the intimacy of a lullaby, his feeling of mingled love and anguish, fear and courage, in such a way that it should speak for itself, almost independently of the words.' Boris/Yury then describes the intricacies of the writing process itself: 'The writing was livelier but still too verbose. He forced himself to still shorter lines. Now the words were crammed in their tetrameters and Yury felt wide awake, roused, excited; the right words to fill the short lines came, prompted by the measure. Things hardly named assumed form by suggestion. He heard the horses' hooves ringing on the surface of the poem as you hear the trotting of a horse in one of Chopin's Ballades. St George was galloping over the boundless spaces of the steppe.'

> Light scattered
> From its blazing mouth.
> It had trapped a girl
> In three coils of its body.
>
> Its neck was swaying
> Over her shoulder
> Like the tail of a whip.
> The custom of that country
>
> Allotted a girl,
> Beautiful
> Prisoner and prey,
> To the monster of the forest.

Pasternak clearly saw himself as the knight riding to the maiden's rescue, traversing 'fords, rivers and centuries' to reach her. He slays the dragon yet is injured in battle. At the end of the poem, the knight and his maiden are bound together for eternity:

At times excess of joy
Triples their tears,
At times a dead sleep
Holds them in its power.

At times his health
Comes home to him,
At times he lies motionless,
Weak with loss of blood.

But their hearts are beating.
Now he, now she
Struggles to awake,
Falls back to sleep.

Eyes closed.
Hills. Clouds.
Rivers. Fords.
Years. Centuries

Inseparable from Olga, Boris now only left her side to go to work. He spent much of his time commuting between his study at Peredelkino and her cramped Moscow apartment. During the winter of 1953, his dacha had been extended and 'turned into a palace', equipped with a gas supply, running water, a bath and three new rooms. Before Olga's release from Potma, Boris had begun to live at the dacha all year round, at the request of his doctors, keen for him to remain in more restful surroundings than Moscow. He gardened keenly; his abundant vegetable patch had always been a source of relaxing pleasure for him, as he once told his father: 'Last year we got out of our spacious kitchen garden, – the fruits of our own, esp Zinaida's labours – half a cellar of potatoes, two casks of sauerkraut, 4,000 tomatoes, and a great deal of peas, French beans, carrots and other vegetables to be consumed in a year.' Yet once Olga was back in Moscow, if Boris had had a particularly productive working day, he would return to her in the evening 'as though to share in some richly earned festivity'.

For Olga, although she now knew she was Boris's 'chosen one', she still was not his official chosen one: his wife. After the loyalty she had shown, did he not owe her that? Their moments of grateful togetherness soon became punctuated by her 'female tantrums'. '[I] longed for recognition and wanted people to envy me,' she wrote. Boris, true to form, placated her with ardent declarations of his inimitable, mystical love, yet refused to leave Zinaida. He claimed that he saw Zinaida as a subject of pity and tried to reassure Olga that she had so much more of him. She may not have had the status of his wife; but she could lay true claim to his heart. She understood the essence of him. Olga oscillated between being content with this and becoming frustrated, yearning for a public acceptance of her role and status in his life. Why couldn't he act decisively, leave Zinaida and publicly claim her? She remembered a typical discussion – or rather, a Boris soliloquy – on the subject:

You are a gift of the spring, my love – how good that God created you a woman ... Let it always be like this: we fly to each other, and never want anything so much as to meet! And we need nothing else. Let's not look ahead, or complicate matters, or hurt other people's feelings ... Would you want to be in the place of that unfortunate woman? For years now we have been deaf to each other ... and of course she is only to be pitied – she has been deaf all her life – the dove tapped at her window in vain ... And now she is angry because something real has come to me – but so late in life! ...

Boris was adamant that they must not force the pace of their relationship. He continued, rather weakly, to rely on external circumstances to shape their lives.

In spite of this, the summer of 1954 became one of the most contented times for the pair. After nearly four years in prison, Olga was 'beginning to take in, with some difficulty, the joy of return to the world after being excluded from it'. As Boris did not wish to force a resolution to his crowded marriage, he was delighted when fate dealt them a new card. Olga found out she was pregnant again. 'This is just as it should be,' he reassured her, relieved. 'It will make everything fall into place, bring things to a head, and a solution will somehow suggest itself. In any case, surely there can be no question that the world is large enough for your and my child?'

As the pregnancy progressed, Olga worried that Irina would take the news badly, that she would disapprove. When it became impossible to hide the fact that she was pregnant any longer, she sent her mother, Irina and Mitia to spend the summer with her aunt in Sukhinichi, west of Moscow. Zinaida conveniently took their son Leonid on holiday to Yalta.

This gave Olga undiluted time with Boris in Peredelkino, providing emotional support as he surged ahead with the novel. Copies of the near-completed manuscript were circulated among various acquaintances; many were awaiting its publication in book form and in serial. The name of an editor was also frequently mentioned, for a larger volume of Pasternak's poetry was being simultaneously prepared for publication.

Pasternak was keen to get what he saw as his life's work read by as many people as possible, partly because he feared the novel might never be published and partly because, like all artists, however brightly they shine, he hungered for external validation. His friend Ariadna Efron once noted that Boris 'had the vanity of any man of true talent who, knowing he will not live to see himself acknowledged by his contemporaries, and hence snapping his fingers at them for their failure to understand him, nevertheless craves *their* recognition more than any other – he knows perfectly well that the posthumous fame of which he is assured is about as much use to him as a wage paid to a worker after his death'. Boris was disquieted when shown a copy of a British newspaper in which there was a double-paged feature under the title 'Pasternak keeps a courageous silence'. It said that if Shakespeare had written in Russian he would have written in the same way that he was translated by Pasternak, whose name was much respected in England, where his father had lived before his death. What a pity, the article continued, that Pasternak published nothing but translations, writing his own work only for himself and a small circle of intimate friends. 'What do they mean by saying my silence is courageous?' Boris asked Olga sadly: 'I am silent because I am not printed.'

Irina recalls the final occasion, in 1954, that Pasternak gave a poetry recital and answered questions in front of an audience. It was in a vast hall in the Moscow School of Engineering and the theme of the evening was 'Hungarian poetry'. The audience consisted of Hungarian poets and translators as well as students. Irina was sitting next to her mother, whom she described as still having 'that bronzed glow with people who spend time in the camps'. Olga was wearing the same dress she had been wearing on the day of her arrest and looked especially slim. They were both, however, 'full of apprehension' for Boris, as the evening was poorly organised, with no posters circulated promoting the event. Irina was 'scandalised by the half-empty room, the thud of conversation and the obvious indifference'. Boris looked 'vulnerable and clumsy in the suit he had inherited from his father', she recalled, 'the one he wore to all special occasions until his very last day. There he was, in this gloomy room, standing on top of a badly lit podium, his only public a handful of students. He reminded me of a big bird thrown onto the shore, its big wings dragging on the floor powerless.' It was a far cry from Pasternak's poetry recitals ten years earlier, when huge, besotted crowds hung on his every word, then roared his poetry in unison back to him.

As Pasternak walked towards the lectern, a man sitting near Irina called Gidas, who had just been released from the labour camps, whispered loudly: 'My God, it is true that Geniuses do not age!'

Pasternak recited some poems that he had translated, his voice heavy. He then delivered his own poems in an equally sombre tone. But most of the students seemed oblivious. There was a weak round of applause, but Pasternak was unable to hide his resentment once he realised that he was not asked to perform more. He clearly expected and was accustomed to a clamouring encore.

\*   \*   \*

Earlier in April 1954, after eight years of his enforced silence, ten of Pasternak's poems from *Doctor Zhivago* were published in the journal *Znamia*. The poems were prefaced by an explanatory note from Boris: 'The novel will probably be completed in the course of the summer. It covers the period from 1903 to 1929, with an epilogue relating to World War II. The hero, Yury Andreyevich Zhivago, a physician, a thinking man in search (of truth), with a creative and artistic bent, dies in 1929. Among his papers written in younger days, a number of poems are found, which will be attached to the book as a final chapter. Some of them are reproduced here.'

Official reaction to the poems was at best lukewarm, yet Boris became jubilant that 'the words "Doctor Zhivago" have made their appearance on a contemporary page – like a hideous blot!' He told his cousin Olga Freidenberg: 'I have to and want to finish the novel, and until it is finished I am a fantastically, manically unfree man.'

At the start of the year, one of Pasternak's 'small circle of intimate friends', the poet and prose-writer Varlam Shalamov, received a copy of the manuscript to read. Shalamov had spent seventeen years in the gulag, later publishing accounts of the most notorious camps of Kolyma in the far north-east of Siberia. He wrote a long letter to Pasternak after reading his work-in-progress: 'I never thought, and could not imagine to myself even in my most distant hopes of the last fifteen years, that I would read your unpublished, unfinished novel, and what is more in a manuscript which I received from you yourself … it has been a very long time since I read a work of Russian literature that lives up to Tolstoy, Chekhov, and Dostoevsky. There is no doubt that *Doctor Zhivago* is of this calibre.'

After observations and reflections on the opening of the book, and Pasternak's descriptions of faith and Christianity, Shalamov devoted page upon page to a detailed discussion of the character of Lara:

So what is the novel, and, moreover, who is Doctor Zhivago, who at least until the middle of the novel does not really exist and is still not apparent when Lara Guichard, the genuine heroine of the first half of these pictures, has already reached her full stature in all her charm, a charm only partly borrowed from Turgenev–Dostoevsky – clear, like crystal, sparkling, like the stones of her wedding necklace. Her portrait is a great success, a portrait of such purity that could not be slandered or soiled by the filth of the Komarovskys of the world.

I used to know such Laras, well not the same, a little less, a little smaller. She is alive in the novel. She knows something more elevated than all the other characters in the novel, including Zhivago, something more real and important than she could share with someone, much as she might want to.

The name you gave her is very good – Lara is the best Russian name for a woman. It is the name of women who suffered a sorrowful Russian fate – the name of the bride without a dowry, the heroine of a remarkable play and it is also the name of a woman, the heroine of my youth, a woman whom I loved to distraction like a boy, with a love that cleansed and lifted me …

But I do not want to talk about her, but about Larisa Guichard. Absolutely everything is upright in her. Even the very difficult scene of Lara's fall does not call up anything except tenderness and purity … Your women come off better for you than your men – it seems this is inherent in our greatest writers …

Your words about the second revolution which is so personal for each of us are very good, as is this whole piece in general. And only Larisa, with her imponderable look, Larisa, inwardly richer than Doctor Zhivago and much more so than Pasha – Larisa is a magnet for everyone, including Zhivago.

I have read 200 pages of the novel – where is Doctor Zhivago? This is a novel about Larisa …

That August the author's real-life Larisa suffered a tragedy worthy of the pages of his novel. Olga was out driving a pick-up, in the countryside west of Moscow, looking for potential dachas to rent, somewhere where she and Boris could spend time together. The drive turned out to be across rough dirt tracks and roads. Feeling unwell, she stopped to ask for help at a pharmacy in Odintsovo. An ambulance was called for her and on the way to the hospital, Olga went into premature labour, but the child was stillborn. 'One might have thought that no one would have been particularly upset by this,' Olga wrote later. 'Ira, whose reaction to my having a child I had feared most of all, would have no cause for concern, or so I imagined. BL had shown no sign of wanting to change his mode of existence and was happy enough for us to live from meeting to meeting – something which would obviously have been complicated by the birth of a child.'

But she was 'quite wrong. Everybody was cross with me. Ira was distressed that I had lost my baby, and Boria sat weeping at the foot of my bed, repeating bitterly what he had said before: "Do you really think there would have been no room in the world for our child? How little faith you have in me!"'

The following spring, after the frustration of going through the long winter without a place of their own – their trips to and from Moscow having been curtailed when the weather was harsh and the snowdrifts particularly bad – Olga did something 'unbelievably foolish'. On the advice of a girlfriend, she rented out a dacha on the Kazan road, leading east out of Moscow, which made it much harder for her and Boris to meet. There was no easy train route and every time Olga arrived at Peredelkino station, Boris would be waiting, miserably pacing the platform.

By the summer Olga decided to take matters into her own hands. She boldly rented half a dacha for her whole family on the lake shores of Izmalkovo, in a village adjacent to Peredelkino; just for a few months initially. The place was idyllic, with canopies of silver birch and weeping willow cascading over the water. Olga's proximity was a welcome relief for Boris, who could walk the twenty minutes from his dacha, over the long wooden plank bridge that crossed the lake. Maria, Irina and Mitia settled into the two rooms of the dacha, while Olga moved into the glassed-in veranda. Gnarled roots provided uneven yet charmingly bucolic steps to the door of the veranda.

On his first visit, Boris was taken aback: 'But I asked you to find us a refuge, not a glass-house – you must admit, it looks very odd, Olia!' Dutifully, Olga hurried back to Moscow to purchase some red and dark-blue chintz to cover the whole of the glass-sided veranda. For Olga, the security of finally having their own domestic space – her first nest with Boris – gave her newfound joy. But Boris was still unhappy. He hated the lack of privacy and the large panes of glass through which you could hear every sound.

Nevertheless, the summer of 1955 was glorious: baking hot and sunny with frequent thunderstorms. The wild roses blossomed luxuriantly. As the summer came to an end Boris began to worry that Olga would move back to Moscow and he would be left in Peredelkino, 'alone' again.

So when Maria and the children returned to the Potapov apartment, Olga decided to stay on at Izmalkovo, where Boris could come to visit her twice a day. She would simply travel to Moscow for necessary visits. She tried to persuade her landlady to let her continue renting part of the house for the winter but she herself advised Olga to take another place nearby which was properly insulated against the cold, and equipped with a cooking stove. Her husband helped Olga move, carrying her blue-painted outdoor table, typewriter and canvas chairs.

Her new landlord was called Sergei Kuzmich. Olga later said that the best years of her life were spent at the Kuzmich property, a little house surrounded by tall poplars. She loved the small room leading out onto a veranda which doubled as a dining room in the summer and a porch in winter. Once furnished, with its ottoman covered in her favourite red and dark blue chintz, matching curtains and a thick red carpet, it was a cosy home with the stove crackling away in the corner. 'If there had been any part of my life which could be described as truly happy, it was during those years between 1956 and 1960,' she said: 'It was the happiness of daily communion with someone I loved, of all the mornings and winter evenings spent together, reading to each other or entertaining people we liked. It seemed like one long, never-ending feast. We shared blissful years of walks together, shared joys and anxieties, working on translations, meeting friends, learning from him and listening to everything he had to say.'

By this stage, with Boris no longer making regular trips into Moscow, the whole of his literary business was entrusted to Olga. She edited his manuscripts, twice retyping the entire manuscript of *Doctor Zhivago* for him. She acted as his secretary and read proofs for him.

Brief separations, such as when Olga needed to go to Moscow, began to alarm the writer. He arranged for a telephone to be installed inside the Potapov apartment, ringing Olga at 9 p.m. sharp to enquire about her day and inform her of his. The children were not supposed to use the phone at this time, leaving the line free for Boris's call. He would always begin the call with: 'Olia, I love you! and ended it with: 'Don't get stuck there tomorrow!'

Every Sunday, Irina, Mitia and Olga's friends from Moscow would visit. Olga and Boris would host these informal Sunday lunches, which soon turned into regular literary gatherings.

For Irina too, the days spent at the 'Little House' at Izmalkovo were among the most blessed times and the source of her fondest memories. 'All it would take for my adolescent melancholy to disappear was for me to see Boris Leonidovich by the village well, wearing his wellies, standing in the mud, wearing his cap and oilskin designed for this kind of weather,' she recalls. 'Whenever I saw him rushing to meet my mother at Kuzmich's house, I would be at peace with myself. "Quickly go and make yourself an omelette" he would tell me with authority, which made him sound even more important. "You need to eat. What did your mother prepare you for lunch?" He thought I was too skinny and would keep on repeating in his humming voice: "Olioucha, you need to make her eat."'

'I loved meeting Boris then, where he looked and felt so well,' continued Irina. 'Someone once said of him "In Pasternak, even his appearance is a piece of art". This even remained true as he aged. It was like some sort of miracle. His grey hair, arranged in a mess would light up his bronzed face which would give him a tanned look all year round. In Peredelkino, with the fresh air of his morning walks no matter the weather, the gardening in his vegetable patch, his swims in the Setourne river – all of this made him into a lively country man who feared inactivity. He was always busy, elegant and driven.'

The summer of 1955 was a 'time of great happiness'. Every evening at six o'clock, Boris would appear, while Olga busily typed up passages of *Zhivago* he had bought over the night before. 'My mother never took the job of typist very seriously,' said Irina, 'her typewriter was not very good and it was not her profession. Boris only asked her to help him when his typist was away or if we needed to see an extract he needed to work on. I was once entrusted with this very sacred task as my mother was busy receiving guests and Boris was due to arrive any minute. But I made so many spelling mistakes, especially with the Siberian characters, that I was never asked again.'

Of their joyful family times together at Kuzmich, on the rush-grown banks of the River Setourne, Olga wrote: 'We had a room of our own, a home, an anchorage. I often reproached myself for not setting up house like this earlier, so we could have lived and worked together from the beginning in complete independence … At Christmas we got a tree which took up almost the whole of the table at which I worked. We laughed when Dinkie, our cat, stole decorations from it and took them off to her hideaway outside. We were so happy at the thought of it all; *our* Christmas tree, *our* table, a place to call our own.'

Sadly, Boris was still torn. Split between the easy-going atmosphere of the Little House and the tensions up at the dacha, the 'Big House'. Although Olga never directly encroached on Zinaida's territory, only visiting the dacha if Zinaida was away, arranging to meet Boris in the woods around Peredelkino, Zinaida would have known instantly about her presence in Izmalkovo. (Years later, however, writing to his sister Josephine, Boris still was happy to declare: 'Z does not know that O is renting a room in a peasant house of a neighbouring village.') When Olga was released from Potma, Zinaida's friends closed ranks, attempting in vain to thwart any further temptation from 'this temptress'. Zinaida, all too aware of her rival's presence across the lake, became ever more hostile to Boris, making 'many demands' on her husband and constantly reminding him about his divided loyalties.

Many nights, Boris would lie alone in his small bed in his study, yearning for the soft comforts of Olga. During one sleepless night, blighted again by his old foe insomnia, he got up to write. The following morning, he brought his fresh poem to Olga – a billet-doux in pencil – for her to type up:

What is the hour? It's dark. Must be three.
Again, I fear, I shall not sleep a wink.
The cowherd in the village will crack his whip at dawn,
And a cold breeze blow through the window
That looks out onto the yard.
And I'm alone.
But no: engulfing me in all your whiteness
You are with me here.

A friend of Boris and Olga's, Nikolai Liubimov, a Spanish and French translator, visited the writer at Peredelkino. Afterwards he told Olga that Pasternak seemed 'heart-rendingly lonely', coming down the stairs from his study to join Liubimov in the drawing room, where Zinaida and her women friends were playing bridge. 'They all cast disapproving glances at him.'

Zinaida's trump card, according to Olga, was that she 'managed to create a kind of "Olympus"' at the Big House in Peredelkino – 'everything there could not have been better arranged for living and working'.

Yet Boris did not want material luxuries. The only luxuries he required were the peace and quiet to write. A desk to work at and a study were essential to him. Not as mere creature comforts but for the sake of his writing, which demanded an orderly way of life.

'I think Zinaida Nikolayevna understood very well that by making a good home for BL, she strengthened her position as his legal wife and the mistress of the "big" house,' said Olga. 'This made it easier for her to reconcile herself to the open existence of the "little" house and she knew that any ill-considered attempt to put pressure on BL would have meant disaster for her.'

Although Boris did the bulk of his writing in his study, he would visit Olga a few times a day, and always early evening, with the pages he had written. Or he would sit at the table with the pages he was working on spread out before him, while Olga curled up with a book on the sofa. This cosy domesticity was in complete contrast to his state of solitude in his large upstairs study in the Big House, which Zinaida only entered to clean. Yet, to Olga's consternation, Boris refused to leave Zinaida or further unsettle the status quo.

'BL was so tormented by compassion and pangs of conscience because he no longer loved Zinaida Nikolayevna,' said Ariadna Efron. She told Olga that 'this uncouth woman who had failed to respond to his love, reminded him of Little Red Riding Hood who had lost her way in the forest, and he wept tears of pity about her'. Speaking about Zinaida, Boris would say to Olga: 'I do not pity you, and I hope to God it will always be like that with you and me. Let us save our pity for others. I saw that ageing woman standing by the fence and thought: "You wouldn't want to change places with her, would you?" So let us bestow the blessing of mercy on those around us.' Olga later wrote of Boris's dual lives – split between the two women and two homes:

It is absurd to imagine that he sat in an ivory tower, preserving an Olympian calm. If he never took desperate steps, it was only because of this sense of pity, particularly in regard to someone he had ceased to love – and thereby wronged, as he felt.

Even at a particularly difficult time, when the alien spirit of the 'big' house had become intolerable, and we both felt so stifled by the hostility emanating from it that we had decided to clear out and settle in Tarusa [a small town south of Moscow, on the River Oka], Boria simply could not bring himself to – again, it was not a question of putting his own well-being first, but of the overwhelming compassion he felt for those who could only suffer uncomprehendingly.

It may well have been a question of not putting himself first and fully considering Zinaida's feelings. More likely though, the novel came first. To upend his domestic status quo would threaten his writing routine. He may not have had ideal working conditions with the tensions between the two houses, but they served his creativity and emotional needs well. He could craft in peace in the day, before bringing his manuscript to his most ardent supporter each evening.

Every conversation with Boris seemed to lead back to *Doctor Zhivago*. Irina paints a sweetly affectionate picture of the way in which she and her mother teased him about his obsession with the novel, mother and daughter catching each other's eye, humorously:

> Before he finished the novel, every conversation brought itself back to the novel. It became a bit of a joke amongst us as he would use any excuse to get back to this subject. All he thought about was that book and everything around him was evaluated through it. My mother would joke: 'Come on, Boris, what has this got to do with Doctor Zhivago? I'm starting to get bored with this book!' They would be standing by a peaceful pond where ducks were paddling around and it would not be long before 'this book' would be brought into the conversation.

For all her gentle ribbing, Olga could hardly have given more of herself, in supporting, loving and encouraging the tortured writer. From the tremendous amount of effort that Olga offered to the creation of *Doctor Zhivago*, she derived almost as much satisfaction as if she had written the novel herself. She was generous to the core in assisting her beloved to fulfil his literary dream. Boris's close friend Alexander Gladkov described Olga's attitude to the book as 'a settlement of accounts with everything she lived through, a devastating blow delivered to a hateful foe ... the apotheosis of her life, her favourite child, delivered in pain and tears'.

Olga was back in the Moscow apartment one evening, attending to business, when she received a call from Boris at Peredelkino. Sounding shaken, he began to speak in a voice choked by tears. 'What's wrong?'

Olga asked him. 'He's dead, he's dead, I say!' Boris groaned several times over.

It turned out that he was talking about the death of Yury Zhivago. 'This harrowing chapter was now over,' concluded Olga crisply.

By the summer of 1955, copies of the first part of the novel had been bound in a handsome brown binding. According to Olga, 'Boris was as pleased as a child with it.' Soon after, the second book was bound as well. The conversations around the supper table in the Little House between Olga, Irina and Boris focused on where the novel would be published. In 1948 Boris had signed a contract with the literary journal *Novy Mir* for publication. However, as his work progressed, due to its 'anti-revolutionary' content, he began to doubt that they would ever be able to publish it. He cancelled the contract and paid back the advance. Now Olga acted as Boris's literary agent, hauling three of the impressive-looking brown volumes round to Moscow publishers. The fully edited and corrected copies were ready for publication.

One warm October evening in 1955, after one of Olga's regular trips to Moscow, Boris met her from the Peredelkino station and walked her back to the Little House. As they crossed the long bridge spanning Izmalkovo Lake, Boris said to her: 'You mark my words, they will not publish this novel for anything in the world. I don't believe that they will ever publish it. I have come to the conclusion that I should pass it round ready to be read by all and sundry – it should be given to anyone who asks for it, because I do not believe it will ever appear in print.' He explained his reasons, having read through the two handsomely bound volumes. 'The Revolution is not shown at all as the cake with cream on top,' he reflected. In his long letter to Pasternak in January 1954, his friend Varlam Shalamov had written:

Your novel raises a great many questions, too many to enumerate and develop in one letter. The first question is about the nature of Russian literature. People learn from writers how to live. They show us what is good, what is bad, they frighten us, they do not allow our soul to bog down in the dark corners of life. Moral pithiness is the distinctive feature of Russian literature.

I do not know how official critics will like the novel. The reader who has not yet been weaned from genuine literature is waiting for just this sort of novel. And for me, an ordinary reader who has long yearned for genuine books, this novel will remain a great event for a long, long time. Here questions which no self-respecting person can ignore are posed with force. Here living heroes of our tragic time, which is after all also my time, have emerged in their full lyric charm. Here the remarkable eye of the artist saw so much that is new in nature, and his brush used the most delicate colours in order to bring out the spirited condition of humanity.

In his conclusion to *An Essay in Autobiography*, which Pasternak was preparing to have published by the Goslitizdat, he wrote: 'I have just finished my chief and most important work, the only one of which I am not ashamed and for which I take full responsibility, a novel with prose with a section in verse, *Doctor Zhivago*. The poems scattered over the past years of my life and collected in the present book are steps preparatory to the novel. And it is as a preparation for the novel that I regard their publication in this book.'

Shortly after completing the manuscript, Boris went for a walk in the woods in Peredelkino with his neighbour, Konstantin Fedin. A veteran Soviet novelist, Fedin would later succeed Alexei Surkov as secretary of the Writers' Union. Hidden amidst the silver birch trees, away from prying eyes and ears, Boris read his friend the novel, chapter by chapter. Fedin listened rapt, even weeping at certain passages. Yet later, when the editorial board of *Novy Mir* voted against the publication of *Doctor Zhivago*, having seen the completed edition, Fedin voted in accordance with his fellow board members.

Goslitizdat never published extracts from the book or the poetry. The journal *Znamia* also turned down the manuscript. By the spring of May 1956, the novel, rejected by the three Russian publishing houses who had been sent the bound manuscripts, remained unpublished. Little did

Boris, Olga and Irina know that the book was to have the most remarkable life of its own.

'The book was going to take us down a spiral,' wrote Irina. 'It would be the centre of a universal glory that would also pillory us; it would lead us both to triumph and to Golgotha. The price of this novel would be humiliation, not to forget my mother's incarceration as well as mine, and it was most certainly responsible for Boris Leonidovich's death too.'

# 8

## The Italian Angel

At the beginning of May 1956, the Italian section of Radio Moscow broadcast the following news: 'The publication of Boris Pasternak's *Doctor Zhivago* is imminent. Written in the form of a diary, it is a novel that spans three quarters of a century, ending with the Second World War.'

A young Italian, Sergio D'Angelo, who had left his native Rome two months earlier to work at the station, translated the cultural news bulletin with heightened interest. The Italian Communist Party had suggested he leave Rome to work at Radio Moscow, as a member of the team involved in Italian-language broadcasts. D'Angelo also agreed to act as a part-time literary agent for a Milanese publisher, Giangiacomo Feltrinelli. The scion of one of the wealthiest business families in Italy, with interests in construction, lumber and banking, Feltrinelli embraced socialism and communism as a young man. He had recently started a publishing company and was particularly interested in contemporary literature from the Soviet Union. His ambitions were to secure worldwide publicity for his publishing house with a major literary coup.

D'Angelo asked a Russian colleague at Moscow Radio, Vladlen Vladimirsky, if he would contact Pasternak to set up a meeting. Vladimirsky, who was not only keen to meet the famous poet but to practise his Italian with D'Angelo, was eager to accompany the handsome emissary on his visit to Peredelkino.

On 20 May, Vladimirsky and D'Angelo took the electric train from Moscow's Kiev station and alighted 50 kilometres south-west at the writer's colony of Peredelkino. They walked along the narrow dirt roads, marvelling at the glories of spring in the countryside. Passing isolated dachas, they eventually found the one they were looking for: Pasternak's dacha, No 3, Pavlenko Street.

Boris was in his vegetable garden, dressed in his work clothes, pruning bushes. When he saw the unexpected visitors he 'approached with a broad smile, threw open the little garden gate and extended his hand'; according to D'Angelo, 'his grip was nice and firm'. He invited the pair to sit with him in the sunshine on a couple of wooden benches. Boris asked about the derivation of Sergio's last name – literally translated as 'of the angel'. D'Angelo explained that it was of Byzantine origin and not that unusual a surname in Italy. This prompted a conversation on his home-land, or more accurately, a Boris soliloquy. Boris explained that he had visited the country in 1912, when he was a student at Marburg University. He had seen Venice and Florence and would have liked to have travelled on to Rome but ran out of money, so had to return to Germany. Characteristically, he then interrupted himself and asked the young men what they wanted to see him about.

D'Angelo launched into his pitch. He spoke proficient Russian, only occasionally turning to Vladimirsky for help with a word or phrase. He explained that he was acting as an agent for Giangiacomo Feltrinelli's new company, Feltrinelli Editore, and that they were interested in publishing Boris's novel. Pasternak interrupted him with a dismissive gesture of his hand. 'In the USSR,' he said, 'the novel will not come out. It doesn't conform to official cultural guidelines.' D'Angelo believed that this prediction was 'far too pessimistic'. He countered that the book's publication had already been announced on Soviet Radio and that since the death of Stalin there had been a relaxation on the restrictions to publishing and a greater receptivity to new ideas. He explained to Boris that everyone in the West was talking about a 'thaw', a loosening of repression and control now Stalin was dead, under the party chairman-ship of Nikita Khrushchev. (The term was coined from Ilya Ehrenburg's novella, *The Thaw*, which found publication in 1954, having originally appeared as 'Ottopel' in *Novy Mir*.)

D'Angelo made his 'reasonable' proposal to Pasternak. 'You will give me a copy of *Doctor Zhivago* to pass on to Feltrinelli, who will immedi-ately begin its translation into Italian, so as to gain advantage over other Western publishers,' he said. 'On his [Feltrinelli's] part, he will agree not to issue the Italian edition until after the Russian version has been published.'

In his eagerness to secure the manuscript and justify his allowance from the wealthy Italian, D'Angelo clearly had no real idea of the risk Pasternak would be taking by placing the manuscript in foreign hands. Boris, however, knew only too well that the unsanctioned publication of the novel in the West, before it had appeared in the Soviet Union, could lead to charges of disloyalty, endangering himself and his family. And, of course, Olga.

Boris fell silent. 'All of a sudden, I realised that the author, who was barely listening to me, was completely lost in his own thoughts,' said D'Angelo. 'I therefore spelt out my proposal once again, this time trying to be even more precise and persuasive.'

After a suspenseful pause, Boris said: 'Let's not worry about whether or not the Soviet edition will eventually come out. I am willing to give you the novel so long as Feltrinelli promises to send a copy of it, shall we say within the next few months, to other publishers from important countries, first and foremost France and England. What do you think? Can you ask Milan?' D'Angelo reassured him that it was not only possible but inevitable, since Feltrinelli would be keen to sell foreign rights to the book.

Boris excused himself and walked slowly towards his dacha. A short time later he emerged carrying a package wrapped in a covering of news-paper. The manuscript was 433 closely typed pages, divided into five parts. Each part, bound in soft paper or cardboard, was held together by twine threaded through rough holes in the paper and knotted. The first section was dated 1948 and the pages were annotated with the author's handwritten corrections.

'This is *Doctor Zhivago*,' Pasternak said, handing the package over. 'May it make its way around the world.' D'Angelo took the package, explaining the good fortune that he would be able to personally deliver the manuscript to Feltrinelli, as he had planned a trip to Europe in the next few days.

It was just before noon, two hours after they initially met, that Pasternak stood at his garden gate and wished the two young men goodbye. As they prepared to leave, Boris looked at Vladirmirsky and D'Angelo with 'an expression of benevolent irony', before saying: 'You are hereby invited to take part in my own execution.'

Early that evening, Olga was returning from a productive visit to Moscow, after doing yet another round with publishers in the city. Boris hurried along the road to meet her from the train. She was buoyed up. *Novy Mir* had confirmed its intention to publish some extracts from the novel. Before she could deliver this cheering news, Boris was saying excitedly to her:

> I had a visit today, Olia, from two young people who arrived here at the house while I was working. One of them was very pleasant – handsome, youthful, and charming … You would have been delighted by him! And, you know, he had such an extraordinary name: Sergio D'Angelo. He came here with someone who is supposedly a member of our Soviet Embassy in Italy – I think he's called Vladimirov. They said that they had heard the announcement on Moscow Radio about my novel and that Feltrinelli, one of the biggest publishers in Italy, was interested in it. D'Angelo is Feltrinelli's *emissario* – of course, that's his private part-time job. He's actually a member of the Communist Party, and he is here in an official capacity with the Italian section of Moscow Radio.

Boris 'obviously realised he had done something a little odd', Olga recalled, 'and was worried about how I would react. From his manner, which was even somewhat ingratiating, I could see that he was pleased and at the same time uneasy, and very anxious for my approval.'

Far from congratulating him for handing over the manuscript, Olga was furious. 'What have you done?' she said reproachfully, not giving in to his blandishments. 'Just think how they'll go for you now! I've been in prison once, remember, and already then, in the Lubyanka, they questioned me endlessly about what the novel would say! Krivitski [a member of the *Novy Mir* editorial board] has good reason for saying the journal can only publish chapters from it. It's because they *can't* accept it all, of course – they simply want to leave out the awkward parts and publish what they needn't be afraid to print. You know how they always try to cover themselves! I'm really amazed you could do this!'

'Really now, Olia, you're overstating things,' Boris remonstrated weakly. 'It's nothing at all. Just let them read it. If they like it, let them do what they want with it – I said I didn't mind!' 'But Boria,' Olga shouted. 'That was giving them permission to publish, don't you understand? They will certainly seize on it! There's bound to be a great furore you'll see.'

Olga, with the traumatic experience of the gulag still fresh in her memory, was not being intentionally prophetic. She knew the great interest Semionov, her interrogator in the Lubyanka, had taken in the still unwritten novel and his suspicions that it would be an expression of literary opposition. She was aware that Goslitizdat's promise to publish the book had been in an atmosphere of growing social liberalisation, but the Hungarian uprising in the autumn of 1956 prompted Moscow to once again tighten the screws, leaving Pasternak and his novel out in the cold.

Boris was put out by Olga's reaction. 'Well then, Olia, you must do what you think best, of course,' he said. 'You can even phone this Italian – because I am not going to make any move without you – you can phone this Italian and ask him to give the novel back, if you're so upset about it. But in that case we should at least play the fool a little; "It's just like Pasternak" tell him, "the way he has given you his novel, but what do you think yourself?'" But Olga knew full well that Boris had made up his mind. After spending twenty years crafting an opus that was so close to his heart, he wanted it to be published. And if it could not be done at home, then let it come out in the West.

The copy that he gave to Sergio D'Angelo was not the only one smuggled out of the Soviet Union. He also gave copies to Ziemowit Fedecki (his friend, and a Polish translator); the Oxford academics Isaiah Berlin and Professor George Katkov, to circulate in England; as well as Hélène Peltier and Jacqueline de Proyart (both French Slavic scholars who later collaborated on the French translation of the novel). Yet foreign publication before a Russian edition was not an outcome he had previously considered or entertained. If it wasn't for the Italian 'angel' it is highly unlikely that *Doctor Zhivago* would have gained such international traction.

Ironically, this created the only occasion where Zinaida and Olga were united. Both lived in fear of the novel being published and considered Boris, as Stalin had once referred to him, to be 'a holy fool'.

The day after D'Angelo's visit, Pasternak gave another copy of the manuscript to Fedecki, whom he had known since 1945, when Fedecki went to Moscow as a press spokesman for the Polish embassy. The encounter was witnessed by the Polish poet Wiktor Woroszylski. Together the men walked from the train station, through the charming countryside past meadows of silver birch to Pasternak's dacha, tracing D'Angelo and Vladimirsky's steps the previous day. Boris invited them inside and over tea, gave them his manuscript. 'This is more important than poems. I have worked on this for a long time,' he told his guests, handing Fedecki 'two thick, bound folios'.

Woroszylski recalled: 'We looked at the doorway – in it, Zinaida Nikolevna was standing, tall, massive, slightly hunched over. We did not hear her walk in, but felt her presence. She looked at Yamomir [Ziemowit Fedecki] with displeasure: "You must know that I am against this! Boris Leonidovich is suffering from thoughtlessness: yesterday he gave a copy to the Italians, today to you. He does not realise the danger and I must look after him."

"'But, Zinaida Nikolaevna,' the poet replied, "everything has changed. It is about time to forget about fears and live normally.'"

A friend of Boris's told Olga that he witnessed a similar conversation at the Big House, between Pasternak and an Italian scholar, Ettore Lo Gatto. Gatto had written a history of Russian literature and the Russian theatre. During their discussion, Boris said that he was ready to face any kind of trouble, as long as the novel appeared. When Zinaida snapped: 'I've had enough of such trouble,' Boris coldly responded: 'I am a writer. I write in order to be printed.'

Sergio D'Angelo took his literary treasure to Germany, flying to East Berlin and taking a room in a hotel in the west of the city, where he rang Feltrinelli in Milan to ask for instructions. He had not been searched when he left Moscow, and the manuscript remained wrapped and undisturbed in his suitcase. Feltrinelli, perhaps more intuitive to the potentially explosive nature of this precious cargo, decided to fly to Germany the following day to collect the manuscript. The following morning, at the small hotel in Joachimstaler Strasse, near the elegant shopping streets, the *Zhivago* manuscript was passed like contraband from one suitcase to the other in the privacy of D'Angelo's room.

The two men then enjoyed two days wandering around Berlin, shopping, eating at outdoor restaurants and chatting about D'Angelo's initial impressions of Soviet life. 'At one point, Feltrinelli asked me if there were any prostitutes in Moscow,' D'Angelo recalled. 'When I told him that I had noticed their presence around the larger hotels (where they also used to spy on foreigners) he seemed very surprised and disillusioned.' The following morning, before the communist publisher flew back to Milan, he embarked on an urgent shopping mission to buy a pair of binoculars for his yacht.

Feltrinelli, who did not read Russian, sent the manuscript to a translator as soon as he returned from Berlin. Pietro Zveteremich, an Italian Slavist, was asked to review the novel for potential publication. His verdict: 'Not to publish a novel like this would constitute a crime against culture.'

The day after D'Angelo's visit, Olga had taken a taxi immediately back to Moscow to see Nikolai Bannikov, Boris's friend and the editor of his forthcoming poetry anthology that Goslitizdat was planning to publish, along with an introduction of autobiographical notes. Part of Olga's frustration when she learned that Boris had handed over the novel was that Bannikov would be furious, putting paid to the publication of the volume of poetry.

She was right. Bannikov was indeed angry and alarmed, crying out: 'But what has he done!' Olga discussed with him the only solution; they must find a way to publish the novel first in Russia. She then went to see another editor, called Vitashevskaya, who was higher up the chain of command at Goslitizdat, at her apartment. Olga found it strange that Vitashevskaya, who had once been the commandant of a forced labour camp, had now been given a job as an editor. Olga told her what had happened: 'Vitashevskaya expressed great sympathy: "I tell you what, Olenka," she said in a soft, purring voice – she was a woman of enormous bulk, covered in rolls of fat – "let me show the novel to someone high up. It is quite possible that everything will then fall into place."'

When an exhausted Olga returned to Potapov Street, she was given a sealed envelope by the building attendant. It was a note from Bannikov that read: 'How can anyone love his country so little? One may have one's differences with it, but what he has done is treachery – how can he fail to understand what he is bringing on himself and us as well?'

From the viewpoint of Boris's friends and editors, his action was treacherous only to the extent that it could scupper their efforts at having his work published in the Soviet Union. Upon their discovery that the novel had been sent abroad, the hierarchy of the Writers' Union was alarmed, as plans for a Soviet edition had not come to fruition. Senior Soviet officials, such as Dmitrii Polikarpov, the head of the Culture Department of the Central Committee of the Communist Party – 'the watchdog for ideological purity' – were concerned that, should an expurgated version of Doctor Zhivago be agreed by a Soviet journal while the Italians published the full text, a politically embarrassing situation might ensue.

The next morning, Olga returned to Peredelkino to show Boris the note. He said that if she was so upset by him handing the novel over and if their friends reacted so badly, she should go and try and get it back from D'Angelo, and gave her the Italian's Moscow address.

D'Angelo's apartment was in a large building near the Kiev train station. Olga was taken aback when his wife, Giulietta, opened the door, a staggering beauty with film-star good looks. She was 'long-legged, dark, with ruffled hair, a sculpted face, and eyes of astonishing blueness'. As she spoke poor Russian and Olga spoke no Italian, they had a comical scene of expansive hand gestures. Yet both were intuitive to what had happened; Olga understood that Giulietta was trying to tell her that her husband had never intended to cause any problems for Boris.

After over an hour of 'much more noise and gesticulation than meaning', the dashing and charismatic D'Angelo appeared. 'He was indeed young and handsome,' wrote Olga. 'A tall man with jet-black hair and delicate features such as one sees on icons.' She was further impressed as he 'spoke Russian magnificently, with only a slight accent'. Nodding sympathetically while Olga explained how serious the ramifications would be for Pasternak if the novel was published in Italy, she beseeched him to return the manuscript.

'You know it is too late,' he replied. 'The novel is already with the publisher. Feltrinelli has already managed to read it and says that he will certainly publish it, come what may.'

Seeing Olga's immediate distress, D'Angelo continued: 'Don't worry. I'll write to Giangiacomo, or even speak to him on the phone. He is my personal friend, and I will be sure to tell him how alarmed you are by this, and perhaps we will be able to find a solution. But you must realise that a publisher who has obtained a novel will be reluctant to part with it! I don't think he will give it up so easily.'

Olga begged him to ask Feltrinelli to delay publication abroad until a Russian edition had appeared first. If D'Angelo did indeed speak to Feltrinelli, it only seemed to hasten the publisher's desire to obtain the novel and secure the rights. In mid-June Feltrinelli wrote to Boris to thank him for the opportunity to publish *Doctor Zhivago*. A courier hand-delivered a letter, setting out royalties and foreign rights, plus two copies of a contract. If Boris had any genuine desire to stop publication, this was his moment to act. Yet, in full view of the potential danger that lay ahead for him, he displayed no second thoughts. He signed the contract. According to D'Angelo, who visited the author again at Peredelkino, Pasternak considered the contract 'the least important' of his concerns.

Characteristically, Boris put his art before commercial considerations. He needed money, yet knew that it was wholly unlikely that he would ever be allowed to receive foreign currency from royalties in Russia. Although he wrote to Feltrinelli that he was not completely uninterested in money, he was aware that geography and politics would make it impossible to receive royalties. Nevertheless, he took a brazen and literally life-threatening publish-and-be-damned approach, writing to his publisher on 30 June: 'If its publication here, promised by several of our magazines, were to be delayed and your version were to come before it, I would find myself in a tragically difficult situation. But this is not your concern. In the name of God, feel free to go with the translation and the printing of the book, and good luck! Ideas are not born to be smothered at birth, but to be communicated to others.'

Feltrinelli had struck literary gold in securing a publishing coup that would earn him millions. (He went on to sell the film rights of *Doctor Zhivago* to MGM for $450,000.) Paradoxically, it was as a capitalist publisher that this Marxist millionaire scored his greatest success, with *Doctor Zhivago*, and a year later with Giuseppe di Lampedusa's *The Leopard*. *The Leopard* had previously been rejected by every significant Italian publisher.

Boris's nephew, Charles Pasternak, met Giangiacomo Feltrinelli and his third wife, the German photographer Inge Schoenthal, in 1963. Inge was the mother of Feltrinelli's son and heir Carlo. The Feltrinellis were in Oxford to visit Charles's mother, Josephine Pasternak, for lunch. 'I will never forget Feltrinelli,' said Charles. 'He was without doubt the most elegant and charming man I have ever met. He dressed superbly, with that understated, exquisite Italian style.' Feltrinelli, who married four times, was a playboy with a keen eye. An astute player in every sense, he was no mere dilettante.

When the Kremlin heard about the contract with Feltrinelli, KGB surveillance around Pasternak tightened. On 24 August the KGB general and head of the secret police, Ivan Serov, wrote a long memo informing the highest command of the Communist leadership of the manuscript's delivery to Feltrinelli. He noted that Pasternak had authorised the rights to be assigned to publishers in England and France.

The KGB had intercepted a parcel that Pasternak had sent to a French journalist, Daniil Reznikov, in Paris. In a letter, Boris had written that permission to publish in the Soviet Union had not been granted: 'I realise perfectly well that [the novel] cannot be published now, and that this is how it is going to be for some time, perhaps forever.' Noting the likelihood of foreign publication, he continued: 'Now they will tear me limb from limb; I have this foreboding, and you shall be a sorrowful witness to this event.'

A week later, the Central Committee's Culture Department prepared a detailed report on the novel. The book was denounced as a hostile attack on the October Revolution and a malicious libel of the Bolshevik revolutionaries, while Boris was castigated as a 'bourgeois individualist'. After criticising *Doctor Zhivago* at great length, the memorandum concluded: 'The novel by B. Pasternak is a perfidious calumny against our revolution, and against our entire way of life. It is obvious that this work, which is not only ideologically unsound, but also anti-Soviet, can never be allowed to be published. In light of the fact that B. Pasternak has given his novel to a foreign publishing house, the Culture Section of the CPSU Central Committee will take the necessary steps, through its friendly relationships with other Communist parties, to prevent this defamatory book from being published abroad.'

Still trying to get publication of the novel authorised in Russia, Olga was 'racing around Moscow like a frantic chicken'. Poor Olga was in an unenviable position. As Pasternak's emissary she was sent to deal with the Moscow officials hostile to her cause, as well as remaining loyal to her beloved Boris and his book. She went to see Vadim Kozhnevnikov, the chief editor of *Znamia*, the journal that had already published some of the verses from *Doctor Zhivago*. They also had a copy of the novel, which she assumed Kozhnevnikov had read. When she appealed to the editor, he sighed: 'How typical of you to get mixed up with the last romantic in Russia.' Comrade Dmitrii Polikarpov was a good friend of his, Kozhnevnikov added. He would arrange for Olga to visit Polikarpov and she must report back what had happened. Shortly afterwards, Olga received a call from the Central Committee to tell her that a pass had been arranged for her to see the head of the Culture Department.

A bleary-eyed and haggard Polikarpov met with Olga in the grim, official Moscow buildings. He insisted that Olga get the manuscript back from the Italians. Olga remonstrated that they probably would not return it and the only answer was to publish in the Soviet Union first, as swiftly as possible. 'No,' Polikarpov replied. 'We must get the manuscript back, because it will be very awkward if we cut out some chapters and they print them. The novel must be returned at all costs.'

After several further conversations with D'Angelo, she went to see Polikarpov for a second time. She told him that she had learned that Feltrinelli had kept the manuscript only to read it, but had stated that he would not part with it. He was ready to take responsibility for this and that the 'crime' would be his. Olga bravely reported to Polikarpov that Feltrinelli did not believe that the Russians would ever publish the manuscript and that he felt it would be an even greater crime to withhold a masterpiece from the world.

Polikarpov picked up the telephone in front of Olga and rang Anatoli Kotov, the director of Goslitizdat. He ordered Kotov to draw up a contract with Pasternak and to appoint an editor. 'The editor should think about what passages to change or cut out, and what can be left unchanged.'

When Olga reported this conversation to Boris, his response was unequivocal. 'I am by no means intent on the novel being published at the moment, when it cannot be brought out in its original form.'

Olga was instructed to keep talking to D'Angelo and to secure the return of the manuscript by offering Feltrinelli first option on a revised text that would be released in Russia. Feltrinelli remained intransigent; he doubted the likelihood of a Soviet edition. 'It seems self-evident that the novel ought to have been published in the Soviet Union,' said Olga.

'But the fact is that those who should have made the crucial decision were simply paralysed by fear.'

Boris clearly felt the same. Despite the KGB closing in on him – from November 1956 to February 1957 almost all of his incoming and outgoing mail was intercepted – he continued to hand over copies of the manuscript to various foreign visitors to Peredelkino. This was reckless in the extreme. When he gave the French scholar Hélène Peltier a copy of the manuscript he entrusted her to take a note from him to Feltrinelli. Typed on a narrow strip of paper, it was undated. 'If ever you receive a letter in any language other than French, you absolutely must not do what is requested of you – the only valid letters shall be those written in French.'

That August, Isaiah Berlin travelled with Zinaida's first husband, Genrikh Neigaus, to Peredelkino, where they were given Sunday lunch. On the train out of Moscow, Neigaus pleaded with Berlin to make Boris see that he should halt foreign publication. He said: 'It was important – more than important – perhaps a matter of life and death.' Berlin agreed that 'Pasternak probably did need to be physically protected from himself.'

Far from being dissuaded from any Western publication, Pasternak pressed the manuscript into Berlin's hands and asked him to read it, before taking it back to England to give to his sisters, Josephine and Lydia, in Oxford. The following day, Berlin read the novel: 'Unlike some of its readers in both the Soviet Union and the West, I thought it was a work of genius. It seemed – and seems – to me to convey an entire range of human experience, and to create a world, even if it contains only one genuine inhabitant, in language of unexampled imaginative power.'

During lunch, Zinaida took Berlin aside and, weeping, begged him to persuade Boris not to publish abroad. Ever the protective mother, she did not want their children to suffer further. She believed that Leonid had been deliberately failed on his exam for entry to the Higher Technical Institute because he was Boris Pasternak's son. She also told Berlin that in May 1950, Boris's eldest son, Evgeny, was prevented from finishing his postgraduate studies at the Moscow Military Academy and sent to

Ukraine for compulsory military service during Stalin's anti-Semitic campaign.

Berlin delicately raised the issue of the consequences for the Pasternak family if Boris continued to defy the authorities. He reassured Boris that even if it were not published in the immediate future, the book would stand the test of time. He said that he would have microfilms of it made and buried in all four corners of the globe so that the novel would survive even nuclear war. Boris was infuriated, retorting that he had spoken to his sons 'and that they were prepared to suffer'. Berlin concluded that Boris chose 'open-eyed' to pursue publication. For all of his affectations of naivety, the writer seemed to be playing his own adroit game of Russian roulette.

On 14 August Boris wrote to Lydia, Josephine and Frederick a joint letter from Peredelkino (this was the first time in almost ten years that Boris was able to do so, restrictions having been eased in 'the Thaw'). He told his family that Isaiah Berlin had visited and would bring one copy of the manuscript back to them in Oxford. He asked that they have it transcribed into no less than twelve copies which he implored them to send to the 'principal Russians over there' and 'very importantly, to [Maurice] Bowra'. (Or 'My dear and more than dear, thrice dear Bowra' as Boris referred to him. The classical scholar, professor of poetry and warden of Wadham College, Oxford was an influential champion of Pasternak's work, who repeatedly nominated the poet for the Nobel Prize for Literature.)

Pasternak told his family about the novel. After repeating his concerns that they would not like much of it, he concluded: 'It's an important work, a book of enormous, universal importance whose destiny cannot be subordinated to my own destiny, or to any question of my well-being. Its existence and publication, where that is possible, are more important and dearer to me than my own existence. That's why the arguments based on caution and common sense which B[erlin] was putting to me, following certain things that had already happened in the book and which he'll tell you about, carry no weight with me.'

\* \* \*

At the beginning of September, Sergio D'Angelo was summoned by the director general of Radio Moscow's foreign news bureau for what he nervously anticipated would be a dressing-down. His 'exalted employer' was seated behind an 'immense desk covered with a variety of cumbersome desktop items in marble and bronze'. He asked D'Angelo, with studied casualness, if he happened to have an unpublished novel by Pasternak in his possession. D'Angelo responded that he had had a copy of *Doctor Zhivago* with him for a few days and then – 'since it was to be published in the USSR, as was announced on the radio, which he will undoubtedly recall' – he gave it to a friend in the Italian publishing business, who was interested in printing it in Italy as well. D'Angelo was surprised by the director general's reaction. Far from castigating him, his boss simply bade him a polite farewell.

He travelled to Peredelkino for a brief visit, where he found Pasternak 'in good spirits and as expansive as ever'. Boris confirmed that he had signed the contract with Feltrinelli before mentioning his meeting with Anatoli Kotov, the director of Goslitizdat, who had assured him that they would publish *Doctor Zhivago*, but only after it had 'literally been picked apart'. Such a compromise was 'completely absurd', shrugged the disgruntled writer. The two men then discussed why Goslitizdat would have concocted such a proposal in the first place. Pasternak remained convinced that the editors knew full well that they would never persuade him to bowdlerise his work. They were merely biding their time in the hope that Feltrinelli would cave in to pressures and abandon the idea of publishing the novel.

D'Angelo reassured Pasternak that Goslitizdat's reasoning had no basis in reality. 'The fact of the matter is that Feltrinelli, who is bound and determined to launch his publishing house on a grand scale, is looking for a major literary coup,' D'Angelo told Boris. 'Should he have any doubts about what this coup will actually be, his colleagues are there to make sure that he understands that it is none other than *Doctor Zhivago*.' D'Angelo also reminded Pasternak that despite his undying loyalty to the Communist Party, Feltrinelli would never subject himself to such a blatant form of censorship. On the contrary, he would proudly claim his right to stand up for the cause of artistic freedom. Pasternak shrugged his shoulders in resignation. "I hope that's the case", was his only response.'

In mid-September, the editorial board of *Novy Mir* formally rejected the novel in a long, stinging rebuke: 'The thing that has disturbed us about your novel is something that neither the editors nor the author can change by cuts or alterations. We are referring to the spirit of the novel, its general tenor, the author's view on life … The spirit of your novel is one of non-acceptance of the socialist revolution. The general tenor of your novel is that the October Revolution, the Civil War and the social transformation involved did not give people anything but suffering, and destroyed the Russian intelligentsia, either physically or morally.'

This hatchet job was written mainly by Olga's former colleague Konstantin Simonov. Four other board members, including Boris's next-door neighbour, Fedin, signed the document. They condemned the 'viciousness' of Yury Zhivago's conclusions on the Revolution: 'There are quite a few first-rate pages, especially where you describe Russian natural scenery with remarkable truth and poetic power. There are many clearly inferior pages, lifeless and didactically dry. They are especially rife in the second half of the novel.'

The letter was hand-delivered to Pasternak's dacha, along with the manuscript. Typical of Boris, who batted the criticism off, was his generous invitation to Fedin for Sunday lunch a week after receiving the toxic letter. He told fellow guests: 'I have also asked Konstantin Aleksandrovich [Fedin] – as wholeheartedly and unreservedly as in previous years – so don't be surprised.' When his neighbour arrived he asked Fedin not to mention the rejection, and the two men embraced.

By the new year, 1957, Soviet officials were increasingly agitated that Feltrinelli had rejected all invitations and commands to return the manuscript. In a bid to increase pressure on the Italian publisher, Goslitizdat sent Feltrinelli a letter saying that the novel would be published in the Soviet Union in September, asking him to delay publication until then. Feltrinelli replied in conciliatory fashion that he had no difficulty in complying with this request. Yet as Olga observed: 'that the letter from

Goslitizdat was nothing more than a manoeuvre to gain breathing space is evident from its timing'.

On 7 January, Pasternak signed a contract with Goslitizdat. Neither he nor Olga believed its editor, Anatoli Starostin, when he said of the novel: 'I shall make this into something that will reflect the glory of the Russian people.' Starostin was a pawn and the contract a ruse to endeavour to get Feltrinelli to return the manuscript. One thing was clear. The Soviet authorities did not want the novel published: in Russia or abroad.

Later that year, on 16 December, Boris wrote to a friend: 'About a year ago Goslitizdat made a contract with me for the publication of the book. If it had been really published, curtailed, and censored, then half the trouble and problems wouldn't have existed. Thus Tolstoy's *Resurrection* and a lot of other books were published here and abroad in two differing editions before the Revolution, and nobody was afraid or ashamed of anything, and people slept quietly and houses didn't come tumbling down.'

In mid-February, as the strain over preventing publication escalated, Boris became ill. He had been suffering a tormenting illness, widely believed to be arthritis in his right knee, the same leg he had fractured in the riding incident in childhood. He was first treated in the Moscow hospital, before being sent to a branch of the Kremlin Hospital at Uzkoe – reserved for eminent Soviet figures – and was away from Peredelkino for over four months.

That winter, the Moscow Art Academic Theatre had begun work on a new production of *Mary Stuart*, the German verse play by Friedrich Schiller, about the last days of Mary Queen of Scots. Pasternak had translated the play at the theatre's request. Before he fell ill it had given him great pleasure to attend rehearsals, with one of Moscow's leading actresses, Alla Tarasova, in the lead role. On 7 May he wrote to Tarasova from the Kremlin Hospital. 'On March 12th I was just going to the city to see one of the last rehearsals, the dress rehearsal. I had already seen you in several scenes, so I rather clearly imagined what a revelation your Stuart as a whole would be. And suddenly, coming down the front step of our cottage porch, I cried out with intolerable pain in the same knee I was going to bend before you in the nearest future, and I couldn't walk another step.'

According to Olga, Boris 'found the terrible physical pain very hard to bear, and thought that he was dying'. (Nevertheless, this still did not prevent him from working on a one-volume edition of verse, whenever the pain died down sufficiently for him to be able to hold a pencil.) Frightened for his own life and that he might never see Olga again, he wrote her nine letters from his hospital bed:

Night of 1–2 April
I will tell you when to visit me. I must see you one last time, give you my blessing for the long years of life you will live in me and without me, and see you make your peace with all the others and look after them. I kiss you. Thank you for an infinity of things. Thank you. Thank you. Thank you.

April 6, 1957
Oliusha dear,
The night was appalling. I couldn't sleep a wink and just twisted and turned, unable to find any position at all bearable. It can't go on like this of course. We have behaved like spoiled children – I am an idiot and a scoundrel without equal, and now I have been given the punishment I deserve. Forgive me, but what else is there I can say? I have a pain in my leg. I feel weak and sick. You really can't imagine how ill I am – not in the sense of danger, but of suffering. If I feel better on Thursday, I'll send for you, but in my present state life is not worth living, and the idea is unthinkable. I kiss you. Don't be cross with me. Thank Irochka for her letter.

[Undated]
Oliousha, tell your mother and the others; I am not afraid to die – I want it terribly, and the sooner the better. Everything is getting worse and worse and more and more difficult. All my vital func-

tions are dying away – except for two: the capacity to suffer pain and the capacity not to sleep. Whatever position I lie in I get no rest. Even you can't imagine what misery it is.

Boris's self-absorption here is breathtaking. How could he question Olga's facility to imagine misery, suffering and pain after her sleep deprivation in the Lubyanka and torturous years in the gulag?

He concluded his letter: 'Keep calm. Don't come here unannounced. I'll send for you again out of the blue – when I don't know. I kiss you. Yesterday you saw for yourself! I have no strength left from the pain.'

Zinaida, who visited Boris every day, was upset during one visit when a hospital official asked who she was. When she presented her identification papers, the employee said that there was a blonde woman in an hour before who had also said that she was Boris's wife.

By July, Pasternak had recovered enough to be moved to the Uzkoye sanatorium, south-east of Moscow, where he received a course of rehabilitation treatment. Before the Revolution, Uzkoye was the estate of the Trubetskoy brothers, acclaimed philosophers. Boris had known their son since school in Moscow. Evgeny Pasternak wrote of a visit with his half-brother, Leonid:

We saw our father in Uzkoye, where he had been sent after hospital. The sight of his face with its black circles under his eyes, his weakness and thinness were a shock to us. But he tried to calm us down, saying that it was just a reaction to penicillin and that he felt much better now. We took walks in the park with him and he told us about Vladimir Soloviev, who had lived here with the Trubetskoys; and showed us the room where he had died. Uzkoye was situated amid fields; a huge city, so familiar from childhood, was seen in the distance. In 1928, Father took Mother here and liked this house and park very much.

Boris returned to Peredelkino in early August. His friend Alexander Gladkov visited him and they took a long, gentle walk together in the woods: 'I remember everything as if it were yesterday,' Gladkov wrote of the encounter:

> the light-grey waters of the lake with the purplish-pink glint on them, the embankment with its branch willows and the black-edged white posts going all the way round, the beautiful old lime trees, cedars and larches in the surviving part of the former estate to which Pasternak took me, and his beloved voice, with the intonation I knew so well.
>
> His manner of talking too had not changed – that is, his sentences piled up rapidly in dense, urgent clusters, he interrupted himself, wandered off into digressions before getting back to the subject – always seeming to lose the thread of what he was saying until you got used to it and understood the relentless logic behind it. He seemed rather agitated and in need of relieving his feelings.

The two men strolled and talked for two hours. Or, as was characteristic, Pasternak talked while his companion listened. At first, Gladkov assumed that Boris must be exaggerating the precariousness of his situation: 'On that beautiful summer morning in the peaceful, familiar countryside near Moscow his forebodings of troubles and persecutions to come seemed to me the product of excessive imagination. A year and two months later I understood that it was not he who had been over-apprehensive but I who had been too complacent. He told me that the storm clouds were gathering over him. His novel was shortly going to appear in Italy.'

Boris recounted how, on the previous Friday, he had been summoned to a meeting of the Secretariat of the Writers' Union. It was supposed to be behind closed doors, he told Gladkov, but because he had refused to attend, they took 'great offence' and 'passed a fearful resolution denouncing' him. 'I suddenly find I have a lot of enemies' Pasternak confided:

I'm in for trouble this time; my turn has come. You really have no idea – it's a very complicated business involving the pride and prestige of all kinds of people. It's a clash of rival authorities. The novel itself is hardly at issue – most of the people concerned with the matter haven't even read it. A few of them would gladly drop the whole affair – not out of sympathy for me, mind you, only because they want to avoid a public scandal. But this is no longer possible. I'm told that someone at the meeting accused me of being hungry for publicity, of wanting to create a great hullabaloo and scandal. If only they knew how foreign and hateful I find such things! I sometimes wake up feeling horror and misery at myself, at this unfortunate character of mine that demands total freedom of spirit, and at the sudden turn of events in my life which is so distressing for those close to me.

Boris had incensed the Writers' Union by not only refusing to attend the meeting but sending along Olga with a note in his stead. Ever loyal to Boris, she dutifully took the somewhat baiting missive to Polikarpov and Surkov. It read:

People who are morally scrupulous are never happy with themselves; there are a lot of things they regret, a lot of things of which they repent. The only thing in my life for which I have no cause for repentance is the novel. I wrote what I think and to this day my thoughts remain the same. It may be a mistake not to have concealed it from others. I assure you I would have hidden it away had it been feebly written. But it proved to have more strength to it than I had dreamed possible – strength comes from on high, and thus its further fate was out of my hands.

Unsurprisingly, an enraged Polikarpov demanded that Olga tear the note up in front of him. He then demanded that Pasternak and Olga must come and see him and Surkov the following day. Two days running the foursome met. Pasternak was told in no uncertain terms that he must send a telegram to Feltrinelli demanding the return of the manuscript. Failure to do so could lead to 'very unpleasant consequences'.

A telegram was produced, written by Polikarpov and Surkov, which Boris was expected to sign. It read:

I have started rewriting the manuscript of my novel Doctor Zhivago, and I am now convinced that the extant version can in no way be considered a finished work. The copy of the manuscript in your possession is a preliminary draft requiring thorough revision. In my view it is not possible to publish the book in its current form. This would go against my rule, which is that the definitive draft of my work may be published. Please be so kind as to return, to my Moscow address, the manuscript of my novel Doctor Zhivago, which is indispensable to my work.

Pasternak was given two days to sign the telegram, or told that he would be arrested. Despite considerable pressure from Olga, who legitimately feared that Boris would be signing their death warrant if he did not send the telegram, to the fiercely proud Boris, this was akin to a death of his creative integrity anyway.

Olga again was left terrified for her life. She went to see D'Angelo, keen to enlist his help in persuading Boris that he must sign the telegram within the next day at all cost. 'This was no easy task,' D'Angelo recalled. 'Anyone who knew Pasternak at all well was aware how warm, kindly, sensitive and broad-minded he was, but also how proud, and how easily moved to anger and indignation.' Pasternak rejected their entreaties, furiously shouting at D'Angelo and Olga that nothing entitled them to speak to him in favour of this move. They clearly did not respect him, he thundered, and were 'treating him like a man without dignity'. What on earth would Feltrinelli think of him, he railed, after he had just written to say that the publication of Doctor Zhivago was the main aim of his life? Wouldn't he think him either a fool or a coward?

Eventually D'Angelo managed to calm and convince Boris that sending the telegram would not mean any loss of face for him in Feltrinelli's eyes. After all, Feltrinelli would not believe the telegram to be genuine, as it would be written in Russian, when Boris had told him to only heed correspondence written in French. Also, it was already too late to stop publication, as many Western publishers had made photocopies of the original manuscript and foreign rights contracts had been signed.

On 21 August the telegram was signed and sent. Immediately Polikarpov informed the Central Committee and suggested that they send a copy of it to the Italian Communist Party to further pressure Feltrinelli not to publish. When a senior official in the Italian Communist Party angrily waved the telegram in the publisher's Milan office, Feltrinelli refused to back down.

Later that day, Boris wrote to Irina, who was on holiday in Sukhumi, Georgia's subtropical beach resort:

Irochka, my treasure,
You have written the most wonderful letter to your mother. She has just read it to me and we are full of admiration. An amazing storm is building against me here but so far, thank God, no bolt of lightning has hit me yet. Because you are not here with me and because you cannot advise me, I was left with no choice but to send a telegram to F asking him amongst other things to slow down his actions. The grumble of thunder was deafening. Your mother will explain everything when you get back. She is sending you a bit of money and will try to send more later on if she is able to. As for you, I hope you are keeping as cheerful as you are in your letter. Don't deny yourself anything and accept these kisses as a goodbye.
    Your BP

Olga also included a letter along with Boris's, which was written, according to Irina, in a 'nonchalant tone'. Olga described the meeting with Surkov and Polikarpov, adding that it was only due to her diplomacy that the whole situation was kept under control: 'Boris came with me and gave them all sorts of lectures as he always does. I was standing behind him, armed with my valerian and camphor drops while he was holding forth. All eventually came back to normal again. While in the middle of this storm, Boris kept on saying in the most touching way: "Shame Irochka is not here. She would have been a great support." I can assure you he was serious.'

The Italian newspaper *L'Unità* reported that at a press conference in Milan on 19 October, Surkov had said: 'Pasternak has written to his Italian publisher asking him to return the manuscript for revision. As I have read yesterday in the *Corriere* and today in the *Espresso*, *Doctor Zhivago* will nevertheless be published against the author's will. The cold war thus invades literature. If this is artistic freedom as understood in the West, then I must say that we have a rather different view of it.'

Weeks later, Boris wrote to his sister Lydia in English, sending the letter via Rome with Sergio D'Angelo. Its strange, stilted form was deliberate. Pasternak had chosen to write in English because his Russian letters frequently disappeared in the post. He purposefully made it confusing due to 'the need for anonymous content'. There was a necessity, he later wrote to Lydia, for this 'broken language'. She understood that his post was being intercepted and monitored, even though he asked her to 'write in your ordinary Russian manner to me'.

1 November 1957.
Peredelkino,
the country house near Moscow

My dear, we have started the disappearing of my letters in the case of their importance. This one will get to you on indirect foreign ways. That is the reason, why I write it in English.

The fulfilment of my secretest dreams, I hope, approaches; the publication of my novel abroad only in translation at first, to my sorrow; in original, some day.

I had pressures to endure here of late, nuisance, menaces, in order to stop the appearance of the novel in Europe. I was forced to sign absurd, false, invented telegrams and letters to my editors. I signed them in the hope, which has not deluded me, that these persons, the unheard baseness of the counterfeit being so transparent, will disregard the feigned demands, – what justly they fortunately did. My triumph will either be tragical or unobscured. In both cases it is joy, victory, I could not have done it alone.

Here must be said about the share, about the part that takes in my last ten years of life Olga Vsevolodovna Ivinskaya, the Lara of the novel, who has undergone four years of imprisonment for me (from 1949) for the sole crime of being the nearest friend of me.

She does enormously much on my behalf. She relieves me from the vexing negotiations with the authorities, she takes the blows of such conflicts on herself. She is the only soul I confer with on what is the tense of age or on what is to be done, or thought, or written, and so on. A translation of her from Rabindranath Tagore was erroneously ascribed to me; it was the only time I left the mistake unobjected.

Zeneide, the mild, terrible, calling forth perpetual compassion, childish-dictatorial and tearful creatress and authoress of the house and garden and the four seasons and our Sunday parties and our family life and domestic establishments is not the woman to suffer hard by another one or ever to betray herself of being aware of it and tolerating it.

And so life goes on, darkened by peril, pity and dissembling – inexhaustible, fathomless, splendid.

You will be so ingenious as to guess, what to touch and what not to touch in your Russian post answer.

I embrace you most tenderly, Your B.

The next day, 2 November, Pasternak wrote to Feltrinelli, thanking him for the imminent Italian publication. He expressed his desire that this would lead to a series of translations: 'But we shall soon have an Italian Zhivago, French, English, and German Zhivagos – and, perhaps, one day geographically distant, yet Russian, Zhivagos!!'

On 10 November, *L'Espresso* published the first instalment of a series of extracts from the novel. It was no coincidence that they chose almost exclusively the anti-Soviet passages. On the 22nd the first edition of the novel appeared in Italian, under the title *Il Dottor Zivago*. Feltrinelli held a grand reception at the Hotel Continental in Milan. *Le tout* Milan attended the glamorous book launch. The first print run of 6,000 copies sold out immediately. It was followed by two other print runs in eleven days. Feltrinelli had achieved his aim. *Doctor Zhivago* was a controversial bestseller. Its progress around the world had begun.

# 9

# The Fat is in the Fire

In the first six months after its November debut, *Doctor Zhivago* was reprinted eleven times in Italian. In the following two years it appeared in twenty-three other languages: English, French, German, Spanish, Portuguese, Danish, Swedish, Norwegian, Czech, Polish, Serbo-Croat, Dutch, Finnish, Hebrew, Turkish, Persian, Arabic, Japanese, Chinese, Vietnamese, Hindi, Gujarati, and in Oriya, spoken in the state of Orissa. But not in Russian, the author's native tongue.

On 22 December 1957, Boris wrote to Nina Tabidze: 'You can congratulate me. Zh[ivago] was published in Italy early in December. In January it will be published in England, and then in Paris, in Sweden, in Norway, and West Germany. Every edition coming before spring. My attitude was dual, as I couldn't be utterly sincere in my attempts to stop the realisation of my most cherished wish and prevent it. A blind opportunity presented itself, and my dream was realised though I was forced to do a lot to prevent it.'

In his letter to his sisters on 14 August 1956, Boris was preoccupied with finding the right translator to do the novel justice in English. No mean feat, given his exacting standards:

A very good translator must be found (an Englishman who is a gifted writer, with a perfect command of Russian), because this thing can't be translated by any-old-how, amateurishly, using whatever resources come to hand. But even then, even if an ideal translator exists, with a perfect command of the literary language, he'll still need advice from experts in Russian folklore and a variety of ecclesiastical nuances and texts, because there's a lot of this sort of thing in the novel, and it's not just in the form of passing references and borrowings which a dictionary or reference-book could explain, but of new formations arising in a live, creative manner against a real and authentic background, in other words everything that would be clear to a knowledgeable person, in a new perspective, different from what has gone before.

Boris had previously asked Josephine and Lydia to send the manuscript to the Russian Jewish émigré, and friend of Bowra and Berlin, George Katkov. When Katkov visited Pasternak in Peredelkino the following month, Boris implored him to ensure the book's translation and publication in England. Katkov mentioned that the *Zhivago* poems would present a spectacular challenge for a translator, and suggested Vladimir Nabokov for the task. 'That won't work,' replied Boris. 'He's too jealous of my position in this country to do it properly.' It apparently infuriated Nabokov that in the West he was being compared to Pasternak. Both men had written hugely successful and controversial books at a similar time. *Lolita* was published in 1955, *Doctor Zhivago* two years later, when it knocked *Lolita* off the top of the American bestseller list. In 1958 Nabokov would refuse to critique *Doctor Zhivago*, claiming it would be a 'devastating review' and in the 1960s called the novel 'vilely written'. '*Doctor Zhivago* is a sorry thing,' Nabokov sneered. 'Clumsy, trite and melodramatic, with stock situations, voluptuous lawyers, unbelievable girls, romantic robbers and trite coincidences …' In a further low blow, he insisted that 'Pasternak's mistress' must have written it.

Katkov now approached Isaiah Berlin's protégé, Max Hayward, a gifted linguist and Oxford University research fellow who had worked as a translator at the British embassy in Moscow. His language skills were so fine that Russians who met him assumed he was a native speaker, though his family hailed originally from Yorkshire. To help speed up the process, Manya Harari, the co-founder of Harvill Press, a division of the publishers Collins in London, aided Hayward with the translation. An émigrée from a wealthy St Petersburg family, Harari had moved to England with her family during the First World War. She would become a staunch defender and ally for Olga after Boris's death.

On 8 July 1957, Harari wrote to Mark Bonham Carter, the publisher at Collins: 'I have written to Max Hayward to try and discover in what state the translation will reach us and to ask him for more of it. I certainly don't think he means merely to produce a draft. But I do think somebody will have to look over what he turns in and it is difficult to judge at this stage how much actual polishing up it will need.' Harari had written informing Hayward that Collins were ready to sign a contract with him for translation, as they had almost finished their contractual negotiations with Feltrinelli. After discussing the fee that Collins proposed to pay him – two guineas per thousand words, 'on the low side for Russian' – Harari debated the technical difficulties of translating the book: the collection of Zhivago poems presented a real headache:

> As for the poetry – I have not yet approached anyone and I don't see how I can until some transliterations have been made. I tried one day to transliterate one of the poems myself and saw how terribly difficult it is. I suppose the ideal solution would have been for you to transliterate the poems and get poets such as Auden and some others to put the finishing touches (except for a few which had better be left to Bowra entirely.) But the last thing we want is to hold you up in translation of the prose – the sooner the book is ready the better.
>
> So we must find some other solution. Perhaps Katkov will transliterate some? This, incidentally, will provide a way of paying him something for his share of work on the book – which is otherwise difficult to define!

Harari and Hayward worked on alternate chapters of the 160,000-word novel, then reviewed each other's work. 'Max would read a page in Russian, and then write it down in English without looking back ... both translators then cross-checked and agreed their combined version against the original.'

On 23 July 1957, Harari wrote to Bonham Carter: 'As to the poetry at the end of the book, Max now suggests that it should be left out, and I must say I am inclined to agree with him. The problems of getting the right translators, not offending Bowra, and getting it all done in reasonable time, seem enormous, and the novel can perfectly well stand on its own feet without the poems, which could always be published separately if the success of the novel were to warrant it. The most pressing thing is obviously to publish the novel as soon as possible.'

*Doctor Zhivago* was published in England the following September, with the Zhivago collection of poems included. The Oxford dons had done Pasternak justice, rising spectacularly to the formidable challenge of transforming 'Yury Zhivago's' poems into English.

While official publication of the novel was making its way around world territories, Pasternak had no idea that the book was also leading a dramatic covert life worthy of a spy thriller. The Russian-language manuscript of *Doctor Zhivago* arrived at the CIA headquarters in Washington DC in early January in the form of two rolls of microfilm. British intelligence provided this copy of the novel. In a memo to Frank Wisner, who ran the clandestine operations for the CIA, the head of the agency's Soviet Russia division described the book as 'the most heretical literary work by a Soviet author since Stalin's death'.

The CIA became interested in producing a Russian edition of the novel as part of its international efforts to distribute works that could counter communist ideology. *Doctor Zhivago* was ideal; partly because of the ban placed on *Zhivago* in the Soviet Union and partly because rumours about the poet's nomination for the Nobel Prize, which had long circulated in the West, were intensified with the Italian publication.

As part of a Cold War initiative, the American and British intelligence services agreed that *Doctor Zhivago* should be published in Russian, but the British requested that it be done in the United States of America. The CIA also calculated that a Russian-language edition produced in the United States would be more easily dismissed in the Soviet Union as propaganda. They decided that if it were published in a small European country then it would be seen as more credible.

The CIA's involvement in printing a Russian-language edition was to draw global attention to the book; but in an internal memo written shortly after the novel appeared in Italy, CIA staff recommended that the novel should be considered for worldwide acclaim and honours such as the Nobel Prize. Their role in operations involving *Doctor Zhivago* was backed at the highest level of government. The Eisenhower White House gave the CIA exclusive control over the novel's 'exploitation'. The Americans feared that if the Russians knew the hand that they were playing it could backfire disastrously on Pasternak and his family. The CIA was ordered from on high to promote the book 'as literature, not as cold-war propaganda'. Books, however, became weapons. If a piece of literature was banned in the USSR for challenging 'Soviet reality', the agency wanted to ensure it was in its citizens' hands.

In 1956, the CIA funded the creation of the Bedford Publishing Company in New York. Its brief was to translate Western literary works and publish them in Russian. Isaac Patch, the first head of Bedford Publishing, said of its covert work: 'The Soviet public, who had been subject to tedious propaganda, was starved for Western books. Through our book program we hoped to fill the void and open up the door to the fresh air of liberty and freedom.' Among the books they translated and distributed were James Joyce's *Portrait of the Artist as a Young Man*, Nabokov's *Pnin* and Orwell's *Animal Farm*. The CIA even planned to set the Russian text in the United States, using an unusual Cyrillic font that could not be traced back to the Americans. One suggestion had been to have the imprint of Goslitizdat on the title page. The American publisher Felix Morrow was put in charge of publication. He worked with Rausen Brothers, a printer in New York, specialising in Russian texts.

The CIA chose as its vehicle for distribution the Brussels World's Fair – 'Expo '58' – which ran from 17 April to 19 October 1958, and which was expected to receive over 18 million visitors. Forty-two nations, including, for the first time, the Vatican, exhibited at the 500-acre site north-west of Brussels, and Belgium issued 16,000 visas to Soviet visitors. 'This book has great propaganda value, not only for its intrinsic message and thought-provoking nature, but also for the circumstances of its publication,' declared a memo to all the branch chiefs of the CIA Soviet Russia Division; 'we have the opportunity to make Soviet citizens wonder what is wrong with their government, when a fine literary work by a man acknowledged to be the greatest living Russian writer is not even available in his own country in his own language for his own people to read.'

During the summer of 1958, the CIA had been under pressure to get copies published in time for the World's Fair. In the end, they collaborated with the Dutch intelligence service, the BVD (Binnenlandse Veiligheidsdienst). The reproduction of *Doctor Zhivago* produced by Felix Morrow was passed to Ruud van der Beek, the leader of the Dutch branch of the anti-communist group Paix et Liberté. In July, van der Beek visited Mouton Press in The Hague with the text ready to be photoprinted and requested a thousand copies. The person he dealt with was Peter de Ridder, one of Mouton's representatives. De Ridder tried to contact Feltrinelli for permission but the publisher was unreachable – holidaying in Scandinavia. De Ridder decided to press ahead, regardless. He tried to protect Feltrinelli's claim to exclusive copyright by printing 'Feltrinelli-Milan 1958' on the title page in Cyrillic. He omitted to include a Feltrinelli copyright notice. The use of Pasternak's full name, including 'Leonidovich' on the title page, further suggested that the book had been produced by a non-native speaker, as Russians would not use the patronymic on a title page.

In the first week of September, the first Russian-language edition of *Doctor Zhivago* was printed in The Hague. The books, dated 6 September 1958, bound in pale blue-linen, and wrapped in brown paper, were taken to the home of Walter Cini, the CIA officer in The Hague. Two hundred copies were then sent to the Washington headquarters. The rest were dispatched to CIA stations across Western Europe – 200 to Frankfurt, 100 to Berlin, 100 to Munich, 25 to London and 10 to Paris. The largest package was sent to Brussels for the World's Fair.

As *Doctor Zhivago* clearly could not just be handed out at the American Pavilion, the CIA arranged an ingenious ally. The nearby Vatican Pavilion agreed to distribute the novel. Russian-speaking priests and lay volunteers – 'ladies with pointed noses and a blessed smile' – handed out religious literature, including bibles, prayer books – and some Russian literature. Three thousand Soviet tourists visited the Vatican Pavilion over the fair's three months. The presence of Rodin's sculpture *The Thinker*, on loan from the Louvre, was also a big part of the lure for Russian visitors, attracting key members of the intelligentsia, scientists, scholars, writers, engineers, collective-farm directors and city mayors.

The CIA triumphed in its aim. Their 'sponsored' edition of the novel made its way into the hands of Soviet citizens. At the end of each day, scores of the book's distinctive blue linen dust-jackets could be found littering the fair-ground floor, the novels having been torn down the spine and stuffed into pockets, making the literary contraband easier to hide. Copies were soon exchanging hands on the black market for around 300 roubles, almost a week's wages for the average Soviet worker.

Later press reports suggested that Russian sailors had smuggled the book into the Soviet Union aboard the ship *Gruzia* and that the Soviet ambassador to Belgium had been removed as a result of events at the Brussels World's Fair. A CIA memo of 9 September 1958 concluded: 'This phase can be considered completed successfully.'

On the 19th, Pasternak wrote to his sisters in Oxford: 'Is it true that an original Russian edition has also appeared? There are rumours that it's on sale at an exhibition in Brussels?'

In the Soviet Union, there had been no official comment in the months following Italian publication. Party figures, including Khrushchev, were fully aware of the international response to the novel and the preparation of various translations. Polikarpov's department was kept up to date via press cuttings from Western media coverage. Due to the official silence and hesitant attitude towards him, it is ironic that in Russia Pasternak depended on his translation work for an income, while Feltrinelli had a lucrative bestseller on his hands.

Several of Pasternak's translations were published that year: Schiller's *Maria Stuart* became the standard translation for Soviet productions of the play. But with the bleak outlook for publication of his novel in Russia in the spring, anxious about his dwindling finances, he suggested to Goslitizdat that they reissue his Shakespeare translations.

The huge strain Boris had been under precipitated a recurrence of his previous illness, with new urological complications, acute pain and a raging temperature. At one point a blood analysis suggested cancer, but this was not confirmed. In the end, a trapped spinal nerve was diagnosed. Hospital treatment was required but nothing suitable was available. The preceding year someone in the Writers' Union ruled that Pasternak was 'unworthy' of treatment in the Kremlin Hospital. And so for the first week of his illness he was forced to remain at Peredelkino, where he read Henry James and listened to the radio between bouts of agonising pain. It took a week of agitating by his family, friends and medical experts before a bed was found for him in the Kremlin clinic. On 8 February 1958 he was carried out of Peredelkino on a stretcher through the heavy snow, blowing kisses to Zinaida, his sons and friends.

Irina observed that towards the end of 1958 and beginning of 1959 it seemed that Boris's 'youth just deserted him'. His former vigour drained away and 'one day he was unrecognisable, grey, distorted. He had become old; he was aching all over. Even his hands, so fine, so lively and astonishingly alive, just slumped down on his knees right in the middle of a monologue.'

As *Doctor Zhivago*'s international success gained momentum, Pasternak was inundated with postal correspondence from abroad containing reader's ecstatic responses, congratulations and press cuttings. This in some ways revived him. By autumn, the Peredelkino postwoman was ferrying up to fifty pieces of post a day up the path to the dacha. It became a source of exasperation between Olga and Irina that Boris squandered so much time trying to respond to all this correspondence.

But after years of enforced isolation, he felt exhilarated and touched by all these messages of support and goodwill.

Since his return from hospital, Boris had feared a relapse. He was required to exercise his leg daily and would sometimes walk around Peredelkino for two to three hours at a time. He also began to work in his study, standing at a bureau, to avoid long periods sitting. That spring and summer he received many foreign visitors, both the expected and the uninvited, from Russia and abroad. In September the Oxford don Ronald Hingley dined at Peredelkino with Boris and Zinaida. He described how Zinaida, 'elderly and clad in black', was silently courteous, but tacitly conveyed her displeasure at these foreign contacts who both protected and compromised her husband. Hingley also noticed how Pasternak was seemingly nonchalant about the constant government surveillance. Yet he watched his host stiffen as a black limousine used by the security police passed slowly down the narrow lane, almost halting by the gate of dacha No 3.

On 12 May 1958, Boris wrote to Josephine:

When D[octor] Zh[ivago] comes out in England, and if you read anything interesting and newsworthy about it, please send me cuttings and write a few words about anything you discover or hear about it (even if it's bad). Don't fear for any consequences for me, excepting only the possibility that what you send may not reach me.

I kiss you warmly, and Fedia, and all your family. After these last two illnesses, and with the continuing pain in my leg and the constant possibility of an acute relapse, I have lost my confidence in the time I have left to me; I just don't know how long I have got – not to mention the permanent (though just temporarily eased) political threat to my position, which also makes it impossible to imagine firm ground beneath my feet.

Alexander Gladkov said of Pasternak at this time: 'I sensed a kind of defiance, the defiance of a very lonely, desperate writer who had grown tired of his own loneliness and despair.' In December, just after the Italian publication of *Doctor Zhivago*, Gladkov saw Boris at a performance of *Faust* by the visiting Hamburg Theatre in Moscow. 'During the interval he was mobbed by a crowd of foreign newspapermen,' recalled Gladkov.

> One of them thrust a copy of his own translation of *Faust* into his hands and they all started taking photographs. The earlier Pasternak would have thought it an unseemly comedy, but this new Pasternak stood there obediently in the foyer of the theatre, posing book in hand before the journalists while the flash-bulbs popped away. He evidently thought he *had* to do this for some reason or other, since I cannot imagine it gave him any pleasure. He had been overtaken by world fame but seemed none the happier for it – one could see the strain in the awkward way he stood there, and in the expression of his face. He looked more of a martyr than a conquering hero.

During the summer of 1958, rumours had been mounting that Pasternak would be awarded the Nobel Prize for Literature. Lars Gyllensten, the Nobel Committee secretary, maintained that Pasternak was put forward for the Nobel Prize each year from 1946 to 1950, in 1953 and in 1957. Albert Camus devoted attention to Pasternak in his acceptance speech in 1957 and nominated him for the prize the following year. This would be Boris's eighth nomination.

In May, Pasternak wrote to Kurt Wolff, his American editor at Pantheon Books, with whom he had struck up a correspondence: 'What you write about Stockholm will never happen, because my government will never give its agreement to any distinction for me. This and much else is grievous and sad. But you will never guess how insignificant is the place that these characteristics of the era occupy my existence. And on the other hand, it's precisely these insurmountable fatalities that give life momentum, depth, and earnestness, and make it quite extraordinary – sovereignly joyful, magic, and real.'

On 6 October, Boris wrote to Josephine, again in stilted English: 'If the N[obel] prize of this year (as sometimes the rumour goes) will be assigned to me, and the necessity for me comes to go abroad (all the matter is still absolutely dark to me) I can see no means not to try and not to want to take with me O[lga] in the voyage, if the permission is only to be obtained, not to say about the probability of my own travel. But, seeing the difficulties, connected with the N. pr., I hope it will be conferred to other competitor, to A Moravia, I believe.

On 23 October the Swedish Academy announced that the Nobel Prize for Literature would be awarded to Boris Pasternak 'for his important contribution to contemporary lyric poetry, as well as to the great tradition of the Russian prose-writers'. Foreign news correspondents flocked to the gates of Boris's dacha, cameras poised, despite persistent rain. When the newsmen asked for his reaction, he replied: 'To receive this prize fills me with great joy, and also gives me great moral support. But my joy today is a lonely joy,' as the camera shutters clicked.

'In one photograph we see BL reading the official telegram from the Swedish Academy,' narrates Olga. 'In another he sits bashfully with raised glass, replying to the congratulations of Kornei Chukovsky and his granddaughter, and of Nina Tabidze … And then, in a photograph taken only about twenty minutes later, he is sitting at the same table, with the same people, but, heavens above, looking so woebegone, his eyes sad and his mouth turned down at the corners.'

What had happened in the intervening twenty minutes? Zinaida, who had refused to get out of bed that morning when Boris first heard he had been awarded the prize, declaring 'nothing good can come of this', was busy downstairs baking: it was her Russian name day. She was trying to ignore the brouhaha of the foreign correspondents outside, when suddenly Fedin, the new secretary of the Soviet Writers' Union, turned up. Without acknowledging Zinaida he walked past her brusquely and upstairs to Pasternak's sanctuary. When he left fifteen minutes later all was silent. Zinaida rushed upstairs and found Boris passed out on the wrought-iron bed in his study.

Fedin had come to tell Pasternak that if he didn't renounce the prize a public campaign would be immediately launched against him. Apparently Polikarpov was waiting next door, at Fedin's house. The Central Committee had decided that since Fedin had some influence with Boris, he should be the one to tell him of the party's decision. 'I'm not going to congratulate you because Polikarpov is at my place and he's demanding that you renounce the prize,' Fedin had told Boris.

'Under no circumstances,' Boris replied. He asked Fedin to give him some time. And then he fainted.

When Boris regained consciousness he hurried across the lane to see another neighbour, Vsevolod Ivanov, a writer of popular adventure stories, to ask his advice. 'Do what seems right to you; don't listen to anyone,' Ivanov told him. 'I told you yesterday and I say it again today; You're the best poet of the era. You deserve any prize.'

An infuriated Polikarpov meanwhile returned to Moscow.

Boris decided to send a telegram of thanks to the Academy. 'He was happy, thrilled with his conquest,' remembered Kornei Chukovsky, who on hearing that Pasternak had been awarded the Prize had hastened with his granddaughter to Peredelkino to congratulate the writer in person. 'I threw my arms around him and smothered him with kisses.' Chukovksy proposed a toast, which was captured by Western photographers in one of the photos Olga described. Later, anxious that his embrace of Pasternak might endanger him and his family, Chukovsky, who had been the victim of an earlier traumatic slander campaign, wrote a hasty note to the authorities denying that he was 'aware that *Doctor Zhivago* contained attacks on the Soviet system'.

Boris excused himself from his visitors and went upstairs to send his telegram to the Academy. It read: 'Immensely grateful, touched, proud, astonished, abashed. Pasternak.' When he had finished writing it, Chukovsky and his granddaughter accompanied Boris part of the way on his walk to see Olga at the Little House. As Zinaida had been nothing but critical over the prize, Boris explained to Chukovsky as they walked, he would not be taking her to Stockholm for the official prize-giving ceremony.

Boris arrived at the Little House in 'an agitated state', remembers Olga. He described Fedin's unexpected visit and explained that the demands from on high insisted that he must 'repudiate' the prize and the novel. He told Olga that he had already sent a telegram of thanks to Stockholm and did not see how he could possibly agree to repudiating his novel. He then rang Irina in Moscow to recount the whole day's events.

'Ah you know already,' Boris said to Irina, in a disappointed tone. 'I have just rung your grandmother and her [new] husband, Sergei Stepanovich answered, so I told him and he didn't even congratulate me. It's starting. The fat is in the fire now. Fedin has been round and tells me I must give it up. He looked as though I'd committed a crime, and didn't congratulate me … Only the Ivanovs did. What marvellous people they are! Tamara Vladimirovna gave me a great kiss – what a nice woman. But those others … I wouldn't speak to Fedin. Was I right?'

Irina later wrote: 'I was probably one of the first people he had told that he would accept the prize and the consequences that would come with it. Mother must have been beside herself. The panic which overtook his entourage must have been the source of great suffering. This crossed my mind very quickly. I answered with exaggerated cheerfulness without expressing any of my concerns. "Of course, of course! Tell them all to go away, the miserable, wretched slaves." "Yes? So, I am right?" BL repeated joyfully.'

After leaving Boris earlier in the day, Chukovsky had called on Fedin, who warned him, 'Pasternak will do us all great harm with all of this. They'll launch a fierce campaign against the intelligentsia now.' Chukovsky was served with a notice to attend an emergency meeting of the Writers' Union the next day. A courier had gone from house to house in Peredelkino with summonses for the writers in the village. After Vsevolod Ivanov received his he collapsed. His housekeeper found him lying on the floor. Diagnosed with a possible stroke, he remained bedridden for a month.

When the courier arrived at the Pasternak dacha, Boris's 'face grew dark; he clutched at his heart and could barely climb the stairs to his room'. He began to experience pain in his arm, which felt as if it 'had been amputated'. Chukovsky wrote: 'There would be no mercy, that was clear. They were out to pillory him. They would trample him to death just as they had Zoshchenko, Mandelstam, Zabolotsky, Mirsky and Benedikt Livshits.'

When Kurt Wolff in America heard about the Nobel Prize award, he wrote immediately to Boris. 'In this case (genius) is being recognised as such. Your book is being read and loved for its remarkable lyric-epic-ethical qualities. (In six weeks, 70,000 copies – that is fantastic – and by the end of the year it will be 100,000 more.)' Wolff added that he was reserving rooms for him in Stockholm for the Nobel Prize ceremonies in December.

'On Saturday 25th October, it all began,' wrote Olga. Radio Moscow immediately denounced 'the award of the Nobel Prize for a mere mediocre work such as *Doctor Zhivago*' as 'a hostile political act directed against the Soviet State'. Two whole pages of Saturday's edition of *Literaturnaya Gazeta* were devoted to a denunciation of Pasternak. The newspaper printed in full the damning 1956 rejection letter written by the editors of *Novy Mir*, along with a leading article and open letter from the newspaper's editors. Accusations included: 'the life-story of a malignant petty bourgeois … open hatred for the Russian people … a paltry, worthless and vile piece of work … a rabid literary snob …' Many Muscovites were reading about *Doctor Zhivago* and the Nobel Prize for the first time. The newspaper's print run of 880,000 ran out within a few hours. The impact of the award on public opinion in Moscow, especially among the intelligentsia, was immense. The award was 'the only topic' of conversation in the capital. The election of Cardinal Angelo Roncalli to the papacy, the death in Leningrad of the eminent physiologist Leon Orbeli, or even the award of the Nobel Prize for Physics to three Soviet scientists received scant attention.

'Spontaneous' protests against Pasternak were held at the Gorky Literary Institute, opposite the Writers' Union on Vorovski Street. Carefully orchestrated, great pressure had been put on the students to attend by the institute director. The stance they took against Pasternak, he said, would be a 'litmus test' for them. The students were instructed to turn up at the demonstration and sign a letter denouncing the writer in the *Literaturnaya Gazeta*. According to Irina, who was studying at the institute: 'The people collecting the signatures came round the dormitories and it was hard to escape them.' Even so, only just over a third of the 300 students signed this letter. 'Some of our girls took refuge in the toilets or in the kitchen, and pretended they weren't in. My friend Alka simply chased them out of her room. But not everybody could afford to do this.' Meanwhile, in Leningrad, three brave students daubed 'Long Live Pasternak!' across the embankment of the River Neva.

The demonstration itself was a 'pitiful display.' Only a few dozen people turned up. They took placards and leaned them against the wall of the Writers' Union. On one of them there was a caricature using anti-Semitic imagery and depicting Pasternak reaching for a sack of dollars with crooked, grasping fingers. Another said: 'Throw the Judas out of the USSR!'

On Sunday 26 October, all the newspapers reproduced in full the materials that had appeared in the *Literaturnaya Gazeta* the previous day. *Pravda*, the official publication of the Communist Party, carried a malicious personal attack on Pasternak written by their favourite hatchet man, David Zaslavsky. Aged seventy-eight, Zaslavsky had been brought out of semi-retirement to savage Boris. The headline read: 'Reactionary Propaganda Uproar Over a Literary Weed'. Zaslavsky decried: 'It is ridiculous but *Doctor Zhivago*, this infuriated moral freak, is presented by Pasternak as the "finest" representative of the old Russian intelligentsia. This slander of the leading intelligentsia is as absurd as it is devoid of talent. Pasternak's novel is low-grade reactionary hackwork.'

'The novel,' he continued, 'was taken up triumphantly by the most inveterate enemies of the Soviet Union – obscurantists of various shades, incendiaries of a new world war, provocateurs. Out of an ostensibly literary event they seek to make a political scandal, with the clear aim of aggravating international relations, adding fuel to the flames of the "cold war", sowing hostility towards the Soviet Union, blackening the Soviet public. Choking with delight, the anti-Soviet press has proclaimed the novel the "best" work of the current year, while the obliging grovellers of the big bourgeoisie have crowned Pasternak with the Nobel Prize.' Zaslavsky concluded: 'The inflated self-esteem of an offended and spiteful Philistine had left no trace of dignity and patriotism in Pasternak's soul. By all his activity, Pasternak confirms that in our socialist country, gripped by enthusiasm for the building of the radiant Communist society, he is a weed.'

Alexander Gladkov was sitting in a barber's shop on Moscow's Arbat Square that afternoon when he heard Zaslavsky's article being read out over the radio. 'Everybody listened in silence – a sullen kind of silence. Only one chirpy workman started talking about all the money Pasternak would get, but nobody encouraged him to go on. I knew that cheap tittle-tattle of this kind would be much harder for Pasternak to bear than all the official fulminations. I had felt very depressed all day, but this silence in the barber's shop cheered me up.'

When Irina read these venomous attacks, she thought how glad she was that Boris did not often read the newspapers:

The monstrous cheapness of it all would have stung him to the quick and wounded him – he would not have been able to treat it aloofly, with contempt, as we could. He might well have taken all this wretched filth to heart, and tried in a desperate (and also comic) manner to justify his actions both to himself and everyone else.

I had often noticed – and it was particularly evident at this time – that he was unable to take an ironical view of things that seemed almost idiotic to others. For example, someone thought to cheer him up during those days by telling him about an exchange between two women in the Metro: 'Why are you shouting at me like that?' said one to the other. 'Do you take me for a *Zhivago* or something?'

When he later re-told the story to us, BL put on a great show of finding it very funny, but I, for one, sensed – and I had an unusually heightened capacity to enter into his feelings during those days – that it was in fact all very painful to him.

Irina left immediately for Peredelkino with two young writer friends from the Literary Institute, Yura and Vania. It was clear that Pasternak was going to be hounded, that a witch hunt had been mounted against him, and it was impossible to say where it might end. Irina's friends, 'afraid and quaking in their shoes' about going to visit Boris Pasternak, nevertheless seemed eager to help.

At the Little House, Olga greeted them at the door. She was not expecting her daughter. Boris was delighted to see Irina but less so her visitors. He wanted to be left alone. He told her guests that he was ready to 'drink his cup of suffering to the end', and despite the terrible weather – it had been raining non-stop for five days – tried to appear cheerful. Irina explained that the members of the Writers' Union had arranged to meet the next day, Monday 27 October, to decide Boris's fate. 'He was devastated,' Irina recalled. 'I could see how much he would have liked to have been spared this trophy. That he wished that all of this was a bad dream and that if only his life could go back to normal; his work, his walks, his correspondences and his visits to my mother.'

Irina and her two friends accompanied Boris back to his dacha. His loneliness was tangible. When he said goodbye and thanked the two young students for coming, he pulled out a checked handkerchief to stem his tears. 'It was a loneliness born of great courage,' remembered Irina. 'He was still dressed in his usual get-up – a cap, a mackintosh, and wellingtons – which Mama and I loved so much. He was wearing this cap and raincoat when he was photographed on the bridge by a Swedish photographer, his hand on his chest. The caption written in our village newsletter read: "Hand on my heart, I can say I have done something for Soviet Literature".'

Later that night, Boris confided to Olga that Irina's two friends, Yura and Vania, had told him that if they refused to sign a letter demanding his expulsion from the country, they would be thrown out of the Literary Institute. They asked Boris what they should do. He had told them to sign it: after all it was an empty formality. When they left him at his dacha, he described watching them walk away hand in hand, 'skipping with joy', clearly relieved that they had Pasternak's personal permission to sign.

Olga saw how much this had hurt Boris. 'How strange young people are now. In our time such things were not done,' he said to her, lamenting their lack of loyalty and backbone.

Mark Twain once wrote that a man is admitted to the Church for what he believes, and is expelled from it for what he knows. 'The time had now come for Boris to be expelled from the Church because of what he knew,' wrote Olga. 'He had broken the basic rule of the age in which we live; the rule that requires you to ignore realities. And he had usurped the right, claimed by our rulers for themselves alone, to have an opinion, to speak and think one's own thoughts.'

# 10

# The Pasternak Affair

At midday on Monday 27 October, 1958, the Writers' Union met to consider 'the Pasternak affair'. Boris went into Moscow early that morning, wearing the cherished three-piece suit he had inherited from his father. He went straight to Olga's Potapov apartment with Vyacheslav 'Koma' Ivanov. He was the son of Boris's Peredelkino neighbour Vsevolod Ivanov, who remained bedridden after the terror of the Writers' Union summons.

Boris and Koma were greeted by Olga, Irina and Mitia. Over strong black coffee they discussed whether Boris should attend his own 'execution' or not. Koma was adamant that he should not. They agreed that Boris would send the committee a letter instead. Boris went into Irina's bedroom and wrote the letter in pencil. 'It was an unusual kind of letter in which he had listed all his points in summary form,' recalled Olga. 'There were twenty-two points. It was quite undiplomatic, without any beating about the bush or compromises, and had been dashed off without a moment's hesitation.'

Boris proceeded to stand in front of them. He read the letter out in his slow, booming voice, gravely pausing after each point. They included:

1. I have received your invitation, and intended to come, but knowing what a monstrous display it will be, I have decided against it.

2. I continue to believe that it was possible to write *Doctor Zhivago* without ceasing to be a Soviet writer – particularly as it was completed at the time of the publication of V. Dudintsev's novel *Not by Bread Alone* – which created the impression of a thaw, of a new situation.

3. I gave the manuscript of *Doctor Zhivago* to an Italian Communist publisher, and expected that the translation would be censored. I was willing to cut out (unacceptable) passages.

4. I do not regard myself as a parasite.

5. I do not have an exaggerated opinion of myself. I asked Stalin to let me write as best I can.

6. I thought that *Doctor Zhivago* would be the object of friendly criticism.

7. Nothing will induce me to give up the honour of being a Nobel Prize winner. But I am ready to hand over the money to the Peace Committee.

8. I do not expect justice from you. You may have me shot, or expelled from this country or do anything you like. All I ask of you is: do not be in too much of a hurry over it. It will bring you no increase of either happiness or glory.

His letter ended with the words: 'I forgive you in advance.'

His audience listened in astonished silence. After he finished there was an anxious pause before Koma, who adored Boris, said encouragingly: 'Well now, it's very good!' Olga suggested that Boris cut out the reference to Dudintsev. Dudintsev's novel had provoked fierce controversy in 1956 due to its outspoken portrait of a Stalinist bureaucrat. But Boris being Boris, he refused to alter his letter in any way. Koma and Mitia took the inflammatory missive to the Writers' Union by taxi, to ensure that it was safely delivered for the start of the meeting.

It was a packed, excitable audience who argued Boris Pasternak's fate at the White Hall on Vorovski Street. All the seats were taken and writers were crammed in, lined up against the walls. Pasternak's letter was read out and greeted with 'anger and indignation'. Polikarpov's summary of the meeting for the Central Committee described it as 'scandalous in its impudence and cynicism'.

The meeting went on for hours yet, in the end, the vote to expel Boris from the Writers' Union was unanimous. A long, formal resolution was printed in the *Literaturnaya Gazeta* the following day, accompanied by a headline in huge print: 'On Actions by Member of the Union of Writers of the USSR B.L. Pasternak Incompatible with His Calling as a Soviet Writer'. The text of the resolution savaging Boris repeated the accusations of his betrayal of the Soviet people. It included coruscating lines such as '*Doctor Zhivago* is the cry of woe of a frightened Philistine who is aggrieved and dismayed because history has not followed the crooked paths which he would have liked to dictate to it ...' and concluded that the board 'divest B. Pasternak of the title of Soviet writer, and expel him from membership of the Union of Writers of the USSR'.

The KGB immediately tightened its grip on Boris and Olga. They were followed wherever they went. 'Our footsteps were dogged by suspicious-looking characters,' said Olga. 'Their methods were extremely crude – they even dressed up as women, and sometimes pretended to hold drunken parties (together with dancing!) on the landing right outside our apartment in Potapov Street.' A bugging device was installed at the Little House. 'Good day to you, microphone!' Boris would say, hanging his cap on a nail next to the place they discovered it had been hidden.

'There was the feeling of being harassed on all sides,' said Olga, 'so we spoke mostly in whispers, frightened of our own shadows, and constantly glancing sideways at the walls – even they seemed hostile to us. Many people turned their backs on us and did not want to know us anymore.'

When Olga returned to her apartment late on 27 October, she could see the KGB agents, some of whom she already knew by sight, hanging around the entrance. Given her previous experience, when the KGB ransacked her apartment before arresting her, she decided that the time had come to try and save some letters and manuscripts and to burn other items. So the following day she and Mitia took as many of her papers as they could out to the Little House. Boris arrived soon after them and began speaking, his voice trembling.

'Olia, I have to say something very important to you, and I hope Mitia will forgive me. I cannot stand this business any more. I think it's time to leave this life, it's too much.' He then proceeded to make the shocking suggestion that he and Olga write a joint suicide note, then take their lives together. 'We'll just sit here this evening, the two of us – and that's how they'll find us. You once said that eleven tablets of Nembutal is a fatal dose – well, I have twenty-two here. Let's do it. It will cost them very dearly. It will be a slap in the face.'

Mitia, understandably upset by the conversation, ran outside. Boris followed after him. 'Mitia, forgive me, don't think too badly of me, my precious child, for taking your mother with me, but we can't live and it will be easier for you after our death … But we can't go on – what's happened already is enough. She can't live without me and I can't live without her. So please forgive me. Now tell me, am I right or not?'

All three of them now stood on the doorstep, oblivious to the snow and the rain. Understandably terrified, Mitia blanched. But such was his regard for Pasternak and love for his mother that he replied stoically: 'You are right, Boris Leonidovich, Mother must do what you do.'

Olga sent Mitia to fetch a basket of wood chips so they could build a fire to burn certain papers. She led Boris inside, sat him down and tenderly asked him to wait a little longer before taking any sort of drastic action. 'Our suicide would suit them very well,' she said, taking him in her arms as he wept against her. 'They will say that it shows we are weak and we knew we were wrong, and they will gloat over us into the bargain.' She gently persuaded Boris to return home to his study and to try and write a little to soothe himself. She reassured him that she would go and find out exactly what the authorities wanted from him, she would start by asking Fedin – 'and if it's something we can laugh at, then better just laugh at it and bide our time. But if not, and I see there is really no way out, then I'll tell you honestly and we'll put an end to it. We'll take the Nembutal. Only wait until tomorrow and don't do anything without me.'

'Very well,' Boris agreed. 'Go wherever it is today, and stay the night in Moscow. I will come out tomorrow morning early with the Nembutal, and we'll decide then. I cannot stand up anymore to this hounding.'

Olga and Mitia accompanied Boris back across the long bridge to Peredelkino, to within sight of his dacha. It was sleeting heavily, but Boris could not make himself go in. He stood in the road, holding Olga tight. She felt desperate for him. Eventually, he was persuaded to go inside.

Olga and Mitia trudged on through deep slush to Konstantin Fedin's house. They arrived soaking wet, their shoes covered in mud. Fedin's daughter, Nina, refused to let them in any further than the hallway. She said her father was ill and was not to be disturbed. When Olga remonstrated that her father would be sorry if he did not see her immediately, Fedin appeared on the upper landing and called them to his study.

Olga told Fedin that Boris was on the verge of suicide. 'Tell me,' she asked Fedin, 'what do they want from him? Do they really want him to commit suicide?' As Fedin walked to the window, Olga thought that she saw tears in his eyes. But then he faced her and his tone was that of an austere party official. 'Boris Leonidovoch has dug such an abyss between himself and us that it cannot be crossed,' he said. Fedin phoned Polikarpov in Olga's presence and arranged a meeting for the following afternoon. As he showed the pair downstairs, he turned to Olga and said: 'You do realise, don't you, that you must restrain him. He mustn't inflict a second blow on his country.' Leaving muddy footprints on Fedin's spotless parquet floor, Olga and her son left, and headed immediately for Moscow.

'Mama came [back] from Peredelkino completely distraught that day,' remembers Irina. 'She looked so old, she looked awful, she was in tears. She came into the apartment, holding herself against the walls, wailing that she would never forgive the people responsible, that the "Classic" had cried. It was horrendous, she said, that he did not feel able to go home anymore, and that they had stayed outside on the road, incapable of parting. She said that they had talked about letting themselves die, that he was determined to die. Mitia and I took her in our arms, she was covered in mud and she just slumped on the couch, her coat still on, sobbing.'

Boris's dacha at
Peredelkino, taken
by the author

Boris and Irina at
Peredelkino, 1957

Olga's 'glass house': her first rental on the shores of Lake Izmalkovo where she spent her happiest summer of 1955

The bridge to the Little House across Lake Izmalkovo. The Little House is in the background

Olga and Boris in the Little House, summer 1958

Olga, Boris and Irina, Peredelkino, 1958

Boris reading the Nobel Prize telegram, with his wife Zinaida sitting on his left, and friend Nina Tabidze on his right. Peredelkino, 23 October 1958

One of Boris's last letters to Olga on 30 April 1960. Boris was ill, lying in bed, writing to Olga 'in defiance of the doctor's orders'.

Boris leaning out of the window in Peredelkino after renouncing the Nobel Prize, 1958

Boris's son Leonid, Charles Pasternak and Rosa, the wife of Alexander Pasternak's son Fedia, at Alexander Pasternak's dacha, Peredelkino, 1961

The funeral procession, Peredelkino, 2 June 1960

Opposite: Olga at the funeral, 2 June 1960

Olga just before her second arrest and deportation, 1960

Olga's identification photograph taken at the Lubyanka during her second incarceration in 1960

ПЧ23 Ивинская Ольга Всеволодовна 1912 гр.

Early the next morning, Olga and Boris argued on the telephone. She accused him of being selfish. She knew that the likelihood was that the authorities wouldn't harm the famous writer and she 'would come off worse'. Later in the day, Boris arrived 'still in his best suit' at the Moscow apartment to 'announce something startling'. He got everyone together – Olga, Irina, Mitia and Ariadna Efron, who was visiting – and told them that earlier that morning he had sent a telegram to the permanent secretary of the Swedish Academy in Stockholm, Anders Österling, renouncing the prize. His brother Alexander had driven him to the Central Telegraph Office near the Kremlin. He had written it in French. It read: 'In view of the meaning given the award by the society in which I live, I must renounce this underserved distinction which has been conferred on me. Please do not take my voluntary renunciation amiss – Pasternak.'

'We were dumbfounded,' Olga later wrote. 'This was just like him – first to act, and only then to speak about it and ask people what he thought. I think it was only Ariadna who went up to him at once and kissed him, saying "Good for you, Boria, good for you!" – not, of course, because this was what she really thought but because it was an accomplished fact and the only thing left was to support him.'

Pasternak had more in store for them. He then announced that he had sent a second telegram to the Central Committee informing the Kremlin that he had renounced the Nobel Prize and asking that Olga Ivinskaya be allowed to work again. He wanted the restrictions lifted so that she could be paid for her translation work, even if he now had no means to earn a living.

That afternoon, Boris took Olga in a taxi to the Writers' Union for the meeting with Polikarpov. He dropped her off and returned alone to Peredelkino to await her news and learn of the union's next move.

'If you allow Pasternak to commit suicide, you will be aiding and abetting a second stab in the back for Russia,' Polikarpov told Olga, echoing Fedin's words. 'This whole scandal must be settled – which we will be able to do with your help. You can help his way back to the people again.

But if anything happens to him, the moral responsibility will be yours.'

Pasternak's renunciation of the prize clearly wasn't enough. They wanted more. Olga thought hard about what exactly the officials sought as she sat on the train out to Izmalkovo that evening. What they really wanted, she understood only later, was to 'humble' Boris, 'to force him to grovel in public and admit his "errors" – in other words, to score a victory for brute force and intolerance. But in moving first as he did, BL took them by surprise'.

The Swedish Academy responded to Pasternak's telegram, saying it had 'received your refusal with deep regret, sympathy and respect'. It was only the fourth time a Nobel award had been rejected. In 1935 Hitler had been incensed when Carl von Ossietzky, a prominent anti-Nazi held by the Gestapo, was awarded the Peace Prize. Hitler subsequently passed a law prohibiting German citizens from accepting Nobel Prizes, thus preventing three other Germans, all scientists, from collecting their awards.

Olga met with Boris in the Little House. Recounting her meeting with Polikarpov, she observed Boris to be in relatively good spirits. At least he seemed to accept that for him to commit suicide was not a feasible way out – there would be no nobility in that. She then left immediately for Moscow, to reassure her children that all was well. 'I had felt that death was very close,' she recalled 'but once I knew that this was the last thing "they" [the Soviet officials] wanted, I was enormously relieved.'

Olga retired to bed early, asking the children not to disturb her. She longed to sleep. The strain was taking its toll and she was physically and emotionally exhausted. To her exasperation she was soon woken from a deep sleep by Mitia. Ariadna was on the telephone, he informed her. Apparently it was urgent that they switch on the television.

Vladimir Semichastny, a high-ranking party official (who was to become head of the KGB a few years later), was making a televised speech before 12,000 people at the Sports Palace in Moscow. The speech, also broadcast live on the radio, was reprinted in various newspapers the following day. The evening before, Semichastny had been summoned to the Kremlin to meet with Khrushchev, who ordered him to include a statement on Pasternak in his forthcoming speech. Khrushchev dictated several pages of notes, laced with insults. He reassured Semichastny that he would visibly applaud when he reached the passage about Pasternak. 'Everyone will understand it,' Khrushchev told him.

Semichastny delivered his diatribe with gusto, pausing to liken Pasternak to a 'mangy sheep' and to a pig: 'As everybody who has anything to do with this animal knows, one of the peculiarities of the pig is that it never makes a mess where it eats or sleeps. Therefore if we compare Pasternak with a pig, then we must say that a pig will never do what he has done. Pasternak, this man who considers himself among the best representation of society, has fouled the spot where he ate and cast filth on those by whose labour he lives and breathes ...' Semichastny was repeatedly interrupted by bursts of applause, as a beaming Khrushchev looked on.

Pasternak read the blistering attack the following morning in *Pravda*. It had become clear what more the Kremlin wanted. 'Why shouldn't this internal emigrant breathe the capitalist air which he so yearned for and which he spoke of in his book?' Semichastny had railed. 'I am sure our society would welcome that. Let him become a real emigrant and go to his capitalist paradise.' The authorities wanted to hound him out of Russia.

Boris discussed with Zinaida the possibility of the family emigrating. She suggested that to live in peace *he* should go. 'With you and Lyonya?' he asked her, surprised, referring to their son Leonid. Zinaida replied that she herself would never go, but she wished him honour and peace for the rest of his life. 'Lyonya and I will have to denounce you, but you'll understand, that is just a formality.'

Boris walked over to the Little House to discuss his situation with Olga and her daughter. Irina was shocked by how grey and thin he looked. 'It was a horrible atmosphere,' Irina recalled. Peredelkino no longer felt safe. 'There was one night [after the Semichastny speech] when people threw stones at the dacha and shouted anti-Semitic abuse.' Pasternak then talked to them about leaving Russia. 'You should go!' Irina declared. 'There is no reason not to.'

'Perhaps, perhaps I should,' Boris agreed. 'And then I'll get you out through Nehru.' (There were rumours that India's prime minister had offered Pasternak political asylum.) Boris sat down and wrote a letter to the Kremlin saying that as he was now regarded as an émigré, he would like to be allowed to leave the country, but did not want to leave 'hostages' behind him. He asked therefore for permission for Olga and her children to accompany him. When he finished the letter, he tore it straight up.

'No, Olia, I couldn't go abroad even if they let us all out together,' he sighed. 'I have always dreamed of going to the West as though on holiday, but I couldn't possibly live like that day in day out. I must have the workaday life I know here, the birch trees, the familiar troubles – even the familiar harassments – and hope. I shall put up with what I have to suffer.'

'During this time, Boris cried a lot,' said Irina. 'We all felt so sorry for him, as he was becoming increasingly vulnerable.' But, she was loath to admit, 'I reproached him for his vulnerability, his lack of character. I no longer saw in him the perfect rigid strength I had seen in him when I was younger. He became increasingly dependent on other people's opinion. He would hang onto the smallest details, from the greeting of the post mistress, to the fact that the wood-burning stove driver was still greeting him "as he used to". I can remember how happy he was the day he had come across a policeman he had known for years and who had taken the initiative of greeting him as if nothing had happened.'

At the height of the most vicious attacks from the Soviet authorities, Pasternak drew immense comfort from the outpouring of respect and support from around the world. A ban on his receiving post had been imposed after he won the Nobel Prize, and Irina now acted as his covert 'postmistress'. She would bring him letters which bore no stamps and sometimes no envelopes: 'People would just slide them under my door, too scared to be identified or convinced their letter would get lost in the post.' Irina would take them from Moscow to Peredelkino, bringing 'boxes after boxes'.

News from the Western press also lifted Boris's spirits. On 30 October both the International PEN Club and a group of eminent British writers sent telegrams of protest to the Soviet Writers' Union. 'International PEN very distressed by rumours concerning Pasternak, asks you to protect the poet, maintaining the right of creative freedom. Writers throughout the world are thinking of him fraternally,' read the PEN Club wire. The telegram from the British writers – whose signatories included T. S. Eliot, Stephen Spender, Bertrand Russell, Aldous Huxley, Somerset Maugham, C. P. Snow and Maurice Bowra – read: 'We are profoundly anxious about the state of one of the world's great poets and writers, Boris Pasternak. We consider his novel, *Doctor Zhivago*, a moving personal testimony and not a political document. We appeal to you in the name of the great Russian literary tradition for which you stand not to dishonour it by victimising a writer revered throughout the entire civilised world.' The British Society of Authors also sent a cable of protest: 'The Society of Authors deeply deplore expulsion of Boris Pasternak by the Soviet Writers' Union and strongly urge his reinstatement.'

That same day, Olga went to see Grigori Khesin, the head of the department for authors' rights at the Writers' Union, to ask for his advice in the wake of the Semichastny speech. In the past he had seemed well disposed towards Pasternak and would always greet Olga warmly and courteously. Now, he was cold, formal and aloof. He bowed stiffly and stared at her. When she asked him, what are *we* to do, he answered loudly, articulating every word. His strange diction left Olga in no doubt that their conversation was being recorded. 'Olga Vsevolodovna, there is now no further advice for us to give you,' Khesin said icily. 'I consider Pasternak has committed an act of betrayal and become an instrument of the cold war, an internal émigré. There are certain things one cannot forgive, for the country's sake. No, I am afraid I cannot give you any advice.'

Olga got up and left, slamming the door. In the corridor, she was approached by a handsome young copyright lawyer by the name of Isidor Gringolts. He was a friend of one of Irina's lecturers. He told an astonished Olga that he would do anything to help, adding 'for me, Boris Leonidovich is a saint!' Grateful for any offer of assistance after the brush-off from Khesin, Olga rashly asked him to come to her Potapov Street apartment in a few hours' time.

Already there were Koma Ivanov, Adriana Efron, Irina and Mitia, anxiously waiting to discuss what to do next. Gringolts's opening words were: 'You must understand that I love Boris Leonidovich and that his name is holy for me.' They all agreed that the campaign against Boris was mounting in a dangerous way. He was receiving threatening letters, rumours were circulating that the house in Peredelkino would be attacked by more mobs, and after Semichastny's speech police reinforcements had had to be called to Peredelkino after a demonstration by young communists looked likely to get out of hand. The group, Boris's most loyal supporters, sat for hours debating what to do for the best, until Olga's 'ears began to ring'. Gringolts was adamant that the only course of action was for Pasternak to write a letter to Khrushchev imploring him not to expel him from the country. Irina was convinced that Boris would baulk at this. She felt that he should not express repentance in any form. Eventually though, genuinely afraid for Boris's life, Olga knew that Gringolts was right: the time had come to 'give in'. There was no other way.

Gringolts drafted a letter, which Olga and Irina reworked to try and make it sound more Boris-like. Irina and Koma then took it straight to Peredelkino for Boris's signature.

'Looking back,' Olga later wrote, 'it seems monstrous that we should have made up this letter, before BL even had any idea of what was going on. But we were in a great hurry, and in the bedlam around us, nothing seemed very extraordinary anymore.'

Boris met Irina and Koma at the gates of his dacha and the three of them walked to the post office, where Boris phoned Olga. He agreed to the letter, adding a line at the end. He signed it and even signed a few blank pages in case they needed to make further revisions. Poignantly, he attached a note in red pencil saying: 'Olia, keep it all as it is, only write that I was born not in the Soviet Union, but in Russia.'

The next day Irina and a friend delivered the letter to the Central Committee building on 4 Staraya Square. They handed it in through a hatch, from which an officer and a soldier leaned out and eyed them with interest.

'Dear Nikita Sergeyevich [Khrushchev],' it read:

I am addressing you personally, the Central Committee of the Communist Party of the Soviet Union and the Soviet Government.

From Comrade Semichastny's speech I learn that the government would not put any obstacles in the way of my departure from the USSR.

For me this is impossible. I am tied to Russia by birth, by life and by work. I can not conceive of my destiny separate from Russia, or outside it. Whatever my mistakes and failings, I could not imagine that I should find myself at the centre of such a political campaign as has been worked up around my name in the West.

Once aware of this, I informed the Swedish Academy of my voluntary renunciation of the Nobel Prize.

Departure from the borders of my country would be tantamount to death and I must therefore request you not to take this extreme measure against me.

It ended with the sentence Pasternak had written himself:

With my hand on my heart, I can say that I have done something for Soviet literature, and may still be of service to it.
Boris Pasternak

Olga would later reproach herself, saying the letter had been a terrible mistake, taking full responsibility and blame for it. However, it is abundantly clear that the trauma of leaving Russia would have been too much for Boris. Already in many ways a broken man, caged in Peredelkino, his only freedom was to continue his daily ritual. Without that and the familiarity of the place he loved so much around him; without his beloved Mother Russia, he had nothing. Exile would have been worse than suicide for him.

Irina remembered that during those days while a 'threat was hanging over his life, he carried out his usual routine as normal as a way to stop any chaos entering his life'. Pasternak was still working; he had decided to translate *Mary Stuart*. This was not the play by Schiller that he had already translated from German, but a drama by the same name by the Polish romantic poet Juliusz Slowacki. 'He had a little nap after his meals whenever possible, went for walks and would read but he was already considered an outlaw, an accused, someone charged awaiting his verdict every hour, not knowing what it would be.' Every evening at nine Boris would go to the Peredelkino Writers' Club to use the phone booth there to make some calls. He would carefully prepare a list of people to ring and the purpose of his call. It could be to discuss a response to a letter, instructions regarding the novel, or to call Irina. 'This is the kind of thing he would say to me. "I am coming to Moscow on Monday, please buy me a 100 non-illustrated envelopes and make sure that the gum adhesive is of good quality. I will also need some stamps. See if you can get me some with a squirrel on it," Irina recalled.

Sometimes the people he phoned would rebuff him, at other times their kindness would floor him. 'That is why those calls were like torture to him. He was scared to hear the voices that might be hesitant or cold, sometimes there were even insults from people he considered friends but despite the hurt that it caused him, he could not stop himself from ringing.'

Irina remembered Boris's call to his friend Lili Brik, widow of the literary critic Osip Brik, at the time of the letter to Khrushchev. It was a dank autumn evening, the wind blowing through the pine trees. 'Mama and I were chatting quietly outside the phone booth while waiting for him, when suddenly we heard a loud sob. We rushed to discover that his conversation had been cut short as his sobs were suffocating him.' As soon as Lili Brik realised it was Pasternak who was calling her, she started 'speaking with a tone full of tenderness as she had been waiting for his call. "Boris, my poor Boris, what is happening to you?" Able to cope with indescribable insults, he was incapable of handling such compassionate concern,' concluded Irina.

The following day, Friday 31 October, Olga returned to Moscow and, worn out, went to the Potapov apartment that afternoon to try and get some sleep. She had just settled into a grateful slumber when her mother woke her. 'You are wanted on the phone,' Maria said. 'They say it is from the Central Committee, on a very important matter.' Clearly Olga had been followed to the apartment. The government officials knew of her every move and whereabouts. Olga took the call. She was surprised that it was Grigori Khesin on the line. He was unusually friendly again, as if their last conversation, when Olga had slammed the door on him, had never taken place.

'Olga Vsevolodovna, my dear, you're a good girl,' he oozed. 'They have received the letter from BL and everything will be alright, just be patient. What I have to say is that we must see you straightaway – we will come right along now.'

Olga, infuriated by Khesin's change of tune, told him that she wanted nothing more to do with him after he refused to help her before. There was a pause before Khesin informed Olga that Polikarpov was also on the line. They were coming to collect her, said Polikarpov, before going to Peredelkino to collect Pasternak, so they could appear before the Central Committee of the Communist Party as soon as possible.

Olga immediately got hold of Irina on the phone and told her to go straight to Peredelkino to warn Boris. It seemed clear to Olga that if Polikarpov was personally coming to collect Boris himself, then Khrushchev intended to meet with him.

By the time Olga had put the telephone receiver down, a black government Zil had pulled up and was waiting outside, honking the horn. Khesin and the fearsome Polikarpov were inside. Olga tried to stall them, to give Irina time to get to Peredelkino first, but in the end she was forced to get in the car. It was hopeless to think that Irina would reach Boris before them, as the limousine raced ahead in a special lane reserved for government cars and did not stop at a single traffic light.

In the back seat of the car, Khesin whispered to Olga that it was he who had sent Isidor Gringolts to her. Olga gasped, realising she had been completely manipulated into persuading Boris to write the letter to Khrushchev. 'They knew BL was stubborn and incapable of taking orders. So they had found a way through me, taking advantage of my fears and thoughtlessness. Knowing that no official person would ever have won me round, they had put this "nice boy", an "admirer" of Pasternak, onto me, and it had worked.'

As Olga battled with her feelings of self-reproach, that she had allowed herself to be so thoroughly duped, Polikarpov turned to her and said to her: 'We're now relying entirely on you. You must set his mind at rest.' Polikarpov seemed unusually concerned that Pasternak might not agree to come to Moscow.

When they reached Peredelkino, dacha No 3, was already surrounded by other official cars, including some from the Writers' Union. Olga was told to wait in another car, as everyone waited for Irina's arrival. Zinaida would not have opened her door to Olga, but she was better disposed towards her daughter. Olga was instructed to afterwards take Boris back to her Potapov apartment, and wait for official passes to be organised for them.

It was already dusk by the time that Irina arrived at Peredelkino, the official cars waiting ominously in the lane outside Pasternak's house. A 'frightened-looking' Zinaida came out to meet her. She told Irina that Boris would get dressed at once. Boris appeared wearing the grey over-coat and hat he often travelled in. Instantly sizing up the situation outside, he agreed to get into the car. He seemed ebulliently cheerful, only complaining that Irina hadn't given him time to change his trousers. He had also concluded that he was about to meet Khrushchev. 'Mama and I sat next to him at the back of the black car and we started our journey to Moscow with our escort,' said Irina.

I remember with elation all the dangers of this trip. BL was in great form. Despite my mother's admonition, who kept whispering to him to keep the volume down as she was pointing to the chauffeur – 'Boris, don't be so loud, he's listening' – we spoke about every-thing without a care in the world.

His excellent sense of humour probably acted as some kind of protection for him. And at that specific time, when such an important decision with potentially dangerous consequences was about to be made, he was like an actor completely engrossed in his part. The discussion which was about to take place at the Central Committee was like a drama reaching its climax, and he was rehearsing his role in the car. 'First, I will tell them that they interrupted my walk, which means that I had to keep on a pair of trousers that were not ironed. I'll tell them that I didn't have time to get changed.' When we told him that nobody would be interested, he continued: 'Not at all, I must tell them otherwise they will think "Here is the scarecrow for which the whole world is boiling."' Left in no doubt that he would say exactly that, we burst into hysterical laughter.

They were followed back to Moscow by a cavalcade of cars, one containing Polikarpov.

Up in the apartment, Boris paced the floor and drank strong black tea while Olga changed. He shouted through to her not to put on any make-up or wear jewellery. They often clashed over this – Boris thought that Olga had such beautiful natural looks that she needed neither adornment nor enhancement. Irina took a 'small vial of valerian, pills for the heart and a bottle of water' – an emergency kit in case the talk became heated. The whole scene was so surreal, remembered Irina, that the three of them were in a mood of 'almost hysterical gaiety'.

When they arrived at Entrance No 5 of the Central Committee, Staraya Square, Boris went up to the guard and started to explain that he had no documents with him except for his writers' card – 'you know, the Writers' Union you and your colleagues have just thrown me out of'. He then went on to talk about his trousers in exactly the way that he had said he would. The astonished guard just mumbled that everything would be fine and waved Boris and Olga through. Irina was left to wait in the hallway in charge of Boris's bottles of medicine, in case he was taken ill.

As they walked upstairs, Boris winked at Olga. 'It will be interesting now, you'll see,' he said, convinced that he was about to enter a room and meet Khrushchev. But when the door to the inner sanctum opened they were astonished to see Polikarpov again. Strangely, he was freshly shaved and had changed his clothes. The whole scene appeared to have been staged so that it looked as if the trip to Peredelkino had never happened, as if he had been sitting at his desk all day.

Polikarpov cleared his throat, rose solemnly to his feet and 'in a voice befitting a town crier' announced that in view of his letter to Khrushchev, Pasternak would be 'allowed to remain in the Motherland'. But, he continued, the writer would have to find a way to make peace with the Soviet people. 'There is nothing we can do at the moment to calm the anger,' adding that in the following day's issue of *Literaturnaya Gazeta* this anger would be sampled across the pages.

This was not the meeting that Boris had anticipated and he erupted in rage. 'Aren't you ashamed, Dmitri Alexeyevich? What do you mean "anger"! You have your human side, I can see, so why do you come out with these stock phrases? "The people! The people" – as though it were something you could just produce from your own trouser pockets! You know perfectly well that you really shouldn't use this word "people" at all.'

Polikarpov was taken aback, but he needed Pasternak's acquiescence. Sucking in his breath, mustering all his patience, he tried again: 'Now look here, Boris Leonidovich, the whole business is over, so let's make things up and everything will soon be all right again ...' and, giving Boris a friendly pat on the shoulder: 'Goodness me, old fellow, what a mess you've landed us in.'

Boris was incensed at being addressed as 'old fellow' in Olga's presence. According to Olga he still thought of himself as 'young and healthy, and the hero of the hour into the bargain'. Impatiently, he pushed Poliparkov's hand aside: 'Will you kindly drop that tone! You cannot talk to me like that.'

Polikarpov continued in his 'friendly' manner: 'Really now, here you go, sticking a knife into the country's back and we have to patch it all up.'

Boris jumped to his feet: 'I will ask you to take those words back. I do not wish to speak with you anymore,' he said, striding for the door.

Polikarpov threw Olga a despairing look: 'Stop him, stop him, Olga Vsevolodovna.'

'You bait him like this and expect me to stop him?' Olga replied. 'You must take your words back.'

Clearly rattled and wary of exciting Pasternak further, Polikarpov mumbled: 'I do, I do.'

Boris hesitated by the door. Olga asked him to come back and the conversation continued more civilly. Boris was told that the only thing that the officials insisted on was that he was to have no contact with the foreign press. As they left, Polikarpov also warned Olga that Pasternak might have to sign another public letter.

In the corridor, on the way back to Irina, Boris said to Olga: 'They should have held their hands out to me and everything would have been different. But they're unable to: they are so mean-spirited. They have no feelings. They are not people but machines. See how terrible they are, these walls here, and everybody inside them is like an automaton.'

Irina, Olga and Boris were driven back to Peredelkino in a government car. Boris was back in high spirits again. He acted out the whole conversation for Irina, ignoring Olga plucking at his sleeve to encourage him to quieten down in front of the chauffeur/informer. During a lull in conversation, Irina quoted some lines from Pasternak's epic poem *Lieutenant Schmidt*. First published in 1926, the poem is based on words spoken by Lieutenant Schmidt, a famous figure in the 1905 Revolution, on the eve of his execution for mutiny. The verses became so frequently quoted in Moscow during the campaign of persecution against Pasternak that some people mistook them to be a new poem written by him in 1958. As Irina recited it, Boris's exuberance drained away. 'Just think – how right, how true it is,' he said mournfully.

In vain, in years of turmoil,
One seeks a happy ending –
Some are fated to kill – and repent –
While others go to Golgotha ...
I suppose you never flinch

From wiping out a man.
Ah well, martyrs to your dogma,
You too are victim of the times ...
I know the stake at which
I'll die will be the boundary mark
Between two different epochs,
And I rejoice at being so elect.

Olga never forgave herself for drafting the letter to Khrushchev. She also berated her and Boris's 'lack of resolve, perhaps even our folly, our failure to recognise "the great moment" which instead turned into one of shame'. She constantly wondered whether the renunciation of the Nobel Prize was more an act of defiance on Boris's part or of their joint faint-heartedness. Yet she recognised that it was only her abject state of panic that prevented her from seeing through Gringolts and acting on his provocation. She later wrote: 'That letter should never have been sent – never! But we sent it. It was my fault.'

# 11

## A Beast at Bay

During his meeting with Polikarpov, Pasternak had asked for the postal ban, which had been reinstated for three days, to be lifted. During the whole vicious campaign against Pasternak nothing depressed him more than being denied access to his correspondence. Eighteen months after the Nobel Prize award, Boris had received approximately 25,000 letters. Now, he found, the post lady at Peredelkino brought two huge bags of mail, which had piled up during the previous few days; the ban had been lifted.

As Polikarpov had predicted, the next edition of the *Literaturnaya Gazeta* lambasted the writer, reflecting the 'wrath of the people'. Yet it was the letters of support which softened these blows. One anonymous but particularly memorable note read: 'Dear Boris Leonidovich, Millions of Russian people are happy at the appearance in our literature of a truly great work. History will not treat you harshly. The Russian People.'

In his overflowing mail bags there were foreign newspapers and magazines containing reactions of public figures and fellow authors to his hounding. 'I shall give him a house to make his life in the West easier,' wrote Ernest Hemingway. 'I want to create the conditions he needs to carry on with his writing. I can understand how divided Boris must be in his own mind just now. I know how deeply, with all his heart, he is attached to Russia. For a genius such as Pasternak, separation from his country would be a tragedy. But if he comes to us, we shall not disappoint him. I shall do everything in my power to save this genius for the world. I think of Pasternak every day.' Jawaharlal Nehru stated: 'We believe that if a well-known writer expresses views which conflict with the dominant ones in his country, he should be respected rather than subjected to any kind of restrictions.' The French journalist Georges Altman concluded: 'I make bold to suggest that Pasternak is a much better representative of the great Russia of yesterday and today than is Mr Khrushchev.'

'The whole world knows that the Union of Soviet Writers would much rather have seen the Nobel Prize go to Sholokhov than to Pasternak,' wrote Albert Camus. 'But this was not something that could influence the Swedish Academy, which was bound to take a detached view of the literary merits of both these writers.' The Academy's choice, 'which is by no means a political one, is simply a recognition of Pasternak's achievements as a writer. It is a long time since Sholokhov has produced anything new, while *Doctor Zhivago* has appeared everywhere in the world as an incomparable work greatly superior to the bulk of the world's literary production. This great novel about love is not anti-Soviet, as some people say – it has nothing to do with any particular party; it is all-embracing.'

According to Pasternak, Albert Camus became a 'cordial acquisition'. Boris also struck up correspondences with T. S. Eliot, John Steinbeck, Thomas Merton, Aldous Huxley, Hemingway and Nehru. Lydia Pasternak wrote that although Boris suffered intensely during this time, 'to a very great extent this triumph of spiritual happiness was due to the spontaneous expression of love and gratitude poured out to him in letters from thousands of individuals from all over the world, overwhelming, unbelievable, unsought for, and completely unexpected after decades of disappointment and frustration'.

On 4 November 1958, Boris was sitting in Olga's Moscow apartment with Irina and Mitia, contentedly going through the latest large batch of postal correspondence. The telephone rang. Olga asked Mitia to say that she was not at home. They were enjoying a rare moment of carefree togetherness, a brief respite from the hostilities around them which she wanted to savour. They heard Mitia say apologetically, as he covered the receiver with his hand: 'Mother, one of the leaders is on the line.'

It was Polikarpov. He announced to Olga that it was time for Pasternak to write an open letter to 'the people'. His letter to Khrushchev was not enough.

Boris diligently wrote a draft letter, which Olga took to the Central Committee the following day. Predictably, Polikarpov said that he and Olga would 'have to do a little work' on the letter. According to Olga, they amended the letter 'like a pair of professional counterfeiters. We took isolated phrases written or said by BL on various different occasions and placed them together in such a way that white was turned into black.'

Reward was instantaneous. Polikarpov promised that Pasternak's translation of *Faust* would come out in a second edition and that he would waive the ban on them working for Goslitizdat. Their translation work would be resumed.

Olga showed Boris the letter 'in which practically all the words but none of the sentiments were his'. He simply waved his hand. Too fatigued to fight any more, he wanted the whole business over. He also desperately needed money to support the two households; the Big and Little Houses, and the many people he gave financial aid to. Olga looked on as Boris, doing 'irreparable violence to himself', signed the second letter. It was published in *Pravda* on Thursday 6 November.

To any discerning *Pravda* reader, it was obvious that Pasternak's hand had been forced. The letter explained why he had renounced the Nobel Prize for Literature, and his constant emphasis that every act that he took was voluntary suggested the complete opposite. Lines included: 'When I saw the dimensions of the political campaign occasioned by my novel, and I realised that the Award was a political move which led to monstrous consequences, I sent my voluntary renunciation on my own initiative and without being forced by anyone.' In the letter, 'Pasternak' concluded:

In the course of this turbulent week I have not been subjected to persecution, and neither my life, freedom, nor anything else at all have been at stake. I wish to emphasise once more that all my actions have been voluntary. People closely acquainted with me know very well that nothing on earth can force me to play the hypocrite or go against my conscience. This has also been the case now. It does not need to be said that nobody has tried to compel me to do anything and that I make this statement with my own free will, with bright faith in the common future and my own, with pride in the age I live in, and in the people around me.

As soon as the furore began to die down, Boris telegraphed his sisters, who he knew would be devastated by the Kremlin's campaign against him: 'Tempest not yet over do not grieve be firm and quiet. Tired loving believing in the future – Boris.' The following month, on 11 December, Boris wrote to Lydia in English a loosely coded message of the scrutiny he was still under. 'All the letters I receive arrive minutely examined of course. But if their number reaches up to twenty daily from abroad (there was a day where there came fifty-four foreign letters at once), your free and frankly written missive will not add or diminish much to or of that pile. I said to a Sw[iss] correspondent I owed my saved life to my far worldwide friends intervening. You owe it, he retorted, to Lara, [Olga] to her courageous activity.'

As the dramatic year of 1958 drew to a close, the year-end tributes to *Doctor Zhivago* began to come in. The London *Sunday Times* Books of the Year review said unhesitatingly that *Doctor Zhivago* was 'the novel of the year'. In Italy *Zhivago* won the 1958 Bancarella Prize – a bestseller award and one of Italy's two most significant literary prizes.

After Pasternak's second 'penitential' letter, he and Olga spent less time in Moscow. Pressures on them eased and once again the Little House became their sanctuary. 'It seemed that we had survived our ordeal, and now we did everything we could to return to our usual way of life,' said Olga. 'Never before had we felt so close and been so at one with each other.' When Irina saw Olga and Boris return to Izmalkovo, she 'understood that all was well and the storm had now passed ... Walking around Peredelkino, which we knew so well by heart, down to the last tree, was our true home. We were breathing again.'

Olga took pleasure in watching Boris drink samogon, a home-distilled vodka, with her landlord Sergei Kuzmich. Boris was fascinated by the 'earthy conversation of the sly, old scoundrel'. Olga and Boris would listen through the wall to Kuzmich's conversations with his wife, who was an invalid. A regularly inebriated Kuzmich enjoyed winding his poor wife up about his conquests with women in his day, even boasting that he could easily get Olga to leave Boris for him. The laughter this provoked provided much-needed light relief for Olga and Boris. The couple would always be grateful to Kuzmich that they had found refuge in his house.

Olga and Boris resumed their normal life. 'Like a fish thrown back into the sea, he rediscovered the world and its daily routine with delight,' wrote Irina. 'He threw himself happily in the open arms of the rest of the world and what he found, I would almost describe as happiness. Before this time, every conversation had led back to *Doctor Zhivago*. From then on, nothing mattered more than his correspondences. He spoke about what his answers would be, he would show us all sorts of touching presents that came through the post – candles, postcards, knick-knacks.'

Boris had promised Polikarpov not to accept requests from foreign correspondents to meet with him: he had written a sign for his door in three languages – English, German and French – which read 'Pasternak does not receive, he is forbidden to receive foreigners.' Although Irina wryly noted: 'this deal took place with some kind of laxity. The press correspondents did not come and see him at his home anymore but nothing stopped them from meeting him when he was out on one of his many walks which were set as clockwork.'

Evenings resumed at the Little House gave Boris relief from tension and anxiety, especially when Irina brought her young friends from Moscow out to see him. 'It was very important for him to learn from them that they still loved and respected him,' said Olga. 'That he still inspired admiration and pride in them.' They would sit on the veranda, talking and laughing. When he left to go back to his dacha, Irina and her friends would walk with him, along the path and over the long bridge across the Izmalkovo Lake. 'BL was always in high spirits, talked a great deal and did not disguise his childlike pleasure at this display of affection.'

According to Olga, he became particularly attached to Irina during this time. 'She's a very clever girl,' he used to say of her. 'She is just the kind I have dreamed of all my life. So many children have grown up around me, but I love only her ...' When Olga reproached him, he'd reply: 'Olia, you mustn't criticise her. The truth always speaks out of her mouth. You always say that she's more mine than yours, so listen to what she says.'

The New Year of 1959 saw Olga and Boris closer than ever. Relieved that they had survived 'their ordeal', they sought to resume their intimate, loving life. But antagonism between the Big and Little Houses was escalating. In no doubt that Boris's health was ailing due to the stress of the turmoil over the Nobel Prize – terrible pains in his shoulder and a general weakening of his nervous system – Zinaida became increasingly protective of her husband. She laid the blame for his deterioration firmly at Olga's door.

Zinaida's daughter-in-law, Natasha, who married Boris's son Leonid two years after Boris died, said that in the Big House they all considered Olga to be 'the source of Boris's decline'. From their perspective, far from saving Pasternak from the authorities, the pressure that Olga put on Boris to be with her was a psychological torment to him.

Olga, on the other hand, firmly believed that it was the authorities and the wrath of the government that weakened Boris. She wrote 'by the time BL found himself being forced to go against all his inclinations and desires, and constantly to violate his own nature, he had evidently passed beyond his own limit. The violence done to him was overwhelming. It broke and then killed him. Slowly but surely his strength was undermined, and his heart and nervous system began to fail.'

That January, Boris announced to Olga that he had finally made up his mind. He would break with Zinaida and marry her. He had made arrangements with his friend Konstantin Paustovski, a novelist and play-wright who lived in Tarusa, for him and Olga to spend the winter there. During the Soviet era, many dissidents settled in Tarusa. This small town, in an area of natural beauty, lay 140 kilometres south-west of Moscow.

As much as Olga wanted to believe that Boris would publicly claim her and take her to Tarusa, intuitively she knew that, aged sixty-nine, he was too old and too weak to 'face the storm that his departure would provoke'. On 20 January, the day they had planned to leave, Boris arrived at the Little House early in the morning, having walked through a bliz-zard to get there. 'Very pale', he announced that he couldn't go through with it.

'What more do you need,' he asked, 'when you know that you are my right hand, and that I am entirely with you?' It was impossible, he contin-ued, to hurt people who were not at fault – Zinaida, his son Leonid and others – and who only wanted to preserve the appearance of the life they were used to. There was nothing he could do, he said, but to go on living in two homes.

Olga exploded with fury. Couldn't he see, she shouted, that she needed the protection of his surname more than anyone else? After all, she had certainly done everything to deserve it. It was only his name that had kept her alive in the labour camps; without it, she would almost certainly have been killed. Why couldn't he see that it was crucial that she had the Pasternak surname now, in case anything happened to him? She shouted at him that he only wanted to preserve his peace of mind at her expense. That all he cared about was keeping the status quo. Feeling betrayed, Olga announced that she was leaving immediately for Moscow. In collapsed, self-pitying tones, Boris conceded that now he was a social outcast, it would be easy for her to drop him.

Incensed that he was missing the point entirely, Olga accused him of being a self-absorbed poseur.

He turned paler and left. Olga, boiling with resentment, but most of all feeling desperately hurt, travelled to Moscow.

That night, when Boris rang with his usual 'Oliusha, I love you' she hung up on him.

Three weeks later, Olga received a call from the Central Committee. It was Polikarpov. 'What Boris Leonidovich has done now is even worse than the business of the novel,' he spat indignantly.

'I know nothing about it,' Olga replied. 'I haven't seen him.'

'Have you two quarrelled?' Polikarpov asked, knowing full well that they had. 'A fine time to do that! Every foreign radio station is broadcasting a poem he handed to a foreigner here. All the fuss had died down but now it has started all over again. Go out there and make things up with him – do everything you can to stop him committing some new act of madness.'

According to Boris, who called Olga later that day from the Writers' Club in Peredelkino – begging her not to put down the receiver – after her departure he went home and wrote a poem about winning the Nobel Prize. In disbelief that she had really left him and gone back to Moscow, he went to the Little House to see if she was there. En route, a journalist, Anthony Brown, who worked for the English newspaper the *Daily Mail*, tracked Boris down. He ended up giving Brown an interview in the woods. 'I am a white cormorant,' he told the journalist. 'As you know, Mr Brown, there are only black cormorants. I am an oddity, an individual in a society which is not meant for the unit but for the masses.'

The *Mail* published the poem on 12 February 1959 under the headline 'Pasternak Surprise: His Agony Revealed in "The Nobel Prize"'.

I am caught like a beast at bay.
Somewhere are people, freedom, light.
But all I hear is the baying of the pack,
There is no way out for me.
Over there is the dark wood, the lake-shore
And the trunk of a felled fir tree,
Everywhere my road is barred.
Let it be so. I care no more.
How dare I write such stuff
– I, scoundrel and evil-doer,

Who made the whole world weep
At the beauty of my native land?

The pursuit draws ever closer,
And now I'm guilty of another thing:
My right hand is no longer with me –
My dear friend is with me no more.

As the noose tightens round my neck,
At the hour when death is so near,
I should like my right hand near me
To wipe away my tears.

When Olga heard the poem, the extent of Boris's pain and anguish laid bare, she went straight back to him in Peredelkino. 'You don't think I would ever leave you, whatever you did?' she told him as they reunited. She might have been bruised that he reneged on his word to marry her, but she would never abandon him. 'Peace,' she said, 'was now restored in our little house by the Izmalkovo Lake.'

Personal harmony may have been re-established but politically, matters were escalating once more. Although Boris repeatedly maintained that 'The Nobel Prize' poem was never meant for publication, and that he had merely asked the *Mail* journalist to pass it on to his French translator, Jacqueline de Proyart, he knew full well that showing such contentious material to a foreign correspondent was an act of pure defiance. 'The falling of a small stone sometimes precipitates an avalanche,' Olga later wrote, 'and it was only in this sense that our quarrel was the cause of "The Nobel Prize" being published. The real reason was the hounding of BL, the fact that he had been put in the situation of a "beast at bay".'

The publication of the poem created a strong current of sympathy for Pasternak among the millions of readers in the world press. The Kremlin was furious with him for his unbowed impudence. The *Daily Mail* commentary that accompanied the poem said that 'sections of the Government and the Soviet Writers' Union press for Pasternak's ejection from his house, forfeiture of all royalties on his poems and translations in the Soviet Union – which would make him penniless – and possible imprisonment for literary deviation'. The article concluded that 'Pasternak has become an outcast'.

The ever-threatening presence of Polikarpov loomed once more. He summoned Olga to tell her that the British prime minister, Harold Macmillan, was coming to Moscow for the last two weeks of February. It was advisable, he said, for Pasternak to leave Moscow during this time. The authorities wanted to prevent foreign journalists from seeking Pasternak out and they knew that they could not guarantee that he would not give controversial and potentially damaging interviews. He was, said Polikarpov, genuinely seen as a danger to himself. Polikarpov also insisted that Olga refuse any contact with the foreign press.

Initially Boris was indignant, saying he had no intention of going anywhere. Then he and Zinaida received an invitation to stay with Nina Tabidze in Tbilisi. Zinaida jumped at the chance; she wanted her husband away from Olga, the foreign press, the stress and the scandal. Olga was outraged, feeling once more cast aside. Olga had strong suspicions that as a friend of Zinaida's, Nina did not like her, nor approve of her relationship with Pasternak. There was a terrible row when Boris rang Olga to say goodbye. She lashed out at him verbally. He kept on repeating: 'Oliusha, it's not you, it's not you saying these things. This is something out of a bad novel. It's not you and me.'

Olga left in a 'cold fury' for Leningrad and refused to take his calls. Boris asked Irina to forward his letters to her mother. Letters, Irina said, he wrote to her in both 'a crafty and sincere way. He did not want to cause pain as he feared an unnecessary upheaval would create an abnormal situation.' Irina decided that as her mother was only to be in Leningrad for a short time, she would not forward the letters but would let her read them all at once when she came back. 'I told her on the phone about the daily letters that were arriving but her reaction remained very cold. She was truly offended.'

Later Olga wrote: 'The misery of this last quarrel in our life still gnaws at me. On all other occasions when he had pleaded with me like this, his voice and hands shaking, I had rushed to his side, covering his hands, his eyes, his cheeks with kisses. How defenceless he was, and how loveable …'

In the fortnight Boris stayed in Tbilisi, from 20 February to 6 March, he wrote Olga eleven letters, including the following:

Oliusha, life will go on as it did before. I wouldn't even know how to live any other way. Nobody thinks badly of you. Only just now Nina's daughter was rebuking me for taking such risks and then evading responsibility, leaving you to bear the brunt – this, she said, is unworthy of me and ignoble.

I give you a big hug. How extraordinary life is. How much we need to love and think. Nothing else should concern us. Your B.

I shall try to phone you today (Sunday 22nd) from the post office. I am beginning to feel that quite apart from the novel, the [Nobel] prize, the articles, scares and scandals, I am also to blame in some other way for our life having recently turned into a bad dream, and that it needn't have been like this. I suppose as D. A. [Polikarpov] said to you, I really should draw in my horns, calm down and write for the future. Yesterday – when I was reproached for it – I clearly understood for the first time that by involving you in all these terrible affairs, I am casting a large shadow on you and putting you in awful danger. It's unmanly and contemptible. I must try to see that it doesn't happen again and that as time goes on only good, joyful, and easy things come your way. I love you and send you lots of kisses. Forgive me. Your B.

Boris spent his days in Tbilisi reading Proust and walking around the pretty town to ease the pain in his leg. His letters to Olga are full of his remorse at the tangled situation he has created. Her silence and her stay in Leningrad rankled with him. It unsettled him that he did not know her movements. Worried that she might not return to him, the sense of his hollowed-out missing, his vaulting fear of losing her, escalates:

[28 February] Oliusha my precious girl, I give you a big kiss. I am bound to you by life, by the sun shining through my window, by a feeling of remorse and sadness, by a feeling of guilt (oh, not towards you of course, but towards everyone), by the knowledge of my weakness and the inadequacy of everything I have done so far, by my certainty of the need to bend every effort and move mountains if I am not to let down my friends and prove an imposter. And the better all those around me are than we two, and the nicer I am to them and the dearer they are to me, the greater and deeper my love for you, the most guilty and sorrowful I feel. I hold you to me terribly, terribly tight, and almost faint from tenderness, and almost cry.

In his letter of 2 March, Boris draws on his deeply held conviction that what he and Olga share is some mythical love that transcends 'all obstacles and adversities'. He refers to their row as having 'a bad effect on' him and challenging her view that if they were married, she would be protected. He will turn out to be completely wrong when he writes:

Even if your fears for yourself were well-founded – well, that would of course be terrible, but no danger hanging over you arises from the circumstances of my private life, any more than my being permanently together with you could ward it off. We are joined together by subtler ties, by higher and more powerful bonds than those of the intimate existence we lead in full view of the world – and everybody is well aware of this.

It is almost unfathomable that someone who could be as astute, strategic and knowingly defiant as Pasternak could equally be this unrealistic and idealistically romantic. It may sound noble to make ardent proclamations of a higher love, but outside the pages of a romantic novel, true love requires everyday acts of mundane sacrifice. No one knew this more than Olga, and while she unfailingly acted on this time and again, her frustrations were understandable that Boris refused to match her. While she always watched his back, it cannot be said that he reciprocated.

On 4 March, home again at Peredelkino, Boris wrote to her:

One day things may be as you (perhaps mistakenly and wrongly) want them to be. But meanwhile, my beloved and adored one, for the very reason that I am pampered by the happiness you give me and lit by the light of your angelic sweetness, for the sake of the charity in which you yourself are always unwittingly instructing me, let us be generous to others – and if needs be, let us be even more generous and forbearing than before – in the name of everything warm and bright that so inseparably and permanently joins us together.

I kiss you, my white marvel, my fond love, you drive me to distraction by making me so grateful to you.

He had every reason to be grateful. On his return from Tbilisi, Olga once again took him straight back into her open, loving arms.

That summer, Boris presented Olga with a copy of the American edition of *Doctor Zhivago* for her birthday. Inside he dedicated it: 'To Oliusha on her birthday, June 27, 1959, with all my poor life. B.P.'.

Despite earning millions in the West for Feltrinelli, Pasternak still had the problem of how to make money. His translation of *Maria Stuart*, which was about to be published, was suspended, while the production of the Shakespeare and Schiller plays he had translated was stopped. No new translation work was commissioned. Pasternak even wrote to Khrushchev to point out that he couldn't even take part in the 'harmless profession' of translation. It is ironic that in a Swiss bank account lay burgeoning funds that Feltrinelli had been depositing from royalty payments from publishers around the world. Despite some Russians carping that Pasternak was a millionaire, Boris knew that if he sought to transfer any of this money to Moscow, he would face 'the perpetual accusation of treacherously living off foreign capital'.

He was forced to borrow money – from friends and even his housekeeper. Contacts of Feltrinelli, such as Sergio D'Angelo and the German correspondent Gerd Ruge, smuggled roubles into Moscow and delivered them to Pasternak, but all these transactions were highly risky. Ruge collected about $8,000-worth of Russian roubles at the West German embassy from Russians of ethnic German origin who had been granted permission to emigrate but could not take the money with them. Ruge took their cash in exchange for the payment of Deutschmarks when they reached Germany. Irina was even once asked by Boris to act as a go-between. Ruge handed her a package of money, wrapped in brown paper, at the metro station Oktyabrskaya, when he amateurishly brushed by her as a signal. Boris knew full well the dangers that both Olga and Irina faced in their secretive efforts to get him money. Yet these precarious ventures continued, like something from a ham-fisted spy caper. For example, Boris told his French translator, Jacqueline de Proyart, that if he wrote and told her that he had 'scarlet fever', it meant that Olga had been arrested, and he wanted de Proyart to raise the alarm in the West.

Feltrinelli also sent seven or eight packages, or 'rolls' as they called them, amounting to about 100,000 roubles, with another German journalist, Heinz Schewe. Schewe, who worked for *Die Welt*, had become friends with Boris and Olga. At the end of 1959 Boris also asked Feltrinelli to transfer $100,000 to D'Angelo, who had assured him that he would purchase roubles in the West and safely smuggle them into Moscow. This money-smuggling was not due to any greed but pure necessity. However, it was typical Boris, as it was reckless. Naturally the KGB were monitoring the situation, watching and biding their time.

During the autumn of 1959, when he wasn't answering all his pressing correspondence, Pasternak began work on his first original work since *Doctor Zhivago*. 'Of course these very letters greatly hindered him in his second source of happiness,' his sister Lydia wrote, 'his new work, which he had begun to write as soon as *Doctor Zhivago* was off his hands with no less zeal and enthusiasm.' This was a play called *The Blind Beauty* – a trilogy set in a manor house in the nineteenth century.

According to Olga, 'BL intended to show what he understood by freedom and the country's cultural tradition. At the beginning of the play –

the time is just before the abolition of serfdom in 1861 – there is much talk among the characters of freedom, particularly the problems of social freedom, as seen from the point of view of Russia's history and the situation at the time. After the reform, it soon becomes clear that the whole idea of social freedom is in general an illusory one, and that, as before, man is only truly free in art.'

That winter, Boris took Irina and Olga to the theatre – one of his passions – for what would be the last time. 'BL loved organising outings to the theatre, no doubt because it reminded him of his youth when all he needed was to see the stage curtains to shake with love and enthusiasm,' remembered Irina. 'He would order a whole load of tickets from the ticket office and would then transform himself into some kind of "ticket booth" as my mother described it.'

A Hamburg theatre was on tour in Moscow. Irina described how Boris 'divided his theatre outings fairly. He went to see *Faust* with his wife, Zinaida, and their son Leonid, and took Mama and me to see *The Broken Jug*.' Irina found the German black comedy by Heinrich von Kleist hard going. The play mocks the failings of human nature and the judicial system in a forgiving way. As Irina didn't really understand German, she was rather bored. Many others in the auditorium clearly felt the same, as there was little laughter. Boris, who spoke 'perfect German', was enthralled. (One of his idiosyncrasies, given his linguistic abilities and fluent French, was that he liked to speak to all foreign correspondents, if possible, in German.) 'He was laughing so loudly and generously, you could hear him at the back of the room,' said Irina. 'By the time the interval came, he was radiant with delight at his admiration of the spirit of the piece and the excellence of the play.' At the end of the performance, the trio went backstage. Pasternak, 'who was now a world-wide celebrity, was surrounded by actors who still had their make-up on and were handing him books and programmes to autograph. He was talking in German and they were drinking his words.'

Afterwards, Boris hailed a taxi. 'We looked like a respectable family,' said Irina, 'the mother wearing the new artificial fur coat she had received from "over there", the daughter showing off in the middle of a group of press correspondents and the father radiant, distributing autographs to delighted Germans. All this was barely a year after he felt relegated to the gutter and all the injuries he had been afflicted with. I was suddenly seized by the feeling of unreality, by all that was surrounding me, its short-lived nature and the feeling that faith had got it wrong when it presented us with this happiness and that it all might just disappear.'

Irina could not shake off her prescient disquiet. Now a fourth-year student at the Literary Institute in Moscow, Irina was in a relationship with a French student called Georges Nivat. He was studying at Moscow University as part of an academic exchange programme. Boris thoroughly approved of Georges and was keen for him to marry Irina. He wanted Irina to have some financial and emotional security by moving with Georges, after their degree studies, to France.

During that winter, Irina and Georges spent a lot of time revising for their exams at the Little House. 'BL would arrive just after seven … even when the evenings were getting darker in the winter,' said Irina. 'He liked to know that in the middle of the snowdrift there was a candle, lighting up a window, (as in *Doctor Zhivago*) where someone was waiting for him. We would rush to meet him, help him take his heavy fur-trimmed coat off and shake the snow off it. He would explain how the hill had caused him to be out of breath. He would say: "I found it hard to control my breathing as I was getting nearer but I kept on thinking it was normal for an eighty-year-old, and then I thought, hold on a minute, I am only seventy." We all laughed together.'

Olga later wrote: 'There was a tacit agreement between us in those days that we must keep our sense of humour, seeing the funny side of things wherever we could, and it seems that we managed to infect BL with out "lighthearted" view of events.' Boris loved to tell comic stories about minor, slapstick incidents – characters in the village who forced their way into the dacha or offered to put the novel into a secret code for him. They were childishly amusing events that Olga could see through. Boris was to a large extent exaggerating his bonhomie when, in reality, everything was very painful to him at this time. Olga knew this, yet to keep his spirits buoyed, said that 'we were constantly laughing, and an outsider might have thought we hadn't a care in the world'.

Irina's fondest and most precious memories of Boris are also from their last New Year's Eve together, 'warm and cosy against the snow' in the glassed-in veranda at the Little House: 'There was a Christmas tree lit with real candles whose bouncing and rippling lights illuminated a Pasternak deep in thoughts, his face full of beauty but whose charms were starting to fade away, a face which was already retiring from the world, just like these wavering lights.' Olga was busy at the table, amusing everyone with her extravagance (they were served three poussins each). 'We drank real French champagne to celebrate New Year's Eve in antici-pation of a New Year full of promises,' Irina recalled. 'For BL, his work, his place, his success and for me, France, a new life, a happy relationship. When it came to serve the chocolates, we were all pretty merry but more from our excitement, than from our consumption of alcohol. We sang 'O Tannenbaum' in German and other Russian songs. It was all very jokey and fun.'

But then, she added soberingly: 'As always our two-faced Pasternak split his evening in two. He stayed with us until eleven p.m. before getting back to his family home where his family and guests were waiting for him. We walked him to the gate of his dacha. We knew our limits.'

As they walked back through the falling snow to the Little House, Irina thought back on the evening. 'BL was in good health but I sensed something was not to last. Often his gaze was above everybody's heads and he was staring as if into eternity. He was brilliant that night; he told brilliant, captivating stories and there was nothing to suggest that anything was wrong. But I had a premonition that he was looking into the future – a future that he was not going to be a part of.'

# 12

## The Truth of Their Agony

During the early months of 1960, life for Olga and Boris seemed to go on 'much as before'. Olga went frequently into Moscow on Boris's literary business, and when she returned to Izmalkovo he would be waiting for her; pacing up and down in front of the Little House, unable to fully settle in himself until his 'right hand' was beside him. On Sundays, Olga would often go out on skis with friends, before entertaining them over lively lunches at the Little House. 'Sometimes BL lunched at the Big House, sometimes with me – there was no hard and fast rule about this,' said Olga.

On Wednesday 10 February, Boris celebrated his seventieth birthday. 'It was astonishing how young and trim he still was at this age,' Olga remembered. 'His eyes shone brightly as ever, he was just as easily carried away, and he was as spontaneous and unreflecting as a child.'

On the morning of his birthday, Boris arrived at the Little House and he and Olga drank brandy together, before exchanging 'fond kisses' in front of the crackling stove. Boris turned to his beloved and said with a sigh: 'How late everything has come for me … but we did get through all our troubles together, Oliusha. And everything is alright now. If only we could live forever like this.' They sat and read 'with huge enjoyment' the piles of birthday greetings and gifts which had arrived from all over the world. Nehru sent an alarm clock in a leather case. Other presents included a little statuette representing Lara, decorative candles and delicate images of saints from Germany.

As winter turned into spring, Boris worked furiously on *The Blind Beauty*. He was in regular correspondence with Feltrinelli over the play's progress – the astute Italian publisher had insisted on exclusive world rights to his entire oeuvre; past, present and yet to come. As part of his own daily ritual, Boris would arrive at the Little House every evening and read aloud his work in progress. 'He put on a show of being in better spirits, fooling both himself and me,' Olga said. 'Three times he read from his play at great length. He spoke the lines with great expression, imitating popular speech with gusto and lingering over the passages he thought funny. He corrected himself and added things in pencil as he went along.'

But Olga began to notice the first, troubling signs that Boris was not well. 'He would sit down to go through some translation or other, but he at once began to feel tired and I would have to do most of the work by myself. He began to complain about a pain in his chest, he was having trouble with his leg again.'

In March, Olga slipped on the staircase in her Moscow apartment, severely tearing a muscle in her leg. It was put in plaster and she had to remain in the city for the month, which distressed Boris. 'This meant a disruption in his usual routine – something that irritated him more than anything.' One morning, when Boris was feeling strong enough, he climbed the stairs to visit Olga. Whilst he was there, the telephone rang. It was Mirella Garritano, the wife of the correspondent who had succeeded Sergio D'Angelo in Moscow. Mirella asked Olga to meet her at the post office and collect some books that had been sent for Pasternak. As Boris was not able to go, and Olga was in plaster, he asked Irina and Mitia to collect them. According to Olga, 'they could not refuse anything he asked'.

Mirella handed them a small suitcase, which Mitia brought back to the apartment. When Olga opened it, they all gasped in surprise. Instead of books, it contained bundles of Soviet banknotes in wrappers, neatly stacked together. These had been sent, indirectly, from Feltrinelli, who referred to them as 'sandwiches'. Boris gave Olga one roll, to cover some expenses, and took the rest of the cash to Peredelkino.

Irina, who was now engaged to Georges, saw little of Boris during these weeks. The last time was at Peredelkino on a beautiful sunny day in March. 'I bumped into BL as he was visiting my grandmother who had moved into a nearby dacha with her third husband,' remembered Irina. 'BL was delighted by the fact that she and her husband were looking so well. They were full of energy and joie de vivre. He did not like anything remotely reminding him of death – he refused to open the *Paris Match* covering Camus's death. Nothing pleased him more than seeing elderly people in good health. The sun was really warm on that spring day and it was impossible to look at the snow. BL screwed up his eyes and kept wiping them as he never wore sunglasses. He seemed tanned, healthy and happy.'

Olga also felt that by April everything augured well. 'April was blissful – as any April always is. Particularly splendid was our small garden with its pine trees, bushes coming into flower, and pale-green birches. Dappled with spots of sunlight it seemed such a safe and splendid haven for us. BL looked to be well and in good heart, and the days resumed their normal measured pace.'

On 4 April, Boris wrote to Feltrinelli in Milan, enclosing a document to be delivered to him by Heinz Schewe. It was entitled *Power of Attorney*.

I entrust OLGA VSEVOLODOVNA IVINSKAYA to place her signature on all instructions related to the publication of my works in those European countries where they have been printed or will be printed, as well as on all financial receipts and financial documents.

I ask that OLGA VSEVOLODOVNA IVINSKAYA's signature be believed as if it were my own and to consider all instructions origi-nating from Olga Vsevolodovna as my own.

The power of attorney which is granted to OLGA VSEVOLODOVNA IVINSKAYA is in effect indefinitely. I entrust her with the potential control over all publications, as well as financial operations in the case of my demise. I ask that all requests for information and receipts to my literary work be addressed to her.

B. Pasternak.

During the third week of April, Olga noticed something 'disturbing about BL's appearance. He was generally fresh and rosy-cheeked in the mornings but suddenly he began to look distinctly sallow.' On Wednesday 20 April, he took a turn for the worse. The doctor was called and said he suspected angina. Boris visited Olga as usual that evening and told her that he would have to stay in bed for a while. He said he would bring his play to her and that she must not let him have it until he was well again. He had already copied out the first half of the play and through sheer willpower, carried on despite attacks of cardiac arrhythmia and acute pain below his shoulder blades. Several times a day he would stop work, lie down and wait for the pain to pass before resuming his writing.

Olga, resigned to not seeing him for ten days or so, was astonished when on Saturday 23 April she suddenly saw Boris coming down the lane to the Little House, dilapidated briefcase in hand. She ran out, ecstatic, to meet him. 'My joy at seeing him so unexpectedly was premature. He looked pale and haggard, a sick man. We went inside the room, where it was cool and shaded.' Initially Boris seemed to be agitated over his financial situation. He was expecting some funds and there was a delay in their arrival. Heinz Schewe had promised to help but he was away. Maybe Sergio D'Angelo would turn up, he wondered, or another Italian courier. Olga started asking questions, similarly concerned.

Without replying, 'Boris kissed me – as though by this he could regain his health, as though it would give him back his strength, courage and will to live.' Olga found herself thinking back to April 1947, the first time Boris had kissed her – at dawn in the Potapov apartment – equally ardent and impassioned.

When he was ready to leave, Olga walked him part of the way back to the Big House. They stopped at the ditch near the dacha, beyond which she never usually went. Just as he was leaving, Boris turned to her.

'Oliousha, I almost forgot – I've brought you the manuscript.' He took a rolled-up sheaf of paper from his briefcase – he always wrapped his work up in the same, neat way – and handed it to her. It was the manuscript of *The Blind Beauty*. 'Keep it,' he said 'and do not let me have it back until I get better. I am going to attend to nothing now except my illness. I know you love me, I have faith in it, and our only strength is in this. Do not make any changes in our life, I beg you.'

It was the last time that Olga and Boris spoke to each other.

Irina also had her last conversation with Boris, on the phone, around this time. 'He answered in a very weak and distant voice. From then on, he no longer had the strength to go to the phone booth anymore.' When there was no further news, Irina went straight to Peredelkino 'to be closer to him'. 'We thought it would be easier to get some news. It rained continuously for the first three days of May and Mama and I stayed on our own, unable to speak.'

On 25 April the doctor diagnosed angina and Boris was ordered to have complete bed rest. He was moved from his upstairs study to the small, rectangular music room downstairs, which looked out onto the veranda and the garden. On the 27th he wrote to Olga, explaining that he was in terrible pain, writing lying down, against doctors' orders. Typically, he wrote that he was looking forward to hearing more of her reactions to the play, which still needed a lot of work: 'There is so much unnatural chit-chat, which must either be cut out or re-done.' He described his excruciating pain and how they would have to 'cross off, two weeks, at the very least, of our life'. He clearly expected to recover. He warned her not to 'take any active steps' to see him. Knowing Olga, he anticipated that she might try to come to the dacha, but strictly warned against it. 'The waves of alarm set off by it would impinge on me and at the moment, with my heart in this condition, it would kill me. Z in her foolishness would not have the wit to spare me.'

Finally he told her: 'If you begin to feel particularly cheated and unhappy in the situation arising from this new complication, take firm hold of yourself and remember: everything, everything crucial that gives meaning to my life is in your hands alone. So be brave and patient. I kiss you and hug you endless times. Don't upset yourself. We have come through worse things than this. Your B.'

Irina observed her mother's despair. 'My mother had a gloomy intuition reinforced by the fact that BL had given her the manuscript of *The Blind Beauty* as a farewell. At the same time, she would hang onto any kind of hope – the dreams she had, the nurses' opinion, the doctors' conversation. Once she shouted out "Oh Irina, how can we carry on afterwards? How can we live without Pasternak?"'

On 5 May, Koma Ivanov came into the garden of the Little House in a state of some agitation. He had brought Olga a package from Boris which contained a number of notes written in pencil. Boris had also sent Olga his treasured 'Diploma from the American Academy of Arts and Letters'. He was tremendously proud of this honorary membership, in recognition of creative achievement in the arts, which he had received three months earlier. He wanted Olga to safeguard it for him. Koma was distressed to report that at best Pasternak might have had a minor heart attack but that treatment was difficult because of asthmatic breathing caused by some other condition.

'These were anxious days,' Olga wrote later. 'I sat waiting for people to bring word from BL, and someone came every day – he sent notes with [their friend] Kostia Bogatyrev, Koma Ivanov, or anybody else who would have been to visit him.'

On Friday 6 May, Boris felt a little better, got out of bed and washed. He then decided to wash his hair, with devastating consequences. He instantly began to feel unwell. His hand shaking, he managed to write Olga one last note. On the night of 7 May, he had another heart attack.

The USSR Literary Fund sent Dr Anna Golodets and two nurses from the Kremlin Hospital to provide care for Pasternak around the clock. Dr Golodets found Boris with a raging temperature and severe lung congestion, which inhibited his breathing. Yet he rarely complained, determined to hide the full extent of his illness from his loved ones. He asked for the window to the garden to be left open. The lilac, one of his favourite flowers, was in full bloom outside.

Boris's instincts about Olga's determination to see him had been correct. At the beginning of his final illness, she had 'wanted to make a direct attack on the fortress'; she wanted to go to the Big House, to see her lover and, quite naturally, to be acknowledged there for who she was to him and what she meant to him. One evening she was discussing this with Irina, Mitia and the poet Konstantin Bogatyrev. She was 'beside herself', accusing her friend Konstantin of being a coward because he refused to take a letter from Olga to Nina Tabidze, who was staying with Zinaida at the time. In the letter, Olga begged Nina to give her some news about Boris's health and to act as a go-between. When Konstantin refused to deliver the letter, Mitia took it instead. He returned straight away to report that Nina had read the letter and warned him that there would be no reply.

Irina's heart ached for her mother. 'My poor Mama had the misfortune to experience what it felt like to be a "stranger". She was faced with the insurmountable barriers which separate those with rights, the legitimate ones, from those without rights. BL tried to reassure her in his last notes but she was at the end of her tether.'

Even when a doctor that Olga had summoned from Moscow, arrived and was giving his diagnosis, she was excluded. 'I remember her elusive silhouette in front of the fence of the Big House,' recalled Irina, sadly. 'She remained there until the last day, staying on the steps of the house shrivelled in front of the door, stubbornly closed behind.'

Boris's eldest son, Evgeny, alarmed that Olga had arranged for a famous cardiologist to visit the house, feared the fracas that Olga's initiative would create, and took it upon himself to ring the Little House daily with updates. Olga and Irina were profoundly touched by this. 'We were so grateful to him,' Irina said. Maybe because Zinaida was his stepmother and his own mother, Evgenia, had been similarly cast aside years before, he was more sympathetic.

Natasha Pasternak was as vociferous in her dislike of Olga as Zinaida. Natasha witnessed the split between the two households as she was staying at the Big House during Boris's last weeks. It is easy to see how his second family closed ranks against the threat of the 'outsider'. 'Olga was an adventuress, who was very sinful,' said Natasha. 'All of Boris and Zinaida's close friends did not like her. They wouldn't shake her hand. This put Boris in a very difficult situation. But at the end of his life he was a sick man and he had a weakness – her.'

Boris was of course fully aware of the simmering cauldron of tensions and jealousies between his family and his lover. Before he realised how ill he was, he had harboured hopes that his sister Lydia would arrive from England and act as an intermediary. 'The nurses in attendance at his bedside reported him as saying "Lydia will come and see to everything",' Olga wrote later. 'The sense of the words was clear: he believed that Lydia was well disposed towards us, his second family, and not unduly prejudiced in favour of the first one, and that she would be able to achieve a "reconciliation" between me and Zinaida Nikolayevna. He very much wanted this.'

On 15 May, when Boris realised that Olga was effectively barred from the Big House and that tensions around her were escalating, he put what Irina describes as 'a communication network' in place. Olga, accompanied by Irina, was told to go to the Kremlin Hospital in Moscow to meet with Marina Rassokhina, one of the nurses who tended Boris day and night. Marina, who was only sixteen years old, came out to talk with them. This sweet young nurse informed Olga that as soon as Boris was able to speak again after his latest heart attack, he had told her of the 'tragic state of affairs' that had arisen from their love for each other; about his 'double life'. He explained it was incredibly painful for him that his true love was banned from his presence at his bedside and asked Marina to visit Olga every day and report on Boris. The nurse 'was always smiling', recalled Irina. 'She told us with her great big smile that BL was dying; all the nurses loved him and that he had a soft spot for her, which is why he had asked her to contact us.'

Marina would go straight to the Little House after she finished her shift, often staying the night there. 'She told me that BL had asked her time and time again to arrange for me to see him – even though nobody was now being allowed to his bedside,' recalled Olga. Zinaida kept the house in a state of deathly silence.

At one stage there had been a plan for Marina to bring Olga to the downstairs window, adjacent to Boris's bed, but it was then postponed due to Boris's vanity. His false teeth had been taken away from him after his heart attack and he was terribly upset by the effect on his appearance. He could not bear for her to see him in any sort of dilapidated state. 'Olyusha won't love me anymore,' he had told Marina. 'I look such a fright now.' Boris was an exceedingly vain man. He did not even like the doctor seeing him unshaven, and when unable to shave himself any more, he asked his son Leonid, or his brother Alexander, to shave him. It is wholly likely that Boris could not bear the thought of Olga seeing him in any decrepit state; that he wanted her to remember him as the robust and shining god that she met in 1946.

Zinaida later claimed to have offered Olga the chance to see Boris one last time, but that Boris had rejected the idea. If indeed, Zinaida did invite Olga, and Boris overruled her, then it would have been chiefly to spare the family distress, and to avoid a 'scene'. It is likely that as his earthly demise took place, he was too tired to fight any more. He had nothing left in him.

News of the gravity of Boris's illness soon filled the European press. Foreign newsmen stood vigil at the gates of his dacha. On 17 May, Josephine and Lydia cabled Peredelkino from Oxford. Their telegram to Zinaida at Peredelkino read: 'VERY WORRIED BORIS ILLNESS WIRE DETAILS ALSO ABOUT YOU. LOVING PRAYING SISTERS FREDERICK.'

Boris's sister-in-law Irina, who was married to Alexander, replied: '19th May 1960. Moscow. BORIS INFARCT. TODAY ELEVENTH DAY ILLNESS ALL MEASURES TAKEN SHURA [ALEXANDER] CONSTANTLY WITH HIM HOPE NOT LOST FAVOURABLE OUTCOME WILL KEEP YOU INFORMED DETAILS BY LETTER KISSES – INA.

Sadly, the doctors' prognosis was wrong. Boris's condition deteriorated and he was diagnosed as having lung cancer.

Olga ceased to get any further notes from him – he was no longer allowed a pencil. 'I begged Marina to let him have the pencil stub she said still lay on the table, but she couldn't bring herself to and there was nobody else to ask,' Olga recalled sadly. 'I lived from one visit of Marina's to the next. I know that on returning to him from me she passed on my words of encouragement, tenderness and love, which were vitally important to him then.'

'We knew that the end was coming soon,' said Irina. 'The latest nurse on the shift, if it wasn't Marina, would wait until she was a reasonable distance from the dacha before briefing us about what had happened during the night. We knew that BL was spitting blood, he kept on losing consciousness and the dacha had been equipped with an oxygen chamber. They had even fitted an x-ray machine which showed that he had cancer on his lungs that was metastasising to other major organs; the heart, liver and bowel.'

On 25 May, Zinaida, and her son Leonid sent the following telegram to Boris's sisters in Oxford: 'CONDITION UNCHANGED MOSCOWS BEST DOCTORS TREATING ALL NECESSARY DRUGS PROVIDED EARNESTLY REQUEST YOU REFUTE FALSE BBC REPORTS OF BORIS UNSATISFACTORY TREATMENT DETAILS BY LETTER – ZINA LYONIA.'

The response was wired back the following day: '26 MAY 1960 OXFORD PASTERNAK PEREDELKINO MOSCOW ASTONISHED BY TELEGRAM BBC GAVE NO SUCH REPORT INDEED NEWSPAPERS AND RADIO STRESS FIRST-CLASS TREATMENT HOWEVER FORWARDED YOUR TELEGRAM TO PRESS GOD PRESERVE YOU.'

As well as the young nurse, Marina, Boris was treated by a more experienced, older woman, Marfa Kuzminichna, who had worked as a nurse on the Eastern front during the Second World War. After coming off duty, she too began to visit Olga, to report on Boris's condition. 'Marfa Kuzminichna, who had seen everything imaginable during the war, spoke with astonishment of the remarkable courage, endurance, and dignity he displayed in his fight with death,' said Olga.

The next day, one of the nurses heard Boris's involuntary cry: 'Zhonia [Josephine], my beloved sister, I'll never see you again!' When he asked again to see his other sister, Lydia, Alexander telegrammed her: '27th May 1960, MOSCOW. SITUATION HOPELESS COME IF YOU CAN – SHURA.' Lydia tried desperately to obtain a visa, even appealing directly to

Khrushchev. She spent a week in London waiting for the Soviet authorities to make their decision.

On 29 May, Boris's pulse dropped perilously low, but the doctors managed to stabilise him. He slept soundly that night. The following morning, he asked to see his son. Evgeny sat with him as his father's heroic strength ebbed away. 'He complained how hard it was for him to realise the insignificance of everything he had done and the ambiguity of his world fame, which was at the same time associated with absolute obscurity in his motherland. He was also distressed that his relations with former friends were severed. He characterised his life as a fight with a reigning and triumphant triteness for a freely playing human talent. "All my life has been spent on it," he concluded sorrowfully.'

'On the day of his death, when the doctor said that he had several hours of life yet, Olga spent all day sitting on the veranda of the dacha,' remembered Natasha Pasternak. 'She asked the family if she could have permission to say goodbye to him but Zinaida, Alexander and Leonid did not answer her. She was crying outside all day, so Zinaida asked Boris if she could come in but Boris did not want her to come in.'

Such anecdotes have been cited as evidence that Olga was not that important, emotionally speaking, in the writer's life; that she wasn't his great love. Yet in Boris's last-ever letter to Olga, written on Thursday 5 May, before he realised he was dying, he told her: 'Everything I possess of value I am passing on to you; the manuscript of the play and now the diploma. Surely it is possible to put up with this brief separation, and even if it requires a certain sacrifice, surely this sacrifice can be borne? If I really were near to death, I should insist that you be called over here to see me. But thank goodness this turns out to be unnecessary. The fact that everything, by the looks of it, will perhaps go on again as before seems to me so undeserved, fabulous, incredible!!'

On the evening of 30 May, Boris had his last blood transfusion. The doctors knew that death was imminent, and Zinaida went in to be with him. His brother Alexander, who had spent a month by his side, told Boris that Lydia was expected at any moment. 'Lydia, that's good,' Boris replied. He then asked for Josephine.

Boris requested to see his two sons alone. At 11 p.m. they stood beside their father's bed. He told them to stand back from the tangled part of his legacy abroad; the novel, the money and the associated complications. He also asked them to take it upon themselves to look after Olga. When they left him, his breathing became more laboured.

As his nurse, Marfa Kuzminichna, attended to him, Boris whispered: 'Don't forget to open the window tomorrow.' As the end drew closer, Marfa took Boris's head in her arms.

At 11.20 p.m. Boris Pasternak died.

The following morning, at six, Olga went to meet Marfa, who was coming off duty. The nurse was approaching a crossroads, walking quickly. When Marfa saw Olga, she bent her head low. Immediately, Olga knew. Weeping, the two women embraced. 'He is dead,' Marfa said. 'He is dead.'

Marfa told Olga that on the day of his death, Boris had said to her: 'Who will suffer the most because of my death? Who will suffer most? Only Oliusha will, and I haven't had time to do anything for her. The worst thing is that she will suffer.'

Seized by a blinding, despairing grief, Olga ran straight to the Big House, up the stairs to the veranda and pushed the door open, forcing her way in. Her actions were purely visceral. 'I don't remember how it happened, but suddenly I found myself in the Big House. Nobody stopped me at the door.' The chambermaid led Olga to where Pasternak lay in the music room.

'Boria was lying there … and his hands were soft. He lay in a small room, with the morning light on him. There were shadows across the floor, and his face was still alive – not at all inert.'

As Olga knelt by her lover's bed, she could hear his voice in her head. The words to his poem 'August', from the Zhivago cycle of poems, washed over her. Olga could not know that the last stanza, which seemed to sound out so clearly, would later be etched in Russian on the Oxford gravestone of Boris's family; his mother, Rosalia, father, Leonid, and sisters, Josephine and Lydia, whose ashes are housed together there.

Farewell, great span of wings unfurled,
The stubborn wilfulness of flight,
Words to illuminate the world,
Creation, wonder-working might!

For half an hour, Olga was left, undisturbed. As she wept beside him, Olga thought how prophetic *Doctor Zhivago* was: 'Yes, it had all come true,' she reflected. 'The very worst had come true. Everything had been marked out beforehand, stage by stage, in the fateful novel – which had indeed played a tragic part in our life, and at the same time totally embodied it.' Lara's farewell to Yury Zhivago, after his death, seemed to echo Olga's final adieu to Boris, as she sobbed helplessly:

So here we are again, Yurochka. The way God brings us together. How terrible, think of it! Oh, I can't bear it! Oh, Lord! I cry and I cry! Think of it! Again something just our kind, just up our street. Your going, that's the end of me. Again something big, inescapable ...
    Good-bye, my big one, my dear one, my own, my pride. Good-bye, my quick, deep river, how I loved your day-long plashing, how I loved bathing in your cold, deep waves.

And in response, his farewell to Lara had been:

'Good-bye, Lara, until we meet in the next world, good-bye, my love, my inexhaustible, everlasting joy. I'll never see you again. I'll never, never, see you again.'

Grief narrows the field of vision, blurring the bounds of consciousness. Olga, vaguely aware of the rest of the family grouped outside the room, stumbled outside the dacha where Mitia and Marina were waiting for her by the gate. Together, they helped Olga home to the Little House.
    Beside herself to know what to do next, Olga and Mitia took a taxi to Moscow, to Irina's apartment. '[Mama] was a lot calmer than I thought she would be. She was crying, but not in a hysterical way,' said Irina. She

kept on repeating, again and again, "'They keep on saying he has changed, but not at all. Not at all. He is as young as ever, still welcoming, still handsome".

Despite the fact that Pasternak's death was international front-page news for every major newspaper, the Soviet press did not report the writer's death. Condolences came in from around the world. But in Moscow, there was silence. Feltrinelli said in a statement from Milan: 'The death of Pasternak is a blow as hard as losing a best friend. He was the personification of my nonconformist ideals combined with wisdom and profound culture.'

The funeral was organised for 4 p.m. on Thursday 2 June. Finally, the day before, a small notice appeared on the bottom of the back page of the *Literary Gazette*. 'The board of the Literary Fund of the USSR announces the death of the writer and member of Litfond [the Literary Fund] Pasternak, Boris Leonidovich, which took place on May 30 in the seventy-first year of his life after a severe and lengthy illness, and expresses its condolences to the family of the deceased.'

Not a word was written about the time and place of the funeral. Notices, written by hand on large sheets of paper, or on pages torn from exercise books, were posted in electric trains and near the ticket offices in Moscow's Kiev station and on the platform at Peredelkino. It is a touching tribute to Boris that when the police kept tearing the notices down, new ones immediately appeared in their place that read: 'Comrades! On the night of May 30–31st, 1960, one of the great poets of modern times, Boris Leonidovich Pasternak, passed away. The civil funeral service will take place at 15.00 at Peredelkino.'

The second of June was a hot summer's day. Boris's beloved garden was awash with pink and white blossom from the apple and lilac trees. Freshly cut pine boughs had been laid across the grass to protect it. From the early morning, people wearing black and carrying sprigs of lilac made the pilgrimage from the train station to the Peredelkino cemetery. The police were already stationed at the approaches to the village, and everybody who arrived by car was made to get out and walk.

'From the early morning the electric trains arriving from the city brought mourners to Peredelkino; wave after wave of friends and strangers, of local peasants and workmen, of all those to whom Pasternak had meant or was beginning to mean so much, old and young – predominantly young people were gathering at his house for the final farewell,' wrote Lydia, who finally got her visa and arrived three days after the funeral. 'How did they know? The sultry air, the clouds, the whispering leaves must have told then. From house to house, over telephone wires, from mouth to mouth the tragic news spread over the whole of Russia. The very silence shouted it.'

The American critic Irving Howe had been proved right when he wrote in 1959: 'What Pasternak's views about the future of the Communist world may be, I do not know. But I believe that if and when freedom is re-established in Russia, the people will regard him as one who, quite apart from political opinions, was faithful to the truth of their agony. And for that they will honour him.' They honoured him that day.

As Olga walked from Izmalkovo to the Big House, she saw the place swarming with people she did not recognise. The road outside his dacha was clogged with Western press; some even climbed into the trees or stood on boxes by the fence for a better view. Inside, the open coffin, almost buried by a vast array of flowers, had been put in the main sitting room. Boris was dressed in his father's favourite grey suit. Artists were taking turns to make drawings of him. Olga watched, just as Boris had watched Leonid sketch Tolstoy at his deathbed. Marina Yudina and Stanislav Neigaus played Chopin – slow, haunting pieces filling the rooms. Olga jostled the throng to see Boris's body, then went and resumed her place where she had spent the last days of his illness, weeping on the veranda outside.

'Inside, people were still taking leave of my beloved who lay there quite impassive now, indifferent to them all, while I sat by the door so long forbidden me,' she wrote. 'I was still in a dazed state and I had been distracted by the trivialities of everyday existence – such as trying on a dress for the funeral – and I found salvation in sheer tiredness, plunging into a sleep which brought hope of waking up to discover that none of it had really happened. I had dreams that Boria was still alive, that he was tapping on my window with a twig. Perhaps I was also dreaming this terrible day with the wind and hot sun?'

Olga watched as, shortly after four, the coffin was borne out of the house, to Chopin's *Marche funèbre*, the music wafting out of the dacha behind the coffin. Boris's sons, Evgeny and Leonid, were among the pallbearers. 'People began passing flowers by the armful through the window, now flung wide open, to others standing in the garden. The wreaths and the lid of the coffin were brought out through the door ... then the open coffin appeared, swaying slightly as it was carried down the steps.'

When Irina looked into Boris's coffin and saw the face of the man who was the closest to a father she had ever had, she thought that he looked like a stranger: adult, severe and distant. She later wrote: 'Sometimes death strips the face of anything superfluous, exposing the essential reality. There was nothing like that with BL. Despite having meditated about death, written about death, prepared for death, death had not entered his life. It was not part of his world. They did not have any common ground. Death had not managed to enter him, it had simply substituted itself to him.'

'There is no death. Death is not for us,' Boris wrote. 'There will be no death because the past has passed. It's almost like this: there will be no death because everybody has already seen it. It is too old and everybody is bored with it, but now the new is in demand and the new life is eternal ...'

Olga followed the procession behind Pasternak's coffin. At one point, Olga became caught up in the crowds. Some friends including Heinze Schewe and Liusia Popova managed to steer her on a shortcut across a newly ploughed field of potatoes to the cemetery.

'The place chosen for the burial could not have been more beautiful,' wrote Alexander Gladkov. 'It was open to all sides on a hillock with three pine trees, in sight of the house where the poet had lived the second half of his life.' Gladkov was amazed by the number of mourners – by his estimation there were over 3,000. 'For everybody present it was a day of enormous importance – and this fact itself turned into yet another triumph for Pasternak.'

The crowd gathered by the grave was interspersed with reporters, photographers and film crews, their cameras whirring, pushing to the front. And of course, KGB informers. 'The procession with the coffin arrived,' remembered Gladkov. 'Before setting it down on the ground, next to the grave, the pallbearers for some reason, lifted it up above the crowd and for the last time I saw the face, gaunt and magnificent, of Boris Leonidovich Pasternak.'

The philosopher Valentin Asmus, a professor at Moscow University and one of Boris's old friends, stepped forward. It is poignant that Pasternak was not accorded the graveside ceremonies normally accompanying the funeral of a member of the Writers' Union. But this was the Russian people's funeral, which would have delighted him far more than anything official and Soviet. 'It was a display of genuine, popular sorrow,' said Olga.

Asmus delivered the eulogy:

We have come to bid farewell to one of the greatest of Russian writers and poets, a man endowed with all the talents, including even music. One might accept or reject his opinions but as long as Russian poetry plays a role on this earth, Boris Leonidovich Pasternak will stand among the greatest.

His disagreement with our present day was not with a regime or state. He wanted a society of a higher order. He never believed in resisting evil with force, and that was his mistake.

I never talked with a man who demanded so much, so unsparingly of himself. There were few who could equal him in the honesty of his convictions. He was a democrat in the true sense of the word, one who knew how to criticise his friends of the pen. He will forever remain as an example, as one who defended his convictions before his contemporaries, being firmly convinced he was right. He had the ability to express humanity in the highest terms.

He lived a long life. But it passed so quickly, he was still so young and he had so much left to write. His name will go down forever as one of the very finest.

An actor from the Moscow Art Theatre followed with a recital of Pasternak's poem 'Hamlet', from the *Zhivago* poems. Although the poem, like the novel, had not been published in the Soviet Union, according to the American correspondent from *Harper's Bazaar*, 'a thousand pairs of lips began to move in silent unison'.

> The noise is stilled. I come out on the stage.
> Leaning against the door-post
> I try to guess from the distant echo
> What is to happen in my lifetime.
>
> The darkness of night is aimed at me
> Along the sights of a thousand opera-glasses
> Abba, Father, if it be possible,
> Let this cup pass from me.
>
> I love your stubborn purpose,
> I consent to play my part.
> But now a different drama is being acted;
> For this once let me be.
>
> Yet the order of the acts is planned
> And the end of the way inescapable.
> I am alone; all drowns in the Pharisees' hypocrisy.
> To live your life is not as simple as to cross a field.*

Copies of Boris's poem 'August' were distributed among the mourners. As one person finished reciting a poem, another would begin. At one

---

* The last line is a Russian proverb.

point, a young worker stood up and shouted: 'Thank you in the name of the working man! We waited for your book. Unfortunately, for reasons that are well known, it did not appear. But you exalted the name of the writer higher than anyone.'

The officials from Litfond, nervous of the rousing, untamed nature of the crowd, moved to bring the funeral to an end. Someone was carrying the lid towards the coffin. Olga, a few steps away from Zinaida, bent down to kiss Boris on the forehead. 'And suddenly the dazed, prostrated feeling of the last few terrible days gave way to tears. I cried and I cried and I cried. I cried without caring about appearance, about what people might say.'

'For a moment she stood still and silent, neither thinking nor crying, bowed over the coffin, the flowers and the body, shielding them with her whole being, with her head, her breast, her heart and her hands as strong as her heart,' Pasternak wrote of Lara's grief for Yury Zhivago. 'The whole of her was shaken by the sobs which she restrained. She fought her tears as long as she could, but at times it was beyond her strength and they burst from her, pouring down her cheeks and falling on her dress, her hands and the coffin to which she clung.'

An official came forward and said in an agitated voice: 'That's enough, we don't need any more speeches. Close the coffin!' People began to shout out from the crowds. 'The poet was killed!' And the crowd roared: 'Shame! Shame on them!' Boris's housekeeper placed a copy of a prayer for the dead on Boris's forehead. Then, as the lid was hammered onto the coffin, more shouts came from the crowd: 'Glory to Pasternak!'

Almost everyone had brought flowers, so when the coffin was lowered into the ground mourners passed the flowers on to each other, over the heads of the crowd. It resembled a magical, undulating sea of flowers floating above the assembled mass. At this moment, quite unexpectedly, the bells of the nearby Church of Transfiguration began to peal. As the coffin was lowered into the grave and the first clods of earth thudded down on it, the crowd began to chant 'Glory to Pasternak! Goodbye! Glory!' The words echoed over the surrounding fields.

For a long time, many of the mourners – students, revolutionaries, young men and women – refused to leave the burial site. They remained near the grave, recited poetry and lit candles. That evening there was a crash of thunder and a heavy downpour. People put their hands over their candles to protect them from the heavy raindrops, and still went on, reciting one poem after another in the flickering candlelight.

A couple of days after the funeral, two senior KGB officials arrived at the Little House and demanded that Olga hand over the manuscript of *The Blind Beauty*. When she put up a valiant fight, saying it was not hers to give, one of the men replied: 'I should not like to have to invite Olga Vsevolodovna to come with us to a place which will certainly be more traumatic for her than this conversation in a private apartment.' His colleague added: 'And you should bear in mind that there are six of us in the car – we can take the manuscript by force if needs be.'

Already it had begun. On 16 August, less than three months after they took *The Blind Beauty*, the KGB arrived at Olga's door once more. A ruddy-cheeked fat man wearing a light-coloured mackintosh burst into her living room and, with a self-assured smile, announced: 'You were expecting us to come, of course, weren't you? You didn't imagine that your criminal activities would go unpunished?' They ransacked the Little House, and confiscated Olga's few remaining precious papers. Olga was then taken to the Lubyanka. Her worst fears that, unless she had the Pasternak surname, she would be vulnerable to attack – possibly death – had come true.

'It was clear that they had decided not to go after Pasternak,' Irina wrote. 'They were after something else. Was it not just pure vengeance? … He had not budged one bit from his views and he had died in his bed. Now he was considered a hero! It was unbearable, but now the machine was switched on to destroy, to humiliate and to flatten. There was no need to kill you. All it took was to make fun of you, to tarnish you in front of the rest of the world, to extract confessions from you and to make you crawl on your stomach.'

'Pasternak was too outstanding a figure to be permanently labelled as an "enemy",' Olga commented later. 'And after his death, therefore, when there was no longer any fear that he might spring some new surprise on them (as he had done with the Nobel Prize poem) the powers-that-be decided it would be better to elevate him to the pantheon of Soviet Literature.' Even his sworn enemy, Surkov, did a complete volte-face, declaring Pasternak 'an honest poet who he personally respected'. Surkov's venom was now turned towards Olga. 'Pasternak's friend Ivinskaya' he declared was 'an adventuress who got him to write *Doctor Zhivago*, and then to send it abroad, so that she would enrich herself'.

On 30 January 1961 the American magazine *Newsweek* reported on Olga's imprisonment:

Obviously justice was less important than revenge, a revenge that the Kremlin's cultural organization men had not dared to take on the world-renowned Pasternak himself just as they had not dared to punish the celebrated pianist Sviatoslav Richter for playing at Pasternak's funeral. Beyond that, most Western experts saw another motive. If Mrs Ivinskaya could be smeared as a 'femme fatale' who had 'corrupted' the ageing author, the government could escape the embarrassment of *Dr Zhivago* and reclaim the younger Pasternak as a great Soviet poet. An official committee in Moscow had already been established to do that, but the world would scarcely accept Pasternak's truth being turned into such a fraud.

Olga was officially arrested on the 18 August 1960. A few weeks later, on 5 September, the KGB came for Irina.

In the Lubyanka, Olga was interrogated by the KGB's deputy chairman, Vadim Tikunov. A rotund figure, he sat behind a huge desk, brandishing a copy of *Doctor Zhivago*: 'You disguised it very cleverly,' he told her, 'but we know perfectly well that the novel was not written by Pasternak, but by you. Look, he says so himself ...' He gestured to the opening page of the book. Suddenly, Olga saw Boris's 'cranes' sailing before her eyes. Boris had written: 'It was you who did it, Oliusha! Nobody knows that it was you who did it all – you guided my hand and stood behind me, all of it I owe to you.'

Tikunov looked at Olga maliciously, 'through tiny slits of eyes buried in puffy rolls of flesh'. Olga stared back at him, before responding boldly: 'You have probably never loved a woman, so you don't know what it means, and the sort of things people think and write at such a time.'

Ignoring her, Tikunov continued: 'The point is that Pasternak himself admits he didn't write it! It was you who put him up to it all. He was not so embittered until you came along. You have committed a criminal offence and established contact with foreigners.'

Three months later, Olga and Irina were tried by a people's court in Moscow. For five days between 13 and 18 December 1960 the farcical trial ran on. 'Not only was the case itself a sham, but even the actual proceedings were bogus – the whole thing was based on falsehood from beginning to end,' said Olga. Mother and daughter were accused of crimes against the state involving smuggling. Tellingly, the court proceedings were never reported in the Soviet press. Twice in foreign broadcasts, however, certain details of the case were leaked. Olga was accused of having received money in Soviet currency illegally imported into the Soviet Union in large quantities at various dates, while Irina was charged with aiding and abetting in these crimes. Her meeting with Mirella Garitano, when she collected the suitcase for Boris, thinking it contained books, was used in evidence against her.

No one who had purchased the Soviet currency abroad and had brought it, presumably illicitly, across the border into the Soviet Union to pass on to Pasternak via Olga and Irina, was prosecuted.

Sergio D'Angelo, anxious to raise awareness of Olga and Irina's plight, published an article in the *Sunday Telegraph* in England in January 1961, in which he confessed to having initiated the scheme to transfer royalties to Pasternak when he was alive and to having obtained Pasternak's authority to do so. He also admitted to having continued the transfers to Olga after Pasternak's death in accordance with Pasternak's instructions.

In his article, D'Angelo himself pointed out that it was remarkable that as the initiator of the operation in which Olga could legitimately be described only as an accessory after the fact, he had visited the Soviet Union in 1960. He questioned how he could have been allowed to have spent a week in Moscow in the last days of August and the first days of September, after Olga's arrest, and was let in and out unmolested by the Soviet authorities.

D'Angelo concluded:

The truth was that Pasternak and Ivinskaya were being far too closely watched for any scheme, for a transfer of funds from abroad, to work without detection. The Soviet police knew what was going on. But they chose to hold their hands until after Pasternak was dead.

It is clear from the above that the Soviet authorities were not interested in catching and punishing the real smugglers of illicitly acquired Soviet currency from abroad, but in using this opportunity to inflict the severest possible punishment on Olga Ivinskaya and her daughter, who became involved in an operation of which the Soviet secret police appears to have been fully informed throughout.

Shortly before his death – when Pasternak wrote to Jacqueline de Proyart in Paris saying that if he sent a telegram saying that someone had caught scarlet fever, it meant that Olga had been arrested – Boris had added: 'in that event, all tocsins should be made to ring as would have done in my place, for an attack on her is in fact a blow at me.' Literary figures in the West tried their hardest to sound the tocsins on behalf of Olga. Graham Greene, François Mauriac, Arthur Schlesinger Jr, all wrote to Soviet authorities, while Bertrand Russell appealed to Khrushchev himself. David Carver, the general secretary of PEN, lobbied Alexei Surkov, who had risen to become the general secretary of the Soviet Writers' Union. Sergio D'Angelo wrote Surkov a stinging open letter in which he said: 'You have always hated Pasternak and, dominated by this feeling, you carried out, as first secretary of the Writers' Union, a series of ill-considered acts which did your country a very poor service.' He went on to sum up: 'Pasternak's death was not sufficient to satisfy your spite, which you are now venting, with invective and slander, on two defenceless women who are, furthermore, *seriously ill*. I have no illusions and I do not think that you will find it possible to change your ways or to show moderation and humanity. But neither should you, on your part, have any illusions about having "closed the futile correspondence on the Ivinskaya affair" as you say in your letter: the conscience of all civilised and honest people will not permit it to be "closed" until justice has been done.'

Olga was sentenced to the maximum penalty of eight years' imprisonment, while Irina was sentenced to three. They were both sent to the gulag, to labour camp 385/14 at Taishet, nearly 5,000 kilometres away from Moscow. There, in the Irkutsk province in Eastern Siberia, the wind was so strong that you had to walk backwards.

'The journey to Siberia was long and terrible,' wrote Olga. 'It was January when the frosts are at their most severe, and the stops on the way, during which we had to spend the night in cold damp cells, were a great torment. Ira was wearing only a light coat intended for spring or autumn (it was made of dark-blue English bouclé) and with her silly mania for keeping in fashion, she had had it shortened. My heart bled for her when I saw her arms sticking way out of her sleeves.'

One month into their sentences, Taishet camp was closed down and Olga and Irina were transferred the thousands of miles back across the USSR – to Potma. In the Khrushchev years, as the huge labour camp complexes of Siberia and the far north were wound down, those in Mordovia became the main centre for the detention of 'political' prisoners. Olga, of course, already knew the hell of Potma; Irina to some extent too, remembering her mother's stories and Boris's fantastical postcards, when 'from the autumn of 1950, the small republic of Mordovia came into our lives never to leave it again'. The two women did not know if being sent to Siberia was due to chaos in the camp system, or if it was another of the regime's sadistic jokes.

'I still cannot think without horror of the final stage of our journey to the camp in Taishet,' wrote Olga, 'which were we forced to do on foot, late at night.'

It was a silvery, Siberian night with a full moon. The pine trees cast their squat, deep-blue shadows across the snow. On either side of the road the grizzled northern fir trees with their spreading branches were bathed in ghostly moonlight, which made them look improbably vast.

The sleigh which should have been waiting for us at the rail junction had not been sent, and our two escort guards had refused to wait, so they had marched us off into the night, to our unknown destination. The two spectral shadows with rifles followed behind us as we stumbled along, shaking all over in this frost which would have seemed nothing much to native-born Siberians, but was unbearable for Muscovites like us who were quite unused to such bitter cold. It penetrated to the marrow of our bones.

In *Doctor Zhivago*, Pasternak grimly prophesised the Soviet state's treatment of Olga: 'One day Lara went out and did not come back. She must have been arrested in the street, as so often happened in those days, and she died or vanished somewhere, forgotten as a nameless number on a list which later was mislaid, in one of the innumerable mixed or women's concentration camps in the north.'

# Think of Me Then

Olga spent three and a half years in prison, half of her sentence. She was released in 1964, aged fifty-two. Irina was released two years earlier, having served half of her sentence also. Olga had written to Khrushchev from the prison camp, appealing for her daughter's early release, describing Irina as 'dying slowly right in front of my eyes'.

The conditions at Potma were 'unbearable, beyond imagination', Irina remembers. 'We were working in the fields in freezing winters and parched, baking summers. There were sixty women in the same barracks, the radio always on, propaganda blaring out from six in the morning until midnight.' Irina had been due to marry Georges Nivat in the summer of 1960. Several weeks after Pasternak's death, the authorities granted Irina a date for the wedding – ten days after Georges's visa expired. He was refused a renewal of his visa and forced to leave Russia.

Georges Nivat campaigned vigorously for Olga and Irina's release from the gulag. Through a friend, he asked Queen Elizabeth of Belgium, the first royal to visit the Soviet Union, in 1958, to appeal directly to Khrushchev. 'Had Boris Pasternak, whom I loved as a father, still lived, this [incarceration] would not have happened,' he wrote.

Irina did not marry Georges, but they remained friends. She met her future husband, Vadim Kosovoi, a political dissident, in Potma. They never once spoke in the camp as the sexes were segregated, but they saw each other from afar and began an exchange of letters, facilitated by prison inmates who created stealthy networks of correspondence. After their release, their romance flourished. Irina has lived in Paris for the last thirty years and had two children. 'France has helped repair many of the wounds of Russia, created thirty years ago,' she says. Olga's beloved son, Mitia, died in 2005.

Leonid Pasternak, Boris's son with Zinaida, died aged thirty-eight. He suffered a fatal heart attack while sitting in his car off Presnya Street in central Moscow – dying at almost the same age and near the exact spot that Yury Zhivago dies of a heart attack in a moving tram in *Doctor Zhivago*. Leonid's wife, Natasha, spoke of a 'mystery' in Boris Pasternak's 'creation': it was 'like he was writing his son's death at a subconscious level. So much of what he wrote held great portent.'

Olga Ivinskaya died in 1995 aged eighty-three in Moscow. Before her death she wrote a pleading letter to the Russian president Boris Yeltsin requesting the return of all Boris's love letters to her and other precious papers which the KGB had taken from the Little House after his death. Her request was not fulfilled.

Khrushchev, who found time to read *Doctor Zhivago* in his retirement, said he regretted his treatment of Pasternak. He admitted that he had had the opportunity to allow publication of the novel, but had 'failed to act'. He expressed regrets about these shortcomings, and acknowledged that the decision to ban the novel in Russia and force Boris to renounce the Nobel Prize 'left a bad aftertaste for a long time to come. People raised a storm of protest against the Soviet Union for not allowing Pasternak to go abroad to receive the prize.'

In 1987, the Soviet Writers' Union posthumously reinstated Boris, a move which gave his work legitimacy in the Soviet Union. This allowed the publication of *Doctor Zhivago* in Russia for the first time, in 1988. Hundreds of people queued outside Moscow bookshops for shipments of the book to arrive.

On 9 December 1989, the Swedish Academy invited Pasternak's eldest son, Evgeny, and his wife to Stockholm to be presented with the gold medal for the 1958 Nobel Prize in Literature, thirty-one years after Boris had been forced to renounce it. Evgeny was overcome with emotion when he stepped forward to accept the prize on behalf of his father.

*   *   *

When I began *Lara*, I was secretly concerned that I would discover that Boris used Olga. As I dug deeper into the story, I was relieved to find that this was far from the case. It was the authorities who used Olga. True, Boris did not save her by publicly 'claiming' her. But he loved her. I believe the depth and passion of his ardour differed from anything he felt for either of his wives. Not just out of gratitude that Olga risked her life in loving and standing by him. But because she understood him; she had a deep inner knowing that in order for him to find a resting place of fulfilment within himself, he needed to write *Doctor Zhivago*.

Although he did not do the one thing Olga desperately wanted – he did not leave his wife for her – from the moment he pledged himself to her, he did his utmost within the constraints of his domestic situation to honour her and her family. He supported them financially, he loved Irina as the daughter he never had, and he trusted Olga with his most precious commodity – his work. He sought her advice, her editing and typing assistance. And what is *Doctor Zhivago*, if not his long and heartfelt love letter to her?

As I wrote *Lara*, I was surprised to develop a more tolerant affection for Boris. I felt like a close friend or relative who overlooks someone's annoying idiosyncrasies – in Boris's case, his self-absorbed soliloquies, his false modesty, his vanity, his addiction to high drama – due to an intrinsic and burgeoning fondness. As Boris began to write *Doctor Zhivago*, refusing to be crushed by the pressure of the Soviet state, I grew in admiration for him. I salute his granite defiance, I applaud his rebellious spirit and I bow down before his monumental courage, especially his publish-and-be-damned attitude to Feltrinelli and the publication of the novel.

As I began to champion him, I mostly forgave him his shortcomings, just as Olga and Irina did. I could see the complexity of the man and his situation. The inconsistency of his character. He was both hero and coward, genius and naïve fool, tortured neurotic and clinical strategist. His loyalty to Russia and her people never wavered. His loyalty to Olga was never steadfast. In spite of everything she did for him, including being prepared to die for him, she could not rely on him.

There were times when I felt immeasurably frustrated by his weakness; his letters to Olga from Tbilisi, when he rejected her desire for marriage, citing their mythical connection as more important than anything as mundane and everyday as marriage, infuriated me. Olga was right; he was wrong. If he had married her, the Soviet authorities would not have dared to treat her so cruelly and unnecessarily after his death.

Yet at other times, I ached for him. When I wrote of the savaging he received after the Nobel Prize award, his pain was palpable, his suffering agonising. If it wasn't for Olga, he might well have committed suicide. She was his strength when his resolution was finally extinguished; she was his guiding light when all around him seemed interminably dark. When they were separated, his letters show the extent of his love, missing and need for her.

But in the end, for all his blistering brilliance, he did not save Olga. I can appreciate that at the conclusion of his life, he did not have the energy to fight any more. Every ounce of his potency was drained in defying the authorities to ensure that *Doctor Zhivago* was published. In this, at least, he ensured that Olga, his Lara, would never be forgotten. While she was fighting for him in the Lubyanka, he was at least exalting her in the pages of his book. She lost two of his children; the legacy of *Doctor Zhivago* is their only child. Both Lara and Yury gain immortality through Yury's poems, the true fruit of their love. Pasternak intended all along to redeem himself by immortalising Olga as Lara. Perhaps on one level he was right; their love would remain everlasting. As he wrote in *Doctor Zhivago*:

It was not out of necessity that they loved each other, 'enslaved by passion', as lovers are described. They loved each other because everything around them willed it, the trees and the clouds and the sky over their heads and the earth under their feet. Perhaps their

surrounding world, the strangers they met in the street, the land-
scapes drawn up for them to see on their walks, the rooms in which
they lived or met, were even more pleased with their love than they
were themselves.

Many years will go by. Many great years. I shall then no longer be alive. There will be no return to the times of our fathers and grandfathers. This would, indeed, be both undesirable and unnecessary. But at last there will appear once more things that have long lain dormant: noble, creative and great things. It will be a time of final accounting. Your life will be rich and fruitful as never before.

Think of me then.

Boris Pasternak, 1958

# NOTES

In most cases the sources of quotations are made clear in the text. The principal narrative sources are: Olga Ivinskaya's *A Captive of Time* (Collins and Harvill, 1978), Irina Emelianova's *Légendes de la rue Potapov* (Fayard, 1997), and author interviews with Pasternak family members (see Acknowledgements). With the help of the Bibliography interested readers will be able to trace any other references without undue trouble.

## PROLOGUE: STRAIGHTENING COBWEBS

xv  'There was in Russia': Boris Pasternak, *Fifty Poems*, translated and with introduction by Lydia Pasternak Slater, Unwin Books, 1963, p. 13.

xvi  'Nothing I have': ibid., p. 16.

xvi  'growing into the revolution': Christopher Barnes, *Boris Pasternak: A Literary Biography, Volume 2, 1928–1960*, Cambridge: Cambridge University Press, p. 4.

xvi  Pasternak wrote: Edith Clowes (ed.), *Doctor Zhivago: A Critical Companion*, Northwestern University Press, 1995, p. 12.

xvi  February Revolution: the Russian Revolution is the collective term for the revolutions in February and October 1917, which dismantled the Tsarist autocracy and led to the eventual rise of the Soviet Union.

xvi  'most celebrated': Boris Pasternak, *Fifty Poems*, p. 13.

xvi  'To read Pasternak's': Peter Finn and Petra Couvée, *The Zhivago Affair: The Kremlin, the CIA, and the Battle over a Forbidden Book*, Harvill Secker, 2014, p. 33.

xvi  'My brother's poems': Lydia Pasternak Slater, *New York Times Book Review*, 29 Oct 1961.

xvii In a poem: Clowes (ed.), *Critical Companion*, p. 12; Evgeny Pasternak, *Boris Pasternak: The Tragic Years 1930–1960*, Collins and Harvill, 1990, p. 298.

xvii 'We drag everyday things': Boris Pasternak, *Safe Conduct: An Early Autobiography and Other Works*, Elek Books, 1959, p. 181, quoted in Clowes (ed.), *Critical Companion*, p. 10.

xviii 'From the bottom of the sea': Boris Pasternak, *Doctor Zhivago*, translated by Max Hayward and Manya Harari, Collins and Harvill, 1958 (henceforward *Doctor Zhivago*), p. 489.

xix 'And now there he was': Olga Ivinskaya, *A Captive of Time: My Years with Pasternak*, Collins and Harvill, 1978, p. 9.

xx 'a terrible man …': Guy de Mallac, *Boris Pasternak: His Life and Art*, University of Oklahoma Press, 1981, p. 204.

xx an estimated 20 million: Simon Sebag Montefiore, *Stalin: The Court of the Red Tsar*, Weidenfeld & Nicolson, 2003, p. 658.

xx 'The immense talent': Finn and Couvée, *Zhivago Affair*, p. 42.

xx 'Revolutionaries who take': *Doctor Zhivago*, pp. 268, 269.

xxi 'a kind of autobiography': Clowes (ed.), *Critical Companion*, p. 20.

xxi 'I've never done anything': Robert Bolt quoted in *Daily Mail*, 25 Nov 2002.

xxi '*Doctor Zhivago* encompasses generations': Omar Sharif quoted in *Daily Express*, Jun 1993.

xxiii 'like cranes': Ivinskaya, *Captive*, p. 15.

xxvi 'How well he loved her': *Doctor Zhivago*, p. 330.


## CHAPTER 1: A GIRL FROM A DIFFERENT WORLD

1 'Boris Leonidovich, let me introduce': Ivinskaya, *Captive*, p. 15.

2 'this God', 'stood there': ibid.

2 He told a friend: Barnes, *Literary Biography*, p. 213.

2 'I've started on a novel': Ivinskaya, *Captive*, p. 10.

3 'Boris Leonidovich started': Boris Leonidovich Pasternak, *Poems*, compiled by Evgeny Pasternak, with a Foreword by Andrei Voznesensky, Raduga, Moscow, 1990, p. 22.

3 'I was simply shaken': Ivinskaya, *Captive*, p. 10.

3 '"She has no coquetry"': *Doctor Zhivago*, p. 264.

4 'dishevelled and on fire': Ivinskaya, *Captive*, p. 7.

5 In 1933 he had written: Clowes (ed.), *Critical Companion*, p. 15.

5 On 26 August: Barnes, *Literary Biography*, pp. 18–19.

6 'The Revolution is': Evgeny Pasternak, *Boris Pasternak*, p. 57.

6 'had to become … for his age': Author interview Evgeny Pasternak, Moscow, Feb 2010.

7 'I think that collectivisation': *Doctor Zhivago*, p. 453.

7 'everything established, settled': ibid., p. 362.

7 'the mental space': Clowes (ed.), *Critical Companion*, p. 16.

7 'The highest incomparable': Boris Pasternak, *Biographical Album*, Gamma Press, Moscow, 2007, p. 309.

8 'tall and trim': Ivinskaya, *Captive*, p. 6.

8 She knew 'instinctively': ibid., p. 11.

9 'But the answers': ibid., p. 12.

9 'magician who had first': ibid., p. 10.

9 'Once again I send': ibid., p. 15.

10 'Don't look at me': ibid., p. 16.

11 'I didn't get … round the town': ibid.

11 'Ivan [Vania] Emelianov': Irina Emelianova, *Légendes de la rue Potapov*, Fayard, 1997, p. 16.

11 'a man from a different era': Emelianova, *Légendes*, p. 18.

12 'I had already gone': Ivinskaya, *Captive*, p. 10.

12 'If you have been': ibid., p. 17.

12 'worn down', 'brilliant and strong-willed': Author interview Irina Emelianova, Paris, Sep 2015.

13 '*Olia*, I love you': Ivinskaya, *Captive*, p. 18.

13 'misery that comes': Author interview Irina Emelianova.

13 'minimalistic option', 'not really … worthy of a man like him': ibid.

13 'Even words I knew': Emelianova, *Légendes*, p. 13.

14 'something remarkable': Author interview Irina Emelianova.

14 'The day came when': Ivinskaya, *Captive*, p. 18.

14 'A little girl of about eight': *Doctor Zhivago*, p. 270.

14 'A divided family': Maya Slater (ed.), *Boris Pasternak: Family Correspondence, 1921–1960*, translated by Nicholas Pasternak Slater, Hoover Institution Press, 2010, p. 321.

15 'What is life if not love?': Ivinskaya, *Captive*, p. 15.

## CHAPTER 2: MOTHER LAND AND WONDER PAPA

16 'shining perennial': Author interview Josephine Pasternak, Oxford, Oct 1990.

16 'You were a real man': ibid.

17 'I wrote to father': Slater (ed.), *Family Correspondence*, p. 366.

17 'He was a genius ... rare thing': Author interview Evgeny Pasternak.

17 'Pasternak's children': *The Museum of Private Collections: Museum Guidebook*, Moscow, 2004, p. 94.

18 'He always wore ... off a canvas': Author interview Charles Pasternak, Oxford, Apr 2015.

18 'I felt more attracted ... purity': Leonid Pasternak and Josephine Pasternak, *The Memoirs of Leonid Pasternak*, translated by Jennifer Bradshaw, Quartet Books Ltd, 1982, p. 44.

18 'One unsolved question': ibid.

18 'I now realise ... existence of Boris': Author interview Josephine Pasternak.

19 'When I think back': Josephine Pasternak, *Tightrope Walking: A Memoir*, Slavica Publishers, 2005, Introduction, p. xi.

19 'From his childhood': Peter Levi, *Boris Pasternak*, Century Hutchinson, 1990, p. 23.

20 'I lacked perfect pitch': Boris Pasternak, *An Essay in Autobiography*, Collins and Harvill, 1959, p. 48.

20 'They offer the squirrel nuts': Leonid Pasternak, Josephine Pasternak, *Memoirs*, p. 133.

21 'Some of the most memorable': ibid., p. 151.

21 'Ah, you express': Author interview Charles Pasternak.

21 'It was from our kitchen': Pasternak, *Essay in Autobiography*, p. 37.

21 'I remember how pressed': ibid.

22 'My imagination was impressed': ibid., p. 38.

22 'Leo Tolstoy's granddaughter': Slater (ed.), *Family Correspondence*, pp. 337–8.

22 'Astapovo. Morning': Leonid Pasternak, Josephine Pasternak, *Memoirs*, p. 177.

23 'In March 1917': Boris Pasternak, *Biographical Album*, p. 175.

24 'The paper was a late extra': *Doctor Zhivago*, pp. 175–6.

25 'Winter was at hand': ibid., p. 168.

26 'They were given spades': Josephine Pasternak, *Tightrope Walking*, p. 127.

26 'But the sun sparkled': *Doctor Zhivago*, p. 208.

27 'Among them was the war': ibid., p. 148.

28 'Everything had changed': ibid., p. 121.

29 'the bitter dregs': Slater (ed.), *Family Correspondence*, p. 289.

29 'If there was a war': Barnes, *Literary Biography*, p. 105.

29 'I do not remember': Josephine Pasternak, 'Patior', *The London Magazine* 6 (Sep 1964), pp. 42–57.

30 'He said: "You know …', ibid.

30 'I could not believe': ibid.

31 'Go to bed': ibid.

31 'Yes … to sleep': ibid.

31 'I'm incapable of doing': Slater (ed.), *Family Correspondence*, p. 285.

31 'This is the first': ibid., p. 346.

32 'When Mother died': Author interview Josephine Pasternak.

32 'an ocean of tears': Slater (ed.), *Family Correspondence*, p. 285.

32 'I'm like someone bewitched': ibid.

32 'This fate of not belonging': Boris Pasternak, *Poems*, p. 309.


CHAPTER 3: THE CLOUD DWELLER

34 'One wanted to bathe': Evgeny Pasternak, *Boris Pasternak*, p. 31.

35 'showered hard cash': Author interview Josephine Pasternak.

35 'people of an artistic nature': Boris Pasternak, *Poems*, p. 314.

35 'We, the family … tearful moods': Author interview Josephine Pasternak.

35 'A child! Slavery!': Josephine Pasternak, *Tightrope Walking*, p. 168.

36 'Germany was cold': Mallac, *Boris Pasternak*, pp. 105–6.

36 'He is so tiny': Josephine Pasternak, *Tightrope Walking*, p. 190.

37 'In many ways the antidote': Ivinskaya, *Captive*, p. 455.

37 'The only bright spot': Slater (ed.), *Family Correspondence*, p. 165.

40 'beauty of the Mary Queen of Scots': Barnes, *Literary Biography*, p. 41.

40 'Her hands astonished him': *Doctor Zhivago*, p. 51.

40 'There is something broken': ibid., p. 358.

41 'I fear for Boris': Mallac, *Boris Pasternak*, p. 126.

41 'undiminished suffering': Slater (ed.), *Family Correspondence*, pp. 195–6.

42 'rinsed out his insides': ibid., p. 210.

42 'Well, are you satisfied?': Barnes, *Literary Biography*, p. 63.

42 'I've fallen in love': ibid., p. 195.

43 'is a very contradictory': ibid., p. 231.

43 'You know, Boris is really': Author interview Isaiah Berlin, Oxford, Oct 1990.

43 'semi-debauched': Author interview Josephine Pasternak.

43 Boris once destroyed: Barnes, *Literary Biography*, pp. 101–2.

43 'Look after her': Author interview Josephine Pasternak.

44 'Dear Borya!': Slater (ed.), *Family Correspondence*, p. 201.

44 'always comes back', 'did more for her than anyone', 'hot-headed': ibid., pp. 203–16.

45 'All this comes … from libraries': ibid.

45 'abundance of sunshine': Mallac, *Boris Pasternak*, p. 126.

45 'Talent radiated from him': Pasternak, *Essay in Autobiography*, p. 113.

46 'crumpled bed': Author interview Josephine Pasternak.

46 'Heavenly colour, colour blue': Finn and Couvée, *Zhivago Affair*, pp. 66–7.

46 'Leave the cloud dweller': ibid., p. 67.

46 'You give me the feeling': Mallac, *Boris Pasternak*, p. 127.

46 When Evgenia finally: Barnes, *Literary Biography*, p. 71.

47 'the walls have ears', 'Because ... people up': Barnes, *Literary Biography*, p. 83.

48 'I'm also writing': Boris Pasternak, *Biographical Album*, p. 277.

48 'Isolate but preserve': Finn and Couvée, *Zhivago Affair*, p. 40.

48 'Stalin said that Mandelstam's': Boris Pasternak, *Biographical Album*, p. 277.

48 'He was quite right': Finn and Couvée, *Zhivago Affair*, p. 41.

49 'All this time': Olga R. Hughes, *The Poetic World of Boris Pasternak*, Princeton, 1972, p. 136.

49 'entrapping writers': Finn and Couvée, *Zhivago Affair*, p. 4.

49 'one of the most remarkable': Evgeny Pasternak, *Boris Pasternak*, p. 74.

50 'Do not make heroes': Levi, *Pasternak*, p. 174.

50 'Zinaida seems to be baking': Barnes, *Literary Biography*, p. 144.

50 'for her immortal phrase': ibid., p. 68.

50 'no one could know': Author interview Natasha Pasternak, Peredelkino, Feb 2010.

51 'Pasternak and Pilnyak', 'I have so much work to do': Rosa Mora, 'The History of Hell', *Independent*, 8 Jan 1995.

51 'Pasternak is going': Boris Pasternak, *Biographical Album*, p. 293.

51 'In those horrendous': Evgeny Pasternak, *Boris Pasternak*, p. 107.

51 'Apart from him': Finn and Couvée, *Zhivago Affair*, p. 46.

52 'I share the feeling': Levi, *Pasternak*, p. 180.

52 'from that moment': Finn and Couvée, *Zhivago Affair*, p. 38.

52 'Following the October': Mallac, *Boris Pasternak*, p. 141.

53 'the lives of people': ibid., pp. 158–9.

53 'I wrote that I had': Barnes, *Literary Biography*, p. 148.

53 'present condition is entirely': Slater (ed.), *Family Correspondence*, p. 322.

53 Zinaida later wrote: Finn and Couvée, *Zhivago Affair*, p. 45.

53 'My wife was pregnant': Mallac, *Boris Pasternak*, p. 59.

54 'We expected': Ivinskaya, *Captive*, p. 142.

54 'Rely only on yourself': Suny Ronald Grigo, *The Making of the Georgian Nation*, Indiana University Press, 1994, p. 272.

54 'The boy was born': Boris Pasternak, *Biographical Album*, p. 299.

55 'He was very drawn': Barnes, *Literary Biography*, p. 130.

55 'She had a very rigid … running a ship': Author interview Natasha Pasternak.

## CHAPTER 4: CABLES UNDER HIGH TENSION

57 'Boris suffered immensely': Author interview Irina Emelianova.

58 'I was so captivated': Ivinskaya, *Captive*, p. 20.

59 'like newlyweds': ibid., p. 19.

59 'My life, my angel': ibid.

59 'Conversation in a half tone': *Doctor Zhivago*, p. 477.

60 'It is impossible': Author interview Irina Emelianova.

60 'slandered the leader': ibid.

60 'would travel in a cattle train': ibid.

61 'No, no, Olia': Ivinskaya, *Captive*, p. 25.

62 'He had decided to cut the knot': *Doctor Zhivago*, pp. 274–5.

63 'an awareness of the sinfulness': Barnes, *Literary Biography*, p. 239.

63 Again I rehearse my excuses: Ivinskaya, *Captive*, pp. 24–5. This poem also appears in *Doctor Zhivago*, p. 475, in a different translation.

64 'by this time Zinaida': Ivinskaya, *Captive*, p. 25.

65 'I love your daughter': ibid., p. 23.

65 'I thought of Boris': ibid., p. 24.

66 'long arguments': Author interview Charles Pasternak.

66 'I started to work': Alexander Gladkov, *Meetings with Pasternak*, Collins and Harvill Press, 1977, pp. 136–7.

66 'little time for Evgeny', 'infrequently': Author interview Natasha Pasternak.

67 'the nearer he was drawn': *Doctor Zhivago*, p. 365.

67 On 6 February 1947: Finn and Couvée, *Zhivago Affair*, p. 58.

67 'Let me take you to see': Ivinskaya, *Captive*, p. 195.

68 'As they drove through': *Doctor Zhivago*, p. 81.

68 'BL was particularly affected': Ivinskaya, *Captive*, p. 196.

68 'Yura was standing absent-mindedly': ibid., p. 84.

69 'It also seems to me': Josephine Pasternak, *Tightrope Walking*, p. 82.

69 'He said that there': Author interview Irina Emelianova.

70 'tired beauty': ibid.

70 'I don't like people who': *Doctor Zhivago*, p. 359.

70 'Here was the very thing': ibid., p. 64.

70 At a reading in May 1947: Finn and Couvée, *Zhivago Affair*, p. 57.

71 'Oh those Peredelkino meals!': Boris Pasternak, *Poems*, p. 21.

71 The secret police were also: Finn and Couvée, *Zhivago Affair*, p. 58.

72 'in the auditorium': György Dalos, *Olga – Pasternaks Letzte Liebe: Fast ein Roman*, Europäische Verlagsanstalt, 1999, sample translation by Patrick Corness, 2003, http://www.new-books-in-german.com/spr2000/book08c.htm.

72 The literary historian Emma Gerstein: ibid.

72 'personally polishes': Slater (ed.), *Family Correspondence*, p. 237.

72 'I personally do not': Finn and Couvée, *Zhivago Affair*, pp. 82, 83.

73 'Nothing was allowed': Boris Pasternak, *Poems*, p. 18.

74 'words and moods': Slater (ed.), *Family Correspondence*, p. 228.

74 'At home he felt': *Doctor Zhivago*, p. 274.

75 'got used to the idea': Author interview Irina Emelianova.

75 'Mum's empty bedroom': Emelianova, *Légendes*, p. 21.

75 'That's life,' wrote Boris: Slater (ed.), *Family Correspondence*, p. 367.

76 'Yesterday Zina and I': Boris Pasternak, *Biographical Album*, p. 327.

76 'When it's a question': Slater (ed.), *Family Correspondence*, p. 309.

76 'heavily built': Author interview Irina Emelianova.

76 'found her appearance': Author interview Irina Emelianova.

77 'ill through loss of blood': ibid.

78 'Dear Irochka, my treasure': Emelianova, *Légendes*, p. 24.

78 'dear Fedia and girls!': Slater (ed.), *Family Correspondence*, p. 376.

78 'Printing it': ibid.

78 'You won't like the novel': ibid.

79 'Your book is above': Boris Pasternak, *Biographical Album*, p. 355.

79 'Ordinarily, people are anxious': *Doctor Zhivago*, p. 235.

80 'Even if you should hear': Slater (ed.), *Family Correspondence*, pp. 376–7.

80 'The impact of their happy': Author interview Evgeny Pasternak.

## CHAPTER 5: MARGUERITE IN THE DUNGEON

81 'By this time our relations': Ivinskaya, *Captive*, p. 89.

82 In her small room on Potapov Street: ibid., p. 30.

82 'The work of our "shop"': ibid., p. 34.

83 'The many books': ibid., p. 92.

84 'expressing anti-Soviet opinions': Emelianova, *Légendes*, p. 36.

84 'At that moment, they broke': Ivinskaya, *Captive*, p. 91.

84 'Everything is finished now': ibid., p. 92.

85 'with his light-blue eyes': ibid., p. 93.

87 'humiliating examination': ibid., p. 96.

87 'What if I don't': ibid., p. 97.

87 'crossed the fateful boundary': ibid.

87 'the prisoners began to feel': ibid., p. 98.

88 'You'll certainly be released': ibid., p. 101.

89 'Nowhere do you come closer': ibid., p. 99.

89 'I struggle with my need': Boris Pasternak, *Biographical Album*, p. 353.

90 'Life literally repeated': ibid.

90 'I am jealous of your hairbrush': *Doctor Zhivago*, p. 360.

91 'What are your initials?': Ivinskaya, *Captive*, p. 102.

91 'handsome, portly figure': ibid.

91 Before torturing his victims: Finn and Couvée, *Zhivago Affair*, p. 68.

92  'handsome, grey-haired': Ivinskaya, *Captive*, p. 103.

92  'To you as a memento': ibid.

92  'the year when our closeness': ibid.

92  'You always worry': ibid.

93  'How did you', 'Take her away': ibid., p. 104.

94  'Ah, but … April 1947 …': ibid., p. 105.

94  'Pasternak sat down': ibid., p. 107.

94  The fact that he had family: Finn and Couvée, *Zhivago Affair*, p. 69.

95  'It became a matter': Ivinskaya, *Captive*, p. 106.

95  *Semionov*: Speak … literary work: Emelianova, *Légendes*, pp. 39–46.

97  'Mary Magdalene': *Doctor Zhivago*, p. 503.

97  'What era does': Ivinskaya, *Captive*, p. 106.

98  'Why are you trying': ibid., pp. 107–8.

98  'Hear that?': Emelianova, *Légendes*, p. 46.

99  In March 1947 a critique: Boris Pasternak, *Biographical Album*, p. 355.

99  'literary bureaucrat': Ivinskaya, *Captive*, p. 221.

99  'hated Boris': ibid.

99  'to become bolder': Zoia Maslenikova, *Portret Borisa Pasternaka*, Sovetskaia Rossiia, Moscow, 1990, quoted in Clowes (ed.), *Critical Companion*, p. 18.

100  'Olga get out of this book': Ivinskaya, *Captive*, p. 221.

100  'It's almost her likeness': Slater (ed.), *Family Correspondence*, p. 403.

100  'There has been much concern': Ivinskaya, *Captive*, p. 84.

100  Writing to his friend: Clowes (ed.), *Critical Companion*, p. 6.

100  'Zina is able to indulge Lyonia': Slater (ed.), *Family Correspondence*, p. 377.

101  'Such a new thing, too': *Doctor Zhivago*, pp. 148–9.

102  'And I would go back to sleep': Ivinskaya, *Captive*, p. 101.

102  'These too exist in hell': ibid.

102  'He was extremely polite': Author interview Irina Emelianova.

103 'overcome with joy': Ivinskaya, *Captive*, p. 110.

103 'Could it be': ibid.

103 'I suddenly felt completely calm': ibid.

104 'Please forgive': ibid.

104 Olga was about to be subjected: Finn and Couvée, *Zhivago Affair*, p. 72.

104 'Do you confirm the evidence': Ivinskaya, *Captive*, pp. 112–13.

105 'I have pondered for a long time': ibid., p. 114.

106 'When I think of my terror': ibid.

106 'It is clear': Author interview Irina Emelianova.

106 A doctor's note in an official document: Finn and Couvée, *Zhivago Affair*, pp. 73n, 286n.

106 'Here Boria's and my child': Ivinskaya, *Captive*, p. 113.

106 'I am not convinced': Author interview Irina Emelianova.

107 The Accusation Act for her case: Emelianova, *Légendes*, p. 46.

## CHAPTER 6: CRANES OVER POTMA

108 'terrible place': Ivinskaya, *Captive*, p. 115.

108 'I just had to put up with it': ibid.

109 Later Semionov used the letter: ibid., p. 116.

109 'In this totally sincere letter': ibid.

109 'They didn't give me the child': ibid., p. 115–16.

110 'The minute he came': Author interview Irina Emelianova.

110 'Oh if only I had known': Ivinskaya, *Captive*, p. 135.

110 'a veritable paradise': ibid., p. 117.

110 'Just as a dossier was kept': ibid.

111 '[Olga] was put in jail': letter dated 7 May 1958, cited in ibid.

111 '1949, 1950, 1951': Author interview Irina Emelianova.

111 'It is thanks': ibid.

112 'Sick at heart': Ivinskaya, *Captive*, p. 118.

112 'Everything will soon be over': ibid.

112 'a small, scrawny woman': ibid.

113 'The camp authorities hated': ibid., pp. 121–2.

114 'The only thing': ibid., p. 119.

114 'Oh for the slush of autumn': ibid., p. 118.

116 'There was one more': ibid., p. 123.

117 'Here is a letter for you': ibid., p. 124.

117 'When the snow … at the corner': ibid.

117 'all those twelve pages': ibid., p. 125.

117 'We are doing everything': ibid.

119 'The small republic of Mordovia': Author interview Irina Emelianova.

119 'My dear Olia': ibid., pp. 127–8.

120 From the threshold: *Doctor Zhivago*, pp. 489–90.

122 'So dark and sad was it': ibid., pp. 397–8.

123 'It's the disease of our time': ibid., pp. 431–2.

123 'a completely unselfish': Clowes (ed.), *Critical Companion*, pp. 128, 129.

123 'I am not writing it': ibid.

124 'Something other than himself': *Doctor Zhivago*, p. 354.

124 'You and I, it's as though': ibid., p. 389.

124 'with a miscellany of mortals': Boris Pasternak, *Biographical Album*, p. 363.

124 Months later: ibid.

124 'When it all happened': ibid.

124 'Was it culpability': Author interview Irina Emelianova.

124 'A verst-long corridor': a *verst* is a unit of length in Russia equal to 1.067 km.

126 'so he can arrange payment': Ivinskaya, *Captive*, pp. 129–30.

126 'Dear Maria Nikolayevna': ibid.

126 'a terrible man died': Mallac, *Boris Pasternak*, p. 204.

126 'On the day of Stalin's death': Ivinskaya, *Captive*, p. 155.

127 'Ivinskaya impressed them': memorandum on the case of Mrs Ivinskaya and her daughter, from the HarperCollins Publishers archives.

127 April 10, 1953: Ivinskaya, *Captive*, pp. 127–8.

128 '[I] saw a dark silhouette': Emelianova, *Légendes*, p. 48.

129  'a typical blend of candour': Author interview Irina Emelianova.

129  'How terrible': Ivinskaya, *Captive*, p. 27.

129  'But then he saw': ibid.

## CHAPTER 7: A FAIRY TALE

130  'seized by a kind': Ivinskaya, *Captive*, p. 27.

130  'It is impossible': ibid.

131  'The position of persons': memorandum, from the HarperCollins Publishers archives.

131  Having spent almost eight years: Clowes (ed.), *Critical Companion*, p. 19.

131  'Even more than by what they had in common': *Doctor Zhivago*, p. 355.

132  'At such moments Yury felt': ibid., p. 392.

132  'It was I who unwittingly': Ivinskaya, *Captive*, p. 27.

133  'Last night he had tried': *Doctor Zhivago*, pp. 394–5.

133  Light scattered: ibid., p. 484.

134  At times excess of joy: ibid., p. 485.

134  'Last year we got out': Barnes, *Literary Biography*, p. 179.

135  'as though to share': Author interview Irina Emelianova.

135  'female tantrums': Ivinskaya, *Captive*, p. 28.

135  '[I] longed for recognition': ibid.

135  'You are a gift': ibid.

135  'beginning to take in': ibid., p. 39.

136  'This is just as it should be': ibid.

136  The name of an editor: Mallac, *Boris Pasternak*, p. 207.

136  His friend Ariadna Efron: Ivinskaya, *Captive*, p. 133.

137  'What do they mean': ibid., p. 38.

137  'that bronzed glow': Emelianova, *Légendes*, p. 68.

137  'My God, it is true': ibid., p. 67.

138  'The novel will probably': Mallac, *Boris Pasternak*, p. 206.

138  'the words "Doctor Zhivago"': Finn and Couvée, *Zhivago Affair*, p. 82.

138 'I have to and want to': ibid.

138 'I never thought': Clowes (ed.), *Critical Companion*, p. 136.

138 'So what is the novel': ibid., p. 141.

140 'One might have thought': Ivinskaya, *Captive*, pp. 39–40.

141 'But I asked you': ibid., p. 40.

141 'If there had been': ibid., pp. 41–2.

142 'Olia, I love you!': ibid., p. 42.

142 'All it would take … make her eat': Emelianova, *Légendes*, p. 57.

143 'time of great happiness': Ivinskaya, *Captive*, p. 41.

143 'We had a room': ibid., pp. 43–4.

143 'Z does not know that O': Slater (ed.), *Family Correspondence*, p. 405.

144 'What is the hour?': Ivinskaya, *Captive*, p. 47.

144 'managed to create': ibid., p. 186.

144 'I think Zinaida Nikolayevna': ibid., pp. 186–7.

145 'BL was so tormented': ibid., p. 187.

145 'I do not pity you': ibid.

145 'It is absurd to imagine': ibid., pp. 187–8.

146 'Before he finished the novel': Emelianova, *Légendes*, p. 86.

146 'What's wrong?': Ivinskaya, *Captive*, p. 208.

146 'a settlement of accounts': Mallac, *Boris Pasternak*, p. 195.

147 'This harrowing chapter': Ivinskaya, *Captive*, p. 208.

147 'You mark my words': ibid., p. 210.

147 'The Revolution is not shown': ibid.

147 'Your novel raises': Clowes (ed.), *Critical Companion*, pp. 36, 140.

148 'I have just finished': Boris Pasternak, *Essay in Autobiography*, p. 119.

149 'The book was going to take us': Emelianova, *Légendes*, p. 87.


## CHAPTER 8: THE ITALIAN ANGEL

150 'The publication': account of Sergei D'Angelo's meeting with Boris Pasternak, www.pasternakbydangelo.com.

151 'his grip was nice and firm': ibid.

151 Characteristically, he then: ibid.

151 'In the USSR': ibid.

152 'You will give me a copy': ibid.

152 Boris, however, knew: Finn and Couvée, *Zhivago Affair*, p. 8.

152 'All of a sudden, I realised': www.pasternakbydangelo.com.

152 'The manuscript was 433': Finn and Couvée, *Zhivago Affair*, p. 12.

152 'Let's not worry': www.pasternakbydangelo.com.

153 'This is *Doctor Zhivago*': ibid.

153 D'Angelo took the package: ibid.

153 It was just before noon: ibid.

153 'I had a visit today': Ivinskaya, *Captive*, p. 212.

154 'obviously realised': ibid.

154 'What have you done?': ibid.

155 He also gave copies: Paolo Mancosu, *Smugglers, Rebels, Pirates: Itineraries in the Publishing History of Doctor Zhivago*, Hoover Institution Press, 2015, p. 2.

155 'This is more important': Mallac, *Boris Pasternak*, p. 210.

155 'We looked': Mancosu, *Smugglers*, p. 27.

156 When Zinaida snapped: Mallac, *Boris Pasternak*, p. 210.

156 'At one point, Feltrinelli': www.pasternakbydangelo.com.

156 'Not to publish a novel like this': Finn and Couvée, *Zhivago Affair*, p. 89.

157 'But what has he done! … fall into place': Ivinskaya, *Captive*, pp. 215–16.

157 'How can anyone love': ibid., p. 216.

158 'long-legged', 'You know', 'Don't worry': ibid.

158 'He was indeed young': ibid., p. 217.

159 According to D'Angelo: www.pasternakbydangelo.com.

159 Although he wrote to Feltrinelli: Finn and Couvée, *Zhivago Affair*, p. 91.

159 'If its publication here': Boris Pasternak, *Biographical Album*, p. 373.

159 'I will never forget Feltrinelli': Author interview Charles Pasternak.

160 'I realise perfectly well': Finn and Couvée, *Zhivago Affair*, p. 92.

160 castigated as a 'bourgeois individualist': ibid.

160 'The novel by B. Pasternak': www.pasternakbydangelo.com.

160 'racing around Moscow': Ivinskaya, *Captive*, p. 219.

161 'How typical of you': ibid., p. 218.

161 When Olga reported: ibid., p. 219.

161 'It seems self-evident': ibid., p. 220.

162 'If ever you receive a letter': Finn and Couvée, *Zhivago Affair*, p. 95.

162 'It was important': Author interview Isaiah Berlin.

162 'Unlike some of its readers': Frances Stonor Saunders, 'The Writer and the Valet', *London Review of Books*, 25 Sep 2014.

163 Berlin concluded that Boris: Finn and Couvée, *Zhivago Affair*, p. 96.

163 'principal Russians', 'dear Bowra': Slater (ed.), *Family Correspondence*, pp. 380–1.

163 'It's an important work': ibid.

164 'exalted employer', 'immense desk': www.pasternakbydangelo.com.

164 'in good spirits', 'completely absurd': ibid.

164 He asked D'Angelo: ibid.

165 Pasternak 'shrugged his shoulders': ibid.

165 'The thing that has disturbed': Boris Pasternak, *Biographical Album*, p. 373.

165 'There are quite a few': Finn and Couvée, *Zhivago Affair*, p.102.

165 'that the letter from Goslitizdat': Ivinskaya, *Captive*, p. 223.

166 'I shall make this into something': Finn and Couvée, *Zhivago Affair*, p. 103.

166 'About a year ago Goslitizdat": Boris Pasternak, *Biographical Album*, p. 373.

166 'On March 12th': ibid., p. 375.

167 I will tell you when: Ivinskaya, *Captive*, pp. 399–400.

168 'We saw our father in Uzkoye': Boris Pasternak, *Biographical Album*, p. 377.

169 'I remember everything … his feelings': Gladkov, *Meetings with Pasternak*, p. 149.

169 'On that beautiful summer morning': ibid.

170 'I'm in for trouble this time': ibid., pp. 148–9.

170 'People who are morally scrupulous': Finn and Couvée, *Zhivago Affair*, p. 108.

171 'I have started rewriting': ibid.

171 'This was no easy task': Ivinskaya, *Captive*, p. 226.

172 'Irochka, my treasure … Your BP': Emelianova, *Légendes*, p. 89.

172 'Boris came with me': ibid.

173 'Pasternak has written': Finn and Couvée, *Zhivago Affair*, p. 112.

173 'the need for anonymous content': Slater (ed.), *Family Correspondence*, pp. 388–9.

173 '1 November 1957': ibid.

174 'But we shall soon have': Mancosu, *Smugglers*, p. 1.

175 On the 22nd the first edition: Mallac, *Boris Pasternak*, p. 271.

## CHAPTER 9: THE FAT IS IN THE FIRE

176 'You can congratulate me': Boris Pasternak, *Biographical Album*, p. 381.

177 'A very good translator': Slater (ed.), *Family Correspondence*, p. 381.

177 'That won't work': Finn and Couvée, *Zhivago Affair*, p. 97.

177 In 1958 Nabokov would refuse: Neil Cornwell, *Pasternak's Novel: Perspectives on 'Doctor Zhivago'*, Keele, 1986, p. 12.

177 'Doctor Zhivago is a sorry thing': Finn and Couvée, *Zhivago Affair*, p. 97.

178 On 8 Jul 1957, Harari wrote: from the HarperCollins Publishers archives.

178 'As for the poetry': from the HarperCollins Publishers archives.

179 'Max would read a page': Ann Pasternak Slater, 'Rereading: Dr Zhivago', *Guardian*, 6 Nov 2010.

179 'As to the poetry': from the HarperCollins Publishers archives.

179 In a memo to Frank Wisner: Finn and Couvée, *Zhivago Affair*, p. 115.

180 The Eisenhower White House: ibid., p. 117.

180 Among the books they translated: ibid., p. 125.

180 The American publisher Felix Morrow: Mancosu, *Smugglers*, p. 9.

180 'The Soviet public': Finn and Couvée, *Zhivago Affair*, p. 125.

181 'This book has great propaganda value': ibid., p. 131.

181 De Ridder decided to press ahead: Mancosu, *Smugglers*, p. 10.

181 In the first week of September: Finn and Couvée, *Zhivago Affair*, p. 138.

182 Later press reports suggested: Mancosu, *Smugglers*, p. 10.

182 A CIA memo of 9 September: Finn and Couvée, *Zhivago Affair*, p. 142.

182 'Is it true that an original': Slater (ed.), *Family Correspondence*, p. 405.

183 On 8 February 1958: Barnes, *Literary Biography*, pp. 333–4.

183 'youth just deserted': Author interview Irina Emelianova.

183 'one day he was unrecognisable': ibid.

184 In September the Oxford don: ibid., p. 337.

184 'When D[octor] Z[hivago] comes out': Slater (ed.), *Family Correspondence*, p. 397.

185 'During the interval': Gladkov, *Meetings with Pasternak*, pp. 152–3.

185 Albert Camus devoted attention: Evgeny Pasternak, *Boris Pasternak*, p. 235.

185 In May, Pasternak wrote: Mallac, *Boris Pasternak*, p. 220.

185 'If the N[obel] prize': Slater (ed.), *Family Correspondence*, pp. 405–6.

186 'to A Moravia': the Italian writer Alberto Moravia.

186 'In one photograph we see BL': Ivinskaya, *Captive*, p. 239.

186 'the congratulations of Kornei Chukovsky': he was a critic and literary scholar who wrote and translated children's books. He translated Rudyard Kipling, Arthur Conan Doyle, Mark Twain and G. K. Chesterton.

187 'I'm not going to congratulate you': Finn and Couvée, *Zhivago Affair*, p. 162.

187 'Do what seems right to you': ibid., p. 163.

187 'He was happy, thrilled': ibid.

187 Later, anxious that his embrace of Pasternak: ibid., p. 163.

188 'I was probably one of the first': Emelianova, *Légendes*, p. 94.

188 'Pasternak will do us all great harm': Finn and Couvée, *Zhivago Affair*, p. 164.

188 'There would be no mercy': ibid.

189 When Kurt Wolff: Mallac, *Boris Pasternak*, pp. 229–30.

189 'On Saturday 25th October': ibid., p. 232.

189 Two whole pages of Saturday's edition of *Literaturnaya Gazeta*: ibid.

190 'Some of our girls took refuge': Ivinskaya, *Captive*, pp. 240–1.

190 'It is ridiculous but *Doctor Zhivago*': Finn and Couvée, *Zhivago Affair*, p. 169.

191 'Everybody listened in silence': Gladkov, *Meetings with Pasternak*, pp. 166–7.

191 'The monstrous cheapness of it all': Ivinskaya, *Captive*, p. 242.

192 'He was devastated': Emelianova, *Légendes*, pp. 96–7.

192 'It was a loneliness': ibid.

193 'How strange young people': Ivinskaya, *Captive*, p. 243.

193 'The time had now come for Boris': ibid.

## CHAPTER 10: THE PASTERNAK AFFAIR

194 'It was an unusual kind of letter': Ivinskaya, *Captive*, p. 245.

195 '1. I have received your invitation': ibid., pp. 245–6.

195 His letter ended: Evgeny Pasternak, *Boris Pasternak*, p. 236.

196 'scandalous in its impudence': Finn and Couvée, *Zhivago Affair*, p. 172.

196 A long, formal resolution: Ivinskaya, *Captive*, p. 247.

196 'There was the feeling of being harassed': ibid., p. 251.

197 'Olia, I have to say something': ibid., pp. 251–3.

197  'Mitia, forgive me': ibid., p. 252.

197  'Our suicide would suit': ibid.

198  'Tell me,' she asked Fedin: ibid., p. 253.

198  'Mama came [back] from Peredelkino': Emelianova, *Légendes*, p. 116.

199  'In view of the meaning': Barnes, *Literary Biography*, p. 346.

199  'We were dumbfounded': Ivinskaya, *Captive*, p. 250.

199  'If you allow Pasternak': ibid., p. 255.

200  It was only the fourth time: Finn and Couvée, *Zhivago Affair*, p. 177. Of the 821 Nobel Laureates who have been awarded the prize since its inception in 1901, just six people have refused it. Boris Pasternak, the three Germans, the Vietnamese politician Le Duc Tho (1973), and Jean-Paul Sartre (1964).

200  'I had felt that death': Ivinskaya, *Captive*, p. 255.

201  'mangy sheep', 'As everybody who': ibid., p. 256.

201  'Everyone will understand it': Finn and Couvée, *Zhivago Affair*, p. 179.

201  'Lyonya and I will have to': ibid., p. 180.

201  'It was a horrible atmosphere': Author interview Irina Emelianova.

202  'No, Olia, I couldn't go abroad': Ivinskaya, *Captive*, p. 256.

202  'During this time, Boris cried': Emelianova, *Légendes*, p. 95.

202  News from the Western press: Mallac, *Boris Pasternak*, pp. 235–6.

202  'People would just slide them': Emelianova, *Légendes*, p. 100.

203  'Olga Vsevolodovna': Ivinskaya, *Captive*, p. 257.

203  'for me, Boris Leonidovich': ibid.

204  'Looking back': Ivinskaya, *Captive*, p. 259.

204  'Olia, keep it all as it is': ibid., p. 259.

205  'Dear Nikita Sergeyevich': ibid.

206  'threat was hanging': Author interview Irina Emelianova.

206  'That is why those calls': ibid.

206  'Mama and I were chatting': Emelianova, *Légendes*, p. 109.

207  'You are wanted on the phone': Ivinskaya, *Captive*, p. 282.

207 'Olga Vsevolodovna, my dear': ibid.

208 'They knew BL was stubborn': ibid., pp. 283–5.

208 'I remember with elation': Emelianova, *Légendes*, p. 129.

209 'It will be interesting now': Ivinskaya, *Captive*, p. 286.

210 'in a voice befitting a town crier': ibid., p. 287.

210 'Aren't you ashamed': ibid.

210 Polikarpov continued in his 'friendly' manner: Ivinskaya, *Captive*, pp. 284–8.

211 'They should have held': ibid., p. 288.

211 'Just think – how right', ibid., p. 289.

211 'In vain, in years of turmoil': ibid.

212 'lack of resolve': ibid., p. 260.

212 'That letter': ibid.

## CHAPTER 11: A BEAST AT BAY

213 'Dear Boris Leonidovich': Ivinskaya, *Captive*, p. 296.

213 In his overflowing mail bags: ibid., pp. 298–9.

214 'The whole world knows … all-embracing': ibid.

214 'Sholokhov': Mikhail Sholokhov was the author of *And Quiet Flows the Don*, regarded as a classic in the Soviet Union. This epic novel was written in four volumes, published between 1925 and 1940. In the earlier parts of the novel, the author is seen to be relatively objective towards the civil war – both Reds and Whites are shown to have committed atrocities. He was awarded the Nobel Prize for Literature in 1965.

214 Boris also struck up correspondences: Evgeny Pasternak, *Boris Pasternak*, p. 238.

214 'to a very great extent this triumph': Boris Pasternak, *Fifty Poems*, p. 22.

215 Lines included: 'When I saw': Ivinskaya, *Captive*, pp. 300–10.

216 'In the course of this turbulent … around me': ibid.

216 'Tempest not yet over': Slater (ed.), *Family Correspondence*, p. 407.

216 'All the letters I receive': ibid., pp. 407–8.

216 'It seemed that we had survived': Ivinskaya, *Captive*, p. 313.

217 'Like a fish thrown back': Emelianova, *Légendes*, p. 135.

217 'Pasternak does not receive': ibid., p. 133.

217 'It was very important for him': Ivinskaya, *Captive*, p. 307.

218 'BL was always in high spirits': ibid., p. 308.

218 'by the time BL found himself': ibid., p. 309.

220 'Have you two quarrelled?': ibid., p. 320.

220 'I am a white cormorant': Finn and Couvée, *Zhivago Affair*, p. 208.

221 'The falling of a small stone': Ivinskaya, *Captive*, p. 322.

221 'sections of the Government': Mallac, *Boris Pasternak*, p. 244.

222 'The misery of this last quarrel': Ivinskaya, *Captive*, p. 323.

223 'Oliusha, life will go on': ibid., pp. 404–12.

223 'I shall try to phone you today': ibid.

224 '[28 February] Oliusha': ibid.

224 'Even if your fears': ibid.

225 'One day things may be': ibid.

225 'To Oliusha on her birthday': ibid., p. 332.

225 'the perpetual accusation': Finn and Couvée, *Zhivago Affair*, p. 202.

226 Boris told his French translator: ibid., p. 203.

226 Naturally the KGB were monitoring: ibid., p. 204.

226 'Of course these very letters': Boris Pasternak, *Fifty Poems*, p. 22.

226 'BL intended to show what he understood': Ivinskaya, *Captive*, p. 333.

227 'BL loved organising outings': Emelianova, *Légendes*, p. 138.

228 'BL would arrive just after seven': ibid., p. 149.

229 'we were constantly laughing': ibid., p. 307.

229 'There was a Christmas tree': ibid., p. 155.

229 'We sang O Tannenbaum': 'O Tannenbaum' is a German Christmas folk song addressed to a fir tree; its evergreen qualities represent constancy and faithfulness.

## CHAPTER 12: THE TRUTH OF THEIR AGONY

230 'Sometimes BL lunched at the Big House': Ivinskaya, *Captive*, p. 336.

230 'It was astonishing': ibid.

231 'He put on a show': ibid., p. 339.

231 These had been sent: Carlo Feltrinelli, *Senior Service: A Story of Riches, Revolution and Violent Death*, Granta Books, 2013, p. 217.

232 'I bumped into BL': Emelianova, *Légendes*, p. 157.

232 'April was blissful': Ivinskaya, *Captive*, p. 339.

232 I entrust: Paolo Mancosu, *Inside the Zhivago Storm: The Editorial Adventures of Pasternak's Masterpiece*, Fondazione Giangiacomo Feltrinelli, Milan, 2013, p. 366.

233 'disturbing about BL's appearance': Ivinskaya, *Captive*, p. 341.

234 'Oliousha, I almost forgot': ibid., p. 343.

234 'There is so much unnatural chit-chat': ibid., p. 413.

234 'If you begin to feel': ibid., p. 413.

235 'he sent notes with [their friend] Kostia Bogatyrev': according to Irina, Konstantin Bogatyrev was a 'fantastic translator who was later assassinated by the KGB'.

235 On Friday 6 May: Barnes, *Literary Biography*, p. 371.

236 'wanted to make a direct attack': Author interview Irina Emelianova.

236 'My poor Mama': Emelianova, *Légendes*, p. 162.

236 'Olga was an adventuress': Author interview Natasha Pasternak.

237 'The nurses in attendance': Ivinskaya, *Captive*, p. 58.

238 'Olyusha won't love me': ibid., p. 344.

238 'VERY WORRIED BORIS ILLNESS': Slater (ed.), *Family Correspondence*, p. 417.

238 '19th May 1960. Moscow': ibid.

238 'BORIS INFARCT': the infarct, a localised area of dead tissue resulting from the obstruction of blood supply to that area, was thought to be in Boris's heart.

238 'I begged Marina': Ivinskaya, *Captive*, p. 344.

239 'We knew that the end': Author interview Irina Emelianova.

239 'CONDITION UNCHANGED': Slater (ed.), *Family Correspondence*, pp. 417–18.

239 '27th May 1960, MOSCOW': ibid., p. 418.

240 'On the day of his death': Author interview Natasha Pasternak.

240 'He complained how hard it was': Boris Pasternak, *Biographical Album*, p. 395.

240 'Everything I possess of value': Ivinskaya, *Captive*, p. 415.

240 'Lydia, that's good': Josephine Pasternak, *Indefinability: An Essay in the Philosophy of Cognition*, Museum Tusculanum Press, 1999, p. ix.

241 'He is dead,' Marfa said: Ivinskaya, *Captive*, p. 348.

242 'Farewell, great span': extract from Pasternak poem 'August' inscribed on Pasternak gravestone in Wolvercote cemetery, Oxford.

242 'Yes, it had all come true': Ivinskaya, *Captive*, p. 348.

242 'So here we are again: *Doctor Zhivago*, p. 448.

242 'Goodbye, Lara, until we meet': ibid., p. 404.

242 '[Mama] was a lot calmer': Emelianova, *Légendes*, p. 169.

243 'The death of Pasternak': Finn and Couvée, *Zhivago Affair*, p. 234.

243 'The board of the Literary Fund': Ivinskaya, *Captive*, p. 350.

243 'From the early morning': Boris Pasternak, *Fifty Poems*, p. 23.

244 Lydia, who finally got her visa: Lydia was granted a visa two days after Boris died. Forty years after she left she travelled back to Russia, and slept that night in the bed where her beloved brother had died.

244 'What Pasternak's views': Clowes (ed.), *Critical Companion*, p. 43.

245 'People began passing flowers': Ivinskaya, *Captive*, p. 354.

245 'Sometimes death strips the face': Emelianova, *Légendes*, p. 174.

245 'There is no death': Boris Pasternak, *Biographical Album*, p. 397.

245 'The place chosen for the burial': Gladkov, *Meetings with Pasternak*, pp. 179–81.

246 'The procession with the coffin': ibid.

246 'We have come to bid farewell': Mallac, *Boris Pasternak*, p. 271.

247 'a thousand pairs of lips': Finn and Couvée, *Zhivago Affair*, p. 241.

247 'The noise is stilled': *Doctor Zhivago*, p. 467.

248 'And suddenly the dazed': Ivinskaya, *Captive*, p. 356.

248 'For a moment she stood still': *Doctor Zhivago*, pp. 446–7.

248 An official came forward: Ivinskaya, *Captive*, p. 357.

249 A couple of days after the funeral: ibid., pp. 359–60.

249 'It was clear that they had decided': Emelianova, *Légendes*, p. 214.

249 'Pasternak was too outstanding a figure': Ivinskaya, *Captive*, p. 366.

250 'an honest poet': ibid., p. 366.

250 'Obviously justice was less important': *Newsweek*, 30 Jan 1961.

251 'You have probably never loved a woman': Ivinskaya, *Captive*, p. 366.

251 'The point is that Pasternak': ibid., p. 370.

251 'Not only was the case itself a sham': ibid., p. 376.

252 'The truth was that Pasternak': from the HarperCollins Publishers archives.

252 'You have always hated Pasternak': ibid.

253 They were both sent: Feltrinelli, *Senior Service*, p. 246.

253 'I still cannot think without horror': Ivinskaya, *Captive*, pp. 382–3.

254 'One day Lara went out': *Doctor Zhivago*, p. 449.

## EPILOGUE: THINK OF ME THEN

255 'dying slowly right in front of my eyes': Finn and Couvée, *Zhivago Affair*, p. 257.

255 'Had Boris Pasternak': ibid., p. 253.

256 'France has helped repair': Author interview Irina Emelianova.

256 'left a bad aftertaste': Mallac, *Boris Pasternak*, p. 235.

258 'It was not out of necessity': *Doctor Zhivago*, p. 447.

261 'Many years': translation from the German original, reproduced in facsimile in Gerd Ruge, *Pasternak*, Munich, 1958, p. 125.

# SELECT BIBLIOGRAPHY

Barnes, Christopher, *Boris Pasternak: A Literary Biography, Volume 2, 1928–1960*, Cambridge University Press, 1998

Clowes, Edith W. (ed.), *Doctor Zhivago, A Critical Companion*, Northwestern University Press, 1995

Cornwell, Neil, *Pasternak's Novel: Perspectives on 'Doctor Zhivago'*, Department of Russian Studies, Keele University, 1986

Emelianova, Irina, *Légendes de la rue Potapov*, Fayard, 1997

Feltrinelli, Carlo, *Senior Service: A Story of Riches, Revolution and Violent Death*, Granta Books, 2013

Finn, Peter, and Petra Couvée, *The Zhivago Affair: The Kremlin, the CIA, and the Battle over a Forbidden Book*, Harvill Secker, 2014

Gladkov, Alexander, *Meetings with Pasternak*, Collins and Harvill Press, 1977

Ivinskaya, Olga, *A Captive of Time: My Years with Pasternak*, Collins Harvill, 1978

Mallac, Guy de, *Boris Pasternak: His Life and Art*, University of Oklahoma, 1981

Mancosu, Paolo, *Inside the Zhivago Storm: The Editorial Adventures of Pasternak's Masterpiece*, Milan, Fondazione Giangiacomo Feltrinelli, 2013

—*Smugglers, Rebels, Pirates: Itineraries in the Publishing History of Doctor Zhivago*, Hoover Institution Press, 2015

Montefiore, Simon Sebag, *Stalin: The Court of the Red Tsar*, Weidenfeld & Nicolson, 2003

*Museum Guidebook: Museum of Private Collections*, Pushkin State Museum of Fine Arts, 2004

Pasternak, Alexander, *A Vanished Present*, Oxford University Press, 1984

Pasternak, Boris, *Biographical Album*, Moscow, Gamma Press, 2007

—*Doctor Zhivago*, translated by Max Hayward & Manya Harari, Harvill Press, 1996

—*An Essay in Autobiography*, Collins and Harvill Press, 1959

—*Family Correspondence 1921–1960*, translated by Nicolas Pasternak Slater, Hoover Institution Press, 2010

—*Fifty Poems*, translated and with an introduction by Lydia Pasternak Slater, George Allen & Unwin Ltd, 1963

—*The Last Summer*, Penguin Books, 1959

—*Zhenia's Childhood*, Allison & Busby Ltd, 1982

Pasternak, Evgeny, *Boris Pasternak: The Tragic Years 1930–1960*, Collins Harvill, 1990

Pasternak, Josephine, *Indefinability: An Essay in the Philosophy of Cognition*, introduction by Michael Slater, Museum Tusculanum Press, 1999

—*Tightrope Walking: A Memoir*, Slavica Publishers, 2005

Pasternak, Leonid, *Memoirs of Leonid Pasternak*, translated by Jennifer Bradshaw, with an introduction by Josephine Pasternak, Quartet Books, 1982

www.pasternakbydangelo.com

Slater, Maya (ed.), *Boris Pasternak: Family Correspondence 1921–1960*, translated by Nicolas Pasternak Slater, Hoover Institution Press, 2010

# ACKNOWLEDGEMENTS AND NOTE ON SOURCES

Two events precipitated my initial interest in Boris and Olga's love story. The first, in 1990, was when I wanted to progress my fledgling career in journalism. To commemorate the centenary of Pasternak's birth, I pitched an article to the *Spectator* magazine, in which I would reveal the real Lara. Knowing embarrassingly little about my family history, I then went to visit my ninety-year-old grandmother, Josephine Pasternak, in her Oxford home. Fifty-five years after she saw her brother Boris for the last time, she vividly brought alive to me that final meeting with him. She died three years later. Josephine also introduced me to her friend, Sir Isaiah Berlin. He invited me to lunch, also in Oxford, and I felt honoured to listen to his fascinating recollections of Boris and the saga surrounding the publication of *Doctor Zhivago*.

When Olga Ivinskaya died in Moscow in 1995, the London *Evening Standard* asked me to research and write her obituary. Having filed the article, I was left with a great feeling of sadness, moved by her story and the haunting sense that there was so much left unsaid about her love affair with Boris.

Fifteen years later I knew that I wanted, and was ready, to write *Lara*. In February 2010 I travelled to Moscow with my father, where Evgeny Pasternak, aged eighty-seven, and his wife, Elena, entertained us. Over homemade lemon digestif, Evgeny patiently agreed to answer my questions about his father, even though he had written extensively on the subject during his life. As I left he presented me with an amazing 'Biographical Album' – a compilation of Boris's life in words, letters and photographs – which their son, Petr, had complied and had privately published, and to which Evgeny had contributed an introductory essay. Later, at Peredelkino, Natasha Pasternak, who was married to Boris's son Leonid, spoke at great length about her father-in-law, his death, and the difficulties for Olga at the end of her life. These are precious memories for me because both Natasha and Evgeny have since died.

Two months after my trip to Moscow, I went to Stanford University in California. The Hoover Institution, which houses all the archive papers donated by my grandmother, Josephine Pasternak, was hosting an international symposium entitled 'The Pasternak Family: Surviving the Storms'. I was invited to give a talk on 'Josephine Pasternak and her Last Meeting with Boris: Berlin 1935'. It was wonderful to meet so many other family members here, especially Petr Pasternak, Boris's grandson. Also, Jacqueline de Proyart, who met regularly with Boris and translated *Zhivago* into French. The conference coincided with the book launch of *Boris Pasternak, Family Correspondence 1921–1960* (edited by Maya Slater), the first English translation of Boris's letters to his family by his nephew, Nicolas Pasternak Slater. I am indebted to Nicolas, as I have drawn heavily on these letters in *Lara* and without them the book would be far poorer. They are a beautifully written and moving account of the writer's life during the forty-two-year separation from his family.

I wish that I had met Olga Ivinskaya, but I consider myself exceptionally lucky to have spent time with Irina Kosovoi, née Emelianova, Olga's daughter. At first, she was reticent about meeting me. She had already written her own account in *Légendes de la rue Potapov* and was sceptical of my motives in writing *Lara*. As a Pasternak, she did not expect me to be sympathetic to her mother. We met twice in Paris and my time spent interviewing her in her apartment is especially meaningful to me. Both *Légendes de la rue Potapov* and her mother's memoir, *A Captive of Time*, have been principal sources of my research.

Another fascinating and valuable source was the fifteen files that the archivist at HarperCollins Publishers found in their Glasgow vaults marked 'Pasternak Correspondence'. Unpublished, these include copies of all the correspondence surrounding the publication of *Doctor Zhivago* in the UK, between the then Collins Publishers and Pantheon Books in the US. There are also many detailed memos and accounts of efforts to free Olga once she was interned in the gulag for the second time, in the 1960s.

My research also took me to Milan, where Carlo Feltrinelli showed me around the exceptional Feltrinelli Foundation. It was an emotional and thrilling moment when he took the original manuscript of *Doctor Zhivago* out of a vault and allowed me to look at it. I felt touched by the care with which the Feltrinelli Foundation has archived the correspondence between Giangiacomo Feltrinelli and Boris Pasternak. These two courageous men had much in common and although they never met, across their many letters their affection for each other is laid bare.

Finally, I feel tremendously blessed and am appreciative of the following who have given so much love, time, help, wisdom, expertise and support during the research and writing of *Lara*. My heartfelt gratitude to all:

Audrey Pasternak, Charles Pasternak, Daisy Pasternak, Josephine Pasternak, Irina Kosovoi, Evgeny Pasternak, Natasha Pasternak, Carlo Feltrinelli, Eugenie Furniss, Arabella Pike, Kate Johnson, Laura Brooke, Lottie Fyfe, Dawn Sinclair, Liz Trubridge, Michael Engler, Betsy Bernardaud, Linda Bernard, Marlene Brand-Meyer, Rafaella de Angelis, Richard Cohen, Ross Clarke, Tina Campbell, Jane Stratton, Jenny Parrot, Neil Cornwell, Minna Fry, Ala Osmond, Daisy Finer, Lucy Cleland, Mark Palmer, Anna Dickinson, Victoria Fuller, Lara Fares, Yvonne Williams, Judith Osborne, Richard Furgerson, Monika Barton, Katya Pilutsky and Linda Matthews-Denham.

# INDEX